God's Love Letter to the Jewish People

To Richard + Sonja

Zechariah 2:10 & 12 Sing and rejoice,
O daughter of Zion: for, lo, I come, and
I will dwell in the midst of thee, saith
the LORD. And the LORD shall inherit
Judah his portion in the Holy land, and
shall choose Jerusalem again

Tilly Steward

Enjoy reading!

Tilly Steward   December 2012

Copyright © 2012 Tilly Steward
All rights reserved.

ISBN: 0615600212
ISBN 13: 9780615600215

Contents

Preface   v

Introduction   vii

Chapter 1 God's Promise to His People   1

Chapter 2 Yeshua Is Our High Priest   81

Chapter 3 My Unexpected Trip to the Holy Land   107

Chapter 4 Biblical Prophecy   153

Chapter 5 The Names of God   170

Chapter 6 The Names of Yeshua   185

Chapter 7 Angels and Demons—Who Are They?   197

Chapter 8 The Difference—Heaven or Hell   215

Chapter 9 The Names of Satan   227

Chapter 10 Who Are the Two Witnesses?   231

Preface

Important Explanation!

For over five months, I waited for a response from several Jewish Bible publishers to whom I had poured my heart out, asking for permission to copy their Scriptures for free. I received only one response—from an Orthodox publisher, who wanted one dollar per Bible verse for the many I requested from their Tanakh. God set me aside to finish writing this book without letting me earn a regular income for over three years. All this time I lived on faith, and somehow Yeshua supplied my need as He spoke to different people to give me a hand.

During a serious prayer at the end of February in 2010, I asked the Lord why I hadn't been able to produce any sales. He instructed me to finish the Manuscript first, then He will bring me business. On March 27, 2011, the Holy Spirit revealed to me that in order to write this book, I would have to trust in Him, that it was between God and me. He alone gets the glory. Then I remembered that when I began my studies to be ordained as a minister of the Gospel over thirty years ago, the Holy Spirit informed me that I would get my orders straight from Him. I would not be instructed by elders who sit around a table in the church office and say things like, "We don't do it this way." In other words, it was He who anointed me and gave me the calling for this task, so I obey Him with the knowledge that He will see me through. He confirmed it in Isaiah 45:2 and 3b: *I will go before thee, and make the crooked places straight: I will break in pieces the gates of brass, and cut in sunder the bars of iron: that thou mayest know that I, the LORD, which call thee by thy name, am the God of Israel.*

Since I could not obtain permission from the publishers, I have copied the Scriptures from the Tanakh and the Brit Chadasha in my King James Bible, for which I need no permission. The overall text is pretty much the same as in the Jewish Scriptures. Many of my quotes from the Brit Chadasha have already been written in the Tanakh.

Romans 10:12-21, *For there is no difference between the Jew and the Greek: for the same Lord over all is rich unto all that call upon him. For whosoever shall call upon the name of the Lord shall be saved. How then shall they call on him in whom they have not believed? And how shall they believe in him of whom they have not heard? And how shall they hear without a preacher? And how shall they preach, except they been sent? As it is written, How beautiful are the feet of them that preach the gospel of peace, and bring glad tidings of good things! But they have not all obeyed the gospel. For Esaias saith, Lord, who hath believed our report? So then faith cometh by hearing, and hearing by the word of God. But I say, Have they not heard? Yes verily, their sound went into all the earth, and their words unto the ends of the world. But I say, Did not Israel know? First Moses saith I will provoke you to jealousy by them that are no people, and by a foolish nation I will anger you. But Esaias is very bold, and saith, I was found of them that sought me not; I was made manifest unto them that asked not after me. But to Israel he saith, All day long I have stretched forth my hands unto a disobedient and gainsaying people.*

In BC. 1451 Moses already told in Deuteronomy 32:21, *They have moved me to jealousy with that which is not God; they have provoked me to anger with their vanities: and I will move them to jealousy with those which are not a people, I will provoke them to anger with a foolish nation.*

This Verse pertains to the Lord turning to the Gentiles. By their rejection of Yeshua and the Cross, the majority of Israelis fashioned themselves into vessels of wrath through their self-will and unbelief.

Introduction

At the end of January 1985, God called me out of Real Estate to serve Him. He had been preparing my heart for some time, so I was ready to give it all up. Had I not obeyed, I would have missed my calling, not knowing at the time that I was about to take a life-changing trip as a tourist that would signal God's glory and completely change my life. I went on this trip with six other people. In chapter 3, I describe the many places we visited during our five-and-a-half-week journey to Israel and eleven days in Egypt.

After our return, God anointed me to write this book. The following year, in 1986, I thought I had the manuscript finished, when God revealed to me to put it up on the shelf, that the last chapter was not written yet. Being on this awesome trip in the Holy Land gave me a greater desire to learn the Scriptures even more. During this time the Holy Spirit would not allow me to attend any kind of Christian meeting, except church services. I also went on a forty day fast during which I drank only water and allowed the Holy Spirit to teach me. Although I did not know anything about lengthy fasting I did know that God called me to do it. I told Him to let me know how long. At sundown on the fortieth day the Holy Spirit revealed to me that I had completed my fast.

Then in October 1986 the Lord allowed me to attend a Christian meeting with between forty and fifty ladies present. The guest speaker was a prophetess from Seattle whom I will mention again later. When my turn came to be ministered to she said: "The Lord gives me Proverbs 21:30, *There is no wisdom, nor understanding, no counsel against the Lord*. The Lord is saying: Daughter, I have a plan for your life. Many people give you advice and they have their own plan for you. You've had to shake that off, you've had to shake off traditions from your background." Then she continued: "I visualize a fish swimming against the stream and you are like that salmon. You have to get upstream, you have eggs to lay. And you say, 'I'll die getting there, but I'm going to make it.' You have a determination inside of you to bring forth life, to lay those eggs out. And you will jump those hurdles, even the hurdles of the fish ladder that have been put up by man. There are a lot of obstacles being put into the stream by man, and when I say man I mean men – males. In other words, your biggest problem will be with the males. They are like that fish ladder. It's not right that they're in; man put those fish ladders there. This was not God's original plan for the river, or the lake, or the reservoir. But the Lord is saying: 'You will swim upstream. You will conquer anything man puts in your way, as you do it in MY strength, in MY wisdom, in MY plan. For nothing can succeed against the Lord.' Thank You Yeshua." You would not believe it, even if I told you my experiences with most of these pastors the Lord sent me to.

After she prayed for a short time in the spirit (tongues) she prophesied to me from Ezekiel 38:23, *Thus will I magnify myself, and sanctify myself and I will be known in the eyes of many nations and they shall know that I am the LORD.* "God is saying, 'Daughter, it's going to be different than it was in the past. There's going to be a sovereign move of God in the days ahead. I see you out in the field when God moves in miraculous ways. It's not like you will have to deliver the words, it's going to be there in the sight of many nations. God is going to shake the heavens and the earth, and nations are going to see it.' I don't know how this is, and who knows? Through a variety of ways there is going to be a shaking, and it has already started, but there are going to be shakings that we do not know about.

"Usually we think of shakings as earthquakes and all that, but I sense that there is going to be a shaking in cults and religions that are not of God, and suddenly there is going to be light coming in, in masses. Suddenly there is revelation of who God really is. And that is what I see, even now as I'm ministering to you, that you are going to be there to nurse the babies, to bring teaching to the babies as God makes Himself known. He's going to do it, but He needs those there to bring the teaching. I even sense that God's going to use your book and have your book there to bring the teaching to the nations. You are going to find yourself giving away most of your books to people who will not be able to pay for it. I sense that God is going to have sponsors to buy a book for someone overseas. He's going to give you a plan on how you will be able to get your word to those that wouldn't hear. The Lord is showing me that one reason why it is not being handled in the stores here is because God intended for that book to go overseas.

"Thank You, Yeshua! Lord, we lift this book, and the books to come, and we ask You Lord, to finance the shipping, mailing, the delivery, the Word that goes forth from those books. Lord, we just pray that any expectation that Your daughter had of it going in a different direction, just take that away and show her that You had a plan for that book that she has not realized yet, and that she freely has been given, so she must freely give this book, now, in Jesus' name, Amen."

I was surprised at her prophecy, because I had no knowledge back then in 1986 that I would minister to the Jewish people. Then the Holy Spirit revealed to me the meaning of it. I shared with a few of the ladies at the meeting there, that these eggs that I have to lay are the new converts that will be birthed. I knew back then that I would be ministering to the Muslims in Egypt some day, but I had absolutely no idea that I will write this book ministering first to the Jewish people.

A week before I returned the edited manuscript to the publisher the Holy Spirit brought to my memory that the prophetic message given to me a few years before in the Foreword contained in my prior book from a local pastor, that I was to include it also in this one: "Jesus Christ is coming soon. Christian men and women of all races must rally around the truth. God's honor is at stake. He has raised Tilly Steward up for such a time as this. In any sport, every good signal caller understands the instructions of the head coach. He perceives, anticipates, and reacts with great precision and daring. As for the body of Christ, Tilly is that woman. I have fellowshipped with her over many years and have watched her move by the leadership of the Holy Spirit in life's difficulties, maintaining her loyalty to her Lord and Savior with true passion and total commitment. Her message crosses all racial and cultural barriers. She has a unique way of bringing different races together for reconciliation and restoration to unity in the body of Christ. With her insight in the spirit realm, she has an eternal perspective. Tilly delivers God's *vision of freedom from the slavery of false religions and denominations.*

"I support and trust her in the vision that God has given her to change the world of false teachings. Her love for God's Word and His people has caused her heart to burn with a godly desire that this generation would know Jesus Christ. To understand her, you will need to read and study her work carefully.

"Several years ago, Tilly and I were talking about the calling that God has given her to write this spiritual masterpiece. Some time later, the Holy Spirit revealed to me that I was to tell Tilly that this book would be used in colleges and universities as a reference book to teach and enlighten the world of false religions. John 8:32 says, *And ye shall know the truth, and the truth shall make you free.* Also Matthew 24:11, *And many false prophets shall rise, and shall deceive many.* I admire this woman of God for being bold enough to obey God. Tilly is attuned to the Holy Spirit, her mind and heart are sensitive to the spiritual needs of humanity.

I am always moved and fascinated as I observe how she focuses on the piercing truth of God's remarkable consistency. Tilly is a strong woman of God. She will look you in the eye and point to the Word of God and its divine purpose. I am standing with her to bring the truth to the generations. This book will set you free and fill you with vision, faith, and courageous insights that will elevate your faith to the next level in your walk with God."

At the time my pastor friend wrote this Foreword, I had over thousand pages in my manuscript which included some of this book, including my next one to come. Since the publisher could not print a book that large, I split it into volume one and two, which this Foreword made reference to. The third volume is not ready yet for publication. I have to wait for the Holy Spirit to tell me when to complete it. It's title: 'Is Mohammed Mentioned in the Bible?' A younger Muslim man from Cairo, Egypt told me here in 1986 that Mohammed was mentioned in our Scriptures and even told me which verse. I cannot remember which one, but it mentioned Kadesh in it which is only mentioned in a few verses. No where could I find his name. Mohammed is absolutely not mentioned in the Tanakh.

By now, this book which had already been twenty-seven years in the making is finally ready for publication. I know that the Holy Spirit will convict many Jewish people at His proper time. Isaiah 65:1a says, *I am sought of them that asked not for me; I am found of them that sought me not.* He speaks to you through me. Recently I have felt an urgent need to complete this manuscript and have been as many as twelve hours in one stretch on the computer day after day till midnight.

Many people think they know God, but they only know about Him. They lack a personal relationship with Him. I would also like to publish this book in the Hebrew, Arabic, Farsi and Russian languages since every fourth person in Israel speaks Russian. Yeshua said in Matthew 10:32–33, *Whosoever therefore shall confess me before men, him will I confess also before my Father which is in heaven. But whosoever shall deny me before men, him will I also deny before my Father which is in heaven.*

The apostle Paul wrote in Romans 1:16, *For I am not ashamed of the gospel of Christ: for it is the power of God unto salvation to every one that believeth; to the Jew first, and also to the Greek.*

We read in Jeremiah 29:11–13,

> *For I know the thoughts that I think toward you, saith the LORD, thoughts of peace, and not of evil, to give you an expected end. Then shall ye call upon me, and ye shall go and pray unto me, and I will hearken unto you. And ye shall seek me, and find me, when ye shall search for me with all your heart.*

> *And we know that all things work together for good to them that love God, to them who are the called according to his purpose* (Romans 8:28).

The following Scriptures are clearly described in Jeremiah 31:31–33,

> *Behold, the days come, saith the LORD, that I will make a new covenant with the house of Israel, and with the house of Judah: Not according to the covenant that I made with their fathers in the day that I took them by the hand to bring them out of the land of Egypt; which my covenant they brake, although I was an husband unto them, saith the LORD: But*

this shall be the covenant that I will make with the house of Israel; After those days, saith the LORD, I will put my law in their inward parts, and write it in their hearts; and will be their God, and they shall be my people.

This New Covenant Scripture - which is the Brit Chadasha reads as follows in Hebrew 8:10, *For this is the covenant that I will make with the house of Israel after those days, saith the Lord; I will put my laws into their mind, and write them in their hearts: and I will be to them a God, and they shall be to me a people.* In other words, you must accept your Messiah first so that the Holy Spirit can convict you of sin, rather than wearing phylacteries on your physical body. This knowledge can be found by confessing Yeshua as your long-awaited Messiah. You just read that God is making a new covenant with you. Why do you refuse what God said? He even proved it to you by having it written in your Scriptures.

You must remove the veil of unbelief from your eyes (spirit). As it is written in Exodus 34:33, *And till Moses had done speaking with them, he put a veil on his face.*

The Brit Chadasha explains it in 2 Corinthians 3:13–17,

And not as Moses, which put a veil over his face, that the children of Israel could not stedfastly look to the end of that which is abolished: But their minds were blinded: for until this day remaineth the same veil untaken away in the reading of the old testament; which veil is done away in Christ. But even unto this day, when Moses is read, the veil is upon their heart. Nevertheless when it shall turn to the Lord, the veil shall be taken away Now the Lord is that Spirit: and where the Spirit of the Lord is, there is liberty.

After Yeshua's resurrection, His beaten body and face were restored but His nail-pierced hands and feet remained visible, as did the wound in His side. They are a sign of the covenant He made with us for the forgiveness of our sins. He gave His life for us by shedding His blood on the cross. A covenant is completed with a meal, which He had in the upper room with His disciples. We have our meal with Him during the seven years of the Rapture, which is called the "Marriage Supper of the Lamb." In the meantime, while we are waiting to see Him face to face the apostle Paul wrote of Yeshua telling us in 1 Corinthians 11:23-26, *For I have received of the Lord that which also I delivered unto you, That the Lord Jesus the same night in which he was betrayed took bread: and when he had given thanks, he brake it, and said, 'Take, eat: this is my body, which is broken for you: this do in remembrance of me.' And after the same manner also he took the cup, when he had supped, saying, 'This cup is the new testament in my blood: this do ye, as oft as ye drink it, in remembrance of me.' For as often as ye eat this bread, and drink this cup, ye do shew the Lord's death till he comes.* I partake of it every morning, by taking unleavened bread and grape juice. To this day in the Middle East, people still make blood covenants.

Galatians 2:16 & 20–21 says,

Knowing that a man is not justified by the works of the law, but by faith of Jesus Christ, even we have believed in Jesus Christ, and not by the works of the law: for by the works of the law shall no flesh be justified. I am crucified with Christ: nevertheless I live; yet not I, but Christ liveth in me: and the life which I now live in the flesh I live by faith of the Son of God, who loved me, and gave himself for me. I do not frustrate the grace of God: for if righteousness come by the law, then Christ is dead in vain.

Yeshua explains in Matthew 5:17–18, *Think not that I am come to destroy the law, or the prophets: I am not come to destroy, but to fulfill. For verily I say unto you, Till heaven and earth pass, one jot or one tittle shall in no wise pass from the law, till all be fulfilled.*

What follows is a sample of the Holy Spirit being present in the Tanakh. Ezekiel 36:26-27,

A new heart also will I give you, and a new spirit will I put within you: and I will take away the stony heart out of your flesh, and I will give you an heart of flesh. And I will put my spirit within you, and cause you to walk in my statutes, and ye shall keep my judgments, and do them. Isn't it time for you to exchange the stony heart for one made of flesh?

I had traveled only one block after the Sabbath service on July 11, 2009, when the Holy Spirit pulled me off the main road into a side street and revealed to me what I was to share with the congregation the following Sabbath: "God wants a family. He sent us His Son Yeshua to be an example."

From 1 Peter 1:15–16, *But as he which hath called you is holy, so be ye holy in all manner of conversation; because it is written, Be ye holy, for I am holy.*

And Ephesians 1:4–5, *According as he hath chosen us in him before the foundation of the world, that we should be holy and without blame before him in love: Having predestinated us unto the adoption of children by Jesus Christ to himself, according to the good pleasure of his will.*

It is confirmed in the Torah in Leviticus 19:1 & 2, *And the LORD spake unto Moses, saying, Speak unto all the congregation of the children of Israel, and say unto them, Ye shall be holy: for I the LORD your God am holy.*

Constantine became Roman emperor in 306 AD. In 321 AD he made Christianity the official religion of the empire, by mixing Roman paganism with Christianity, and excluding all other religions. This signaled the end of the persecution of the Christians but the beginning of discrimination and persecution against the Jewish people. He stopped Passover and changed the day of worship to Sunday—without God's approval.

In my last book *Revival In The Land—Are You Ready For It?* published in December 2008 by Creation House, I quote different prophesies of God's call upon my life. For example, in 1983, an evangelist from Canada whom I had not met before was the guest speaker in a prayer meeting I attended. He prophesied to me that God is beginning to open some doors for you so that you will be able to travel and do outreach in an area of the ministry that God will establish. I see you holding hands and supporting somebody else's arms. He is calling you to an area of helps in government. He is calling you to be a strength and support, to be a help, to uplift, uphold – like a strengthener. Cause that anointing to be birthed in to her new ministry to the work You called her to do. The Lord is saying, 'I'm preparing the way for you; and be ready to walk when the time comes. I'm going to cause you to be a yielded vessel. Thine heart will be soft toward others. This time, you are going to be able to do the praying because you're the one who will bring them into the kingdom of God.' Don't stop. You will alter and change many lives and that is really where God has placed you right now. God is going to give you the ability to stand before multitudes of people and preach His word. You will find that many will come into salvation who have never known God. God is going to do that because He will answer what you have promised. You said that you are willing to go forth to preach the gospel of Jesus Christ. God will anoint you as a minister of the gospel, and signs and wonders shall follow the preaching of your words. You will see many lives changed and altered by what God is going to do.

Afterwards Satan whispered many, many times in my ear: 'Who do you think you are little girl, trying to convert a whole nation?' Instead of panicking I got my prophesies out each time and read them to him out loud. When Satan does not get you to listen to him he gives up after a while looking for his next victim. All along I assumed that I was going to be used by God in Egypt, because there was no thought yet about Israel.

I will copy a few prophesies from chapter 10 in my last book that were given to me between 1986 and 2008 so that you can see the sincerity of my calling to the Jewish people.

On June 4, 1996, a Seattle prophetess, who has been used by God around the world prophesied to me:

The Lord gave me an interesting Scripture for you.

Go throughout the city of Jerusalem and put a mark on their foreheads of those who grieve and lament over all the detestable things that are done in it (Ezekiel 9:4). What I see is that God sends you to places to destroy the idolatry. Whether it's in Jerusalem or wherever He sends you, to Muslims, to different places.

The Lord says, "*As you go through the city, even as you pray or speak, putting a mark on their forehead means changing their thinking, giving them truth, taking out the lie as you see the detestable thing that are in the minds of the people.*" I see you placing God in there, as you speak, as you minister, as you send materials or leave materials behind. It's as though you are putting a mark on their forehead, and directly behind their forehead are their brains. The marking shows their understanding of the idolatry.

He who turns a deaf ear to instruction—his prayer is an abomination (Proverbs 28:9). *Thou shalt have no other gods before me* (Exodus 20:3). I see you taking away the false gods and putting in the real God. Thank You, Yeshua. In this country, many, including some pastors, will realize that they've only been exposed to a partial gospel, not the full gospel's preaching and teaching!

The Lord says, "Make sure that you are fully armed with the armor of God, because you're on the frontlines doing battle and not everyone understands this; not everyone understands the demonic powers that come against you." It's as though you were before your time. You had a vision and you're a "goer." A lot of people need years to get ready to do what the Lord is telling you to do. You heard what He said and you went ...

So shall my word be that goeth forth out of my mouth: it shall not return unto me void, but it shall accomplish that which I please, and it shall prosper in the thing whereto I sent it (Isaiah 55:11).

We sing, "Nothing is impossible when you put your trust in God."

Will Yeshua ask us one day, "Did you do your best to reach the world for Me?"

CHAPTER 1

God's Promise to His People

"Shema!" Hebrew for *hear* or *listen*. God said to your forefathers in Deuteronomy 7:7–9,

> *It is not because you are the most numerous of peoples that the LORD set his heart on you and chose you—indeed, you are the smallest of peoples; but it was because the LORD favored you and kept the oath he made to your fathers that the LORD freed you with a mighty hand and rescued you from the house of bondage, from the power of Pharaoh king of Egypt. Know, therefore, that only the LORD your God is God, the steadfast God who keeps his covenant faithfully to the thousandth generation of those who love him and keep his commandments.*

The Lord even confirms His loyalty to us by declaring a marriage between us.

The LORD is my strength and song, and he is become my salvation; he is my God, and I will prepare him an habitation; my father's God, and I will exalt him (Exodus 15:2). *Turn, O backsliding sons, says the LORD; for I am married to you; and I will take you one from a city, and two from a family, and I will bring you to Zion* (Jeremiah 3:14). God is a man of His word. He keeps the oath He swore to your forefathers. His revelation in the Torah cannot be shaken. Number 23:19 tells us, *God is not a man, that he should lie; neither the son of man, that he should repent: hath he said, and shall he not do it? or hath he spoken, and shall he not make it good?* God told Abraham in Genesis 17:7–8 & 19,

> *And I will establish my covenant between me and thee and thy seed after thee in their generations for an everlasting covenant, to be a God unto thee, and to thy seed after thee. And I will give unto thee, and thy seed after thee, the land wherein thou art a stranger, all the land of Canaan, for an everlasting possession; and I will be their God. And God said Sarah thy wife shall bear thee a son indeed, and thou shalt call his name Isaac: and I will establish my covenant with him for an everlasting covenant and with his seed after him.*

This everlasting covenant also applies today. Israel is a country of nations, comprised of people from over hundred different nations. God has not changed; it is you who have distanced yourself from Him. We read in Romans 2:28–29, *For he is not a Jew, which is one outwardly; neither is that circumcision, which is outward in the flesh: But he is a Jew, which is one inwardly; and circumcision is that of the heart, in the spirit, and not in the letter; whose praise is not of men, but of God.* You are still His chosen people.

Because of the Israelites' apostasy, God had to pronounce fierce judgment and chastise the people. But today He presents a wonderful promise of restoration. He says He will bring forth your righteousness at the noonday and you will become a watered garden. He will take away your iniquity, heal your apostasy, and love you freely. Between His voice of judgment and His promise of restoration, however, God's prophets consistently impose one vital exhortation: repent! What applied in the olden days remains true today. He judged the surrounding nations. In Zephaniah 2:4–7,

> *For Gaza shall be forsaken, and Ashkelon a desolation: they shall drive out Ashdod at the noon day, and Ekron shall be rooted up. Woe to the inhabitants of the sea coast, the nation of the Cherethites! The word of the LORD is against you; O Canaan, the land of the Philistines, I will even destroy you, that there shall be no inhabitant. And the sea coast shall be dwellings and cottages for shepherds, and folds for flocks. And the coast shall be for the remnant of the house of Judah; they shall*

feed thereupon: in the houses of Ashkelon shall they lie down in the evening: for the LORD their God shall visit them, and turn away their captivity.

Modern Palestinians presently occupy this area and expect a Palestinian state. Despite every effort made on the behalf of the Palestinian people, the question will not be solved or fulfilled until the return of the Messiah, when He will rule the world from Jerusalem.

God sent the prophet Nathan to see David after he had sinned with Bathsheba. I'm sure you're familiar with what happened. David repented and wrote Psalm 51. He writes in verses 10, 16, and 17, *Create in me a clean heart, O God; and renew a right spirit within me. For thou desirest not sacrifice; else would I give it: thou delightest not in burnt offering. The sacrifices of God are a broken spirit: a broken and contrite heart, O God, thou wilt not despise.*

He is calling me to invite you to repent so that you, too, can take part in our impending worldwide revival. Over twenty years ago, the prophetess from Seattle whom I mentioned earlier spoke the following words to me from Ezekiel 33:7, *I made you a watchman for the house of Israel. So hear the words I speak and give them warning from me.* God has made you a watchman, too. You're a watchman for the people of God. He gives you words of warning. The Lord is encouraging you. You have been chosen by God to speak His Word.

He tells you in Hosea 14:1, *O ISRAEL, return unto the LORD thy God; for thou hast fallen in thine iniquity.*

We read where God calls the Israelites rebellious children in Isaiah 30:1–3,

Woe to the rebellious children, saith the LORD, that take counsel, but not of me; and that cover with a covering, but not of my spirit, that they may add sin to sin: That walk to go down into Egypt, and have not asked of my mouth; to strengthen themselves in the strength of Pharaoh, and to trust in the shadow of Egypt! Therefore shall the strength of Pharaoh be your shame, and the trust in the shadow of Egypt your confusion.

The plea has always been for you to turn to God Himself—to allow Him to cleanse and restore you. The same applies for today. Numerous trips made by government officials to other nations to bring about peace treaties have accomplished nothing. Why? They did not fit into God's "timetable." Intellect and outside influence will not bring it to pass. You must repent and accept Yeshua as your Messiah and receive the baptism in the Holy Spirit. Then you can ask in prayer and await the answers from the Holy Spirit, even answers to personal concerns or questions regarding government affairs, as described in Matthew 6:7, *But when ye pray, use not vain repetitions, as the heathen do: for they think that they shall be heard for their much speaking.*

Here are a few Scriptures from the Tanakh and Brit Chadasha pertaining to baptism in the Holy Spirit. Do you practice them? *For with stammering lips and another tongue will he speak to this people* (Isaiah 28:11). Nearly eight hundred years before Yeshua, Isaiah uttered this prophecy concerning baptism in the Holy Spirit with evidence of speaking in other tongues. Paul, the apostle to the Corinthians taught them: *Wherefore tongues are for a sign, not to them who believe, but to them who believe not: but prophesying serves not for them who believe not, but for them which believe. Wherefore, brethren, covet to prophesy, and forbid not to speak with tongues* (1 Corinthians 14:22 & 39). Then, as Paul came to Ephesus, he asked certain disciples in Acts 19:2 & 6, *He said unto them, Have you received the Holy Spirit since you believed? And they said unto him, we have not so much as heard weather there be any Holy Spirit. And when Paul had laid his hands upon them, the Holy Spirit came on them; and they spoke with tongues, and prophesied.*

In my last book, I explain in detail the nine gifts of the Holy Spirit: wisdom, knowledge, faith, healing, the working of miracles, prophecy, discerning of spirits, diverse tongues, and the interpretation of tongues.

If his children forsake my law, and walk not in my judgments; If they break my statutes, and keep not my commandments; then will I visit their transgression with the rod, and their iniquity with stripes. Nevertheless, my lovingkindness will I not utterly take from him, nor suffer my faithfulness to fail. My covenant will I not break, nor alter the thing that is gone out of my lips. Once have I sworn by my holiness that I will not lie unto

David? His seed shall endure for ever, and his throne as the sun before me.
It shall be established forever as the moon, and as a faithful witness in
heaven Selah (Psalm 89:30-37).

We read of another promise of God on Joshua 1:1-6,

Now after the death of Moses the servant of the LORD it came to pass, that
the LORD spake unto Joshua the son of Nun, Moses' minister, saying, Moses
my servant is dead; now therefore arise, go over this Jordan, thou, and all
this people, unto the land which I do give to them, even to the children of
Israel. Every place that the sole of your foot shall tread upon, that have I
given unto you, as I said unto Moses. From the wilderness and this Lebanon
even unto the great river, the river Euphrates, all the land of the Hittites,
and unto the great sea toward the going down of the sun, shall be your coast.
There shall not any man be able to stand before thee all the days of thy life:
as I was with Moses, so I will be with thee; I will not fail thee, nor forsake
thee. Be strong and of good courage: for unto this people shalt thou divide
for an inheritance the land, which I sware unto their fathers to give them.

The land that God gave to Abraham stretched from the Brook
of Egypt—they call it Wadi el-Arish—to the Euphrates River, as
described in Genesis 15:18, *In the same day the LORD made a covenant*
with Abraham, saying, Unto thy seed have I given this land, from the river of
Egypt unto the great river, the river Euphrates.

Will Israel's borders once again stretch as far as described in
Ezekiel 47:13–21? The northern border of the Promised Land will
begin on the coast of the Mediterranean Sea to include Damascus
on the other side and all of modern day Syria. The eastern border
includes all of modern day Jordan and extends to the Euphrates
River, even part of Iraq.

Does this next Scripture answer some of the disputes faced by
Israel today? God said in Leviticus 25:23, *The land shall not be sold for-*
ever: for the land is mine; for ye are strangers and sojourners with me. Then
Ezekiel gave a Messianic prophecy in chapter 37:25–28,

And they shall dwell in the land that I have given unto Jacob my servant,
wherein your fathers have dwelt; and they shall dwell therein, even they,

and their children, and their children's children for ever: and my servant David shall be their prince for ever. Moreover I will make a covenant of peace with them; it shall be an everlasting covenant with them: and I will place them, and multiply them, and will set my sanctuary in the midst of them for evermore. My tabernacle also shall be with them: yea, I will be their God, and they shall be my people. And the heathen shall know that I the LORD do sanctify Israel, when my sanctuary shall be in the midst of them for evermore.

If more people had become familiar with the Word of God and obeyed it, many lives could have been spared over the years. He will tabernacle among you when His sanctuary is in your hearts. In the last book of the Bible, John recorded in Revelation 21:3, *And I heard a great voice out of heaven saying, Behold the tabernacle of God is with men, and he will dwell with them, and they shall be his people, and God himself shall be with them, and be their God.*

In 1987, a friend prophesied over me at an intercessory prayer meeting that I have the anointing of tabernacles upon me. I also was to read chapter 40 of the book of Exodus and that I would estab-lish the body of Yeshua. The footnotes of the Torah explain that God's glory filled the tabernacle; without His glory and presence, the work was unfinished and the tabernacle useless. As the cloud of the Lord's presence covered the tent of the congregation, His glory filled His temple, and only when the cloud lifted would the children of Israel continue their journey. By day the cloud was above the tabernacle but by night fire, so they were able to see. Just as He was personally present with them, so is His desire to personally know and guide you now. Are you ready to let go of your traditions and obey what God says in the Scriptures? He is in the process of gathering you to Himself, as told by Ezekiel in 34:13, *And I will bring them out from the peoples and gather them from the countries, and will bring them to their own land; I will feed them on the mountains of Israel, in the valleys and in all the inhabited places of the country.* He is seeking to restore Israel according to the promise of your Messiah, who shed His blood on the cross for all our sins approximately two thousand years ago.

On Pentecost in 2009, the Holy Spirit moved upon me. I became emotional and teary eyed as I made my way by car to a church picnic and water baptism in the lake. Later that day, He revealed to me that I was to bring the Jewish people and the believers in Yeshua together to worship on the same day. I replied, "Okay, Lord. You put it together and I will implement it". When Yeshua comes to rapture us, He will come for a bride in a white garment, but He has to clean us up first. This certainly means that we should obey Him and worship on His ordained Sabbath day. He could have returned earlier, then many would have been denied to enter heaven if they had not yet accepted Yeshua as Savior. We read in 2 Peter 3:9, *The Lord is not slack concerning his promise, as some count slackness; but is longsuffering to us-ward, not willing that any should perish, but that all should come to repentance.* In the Tanakh, there are 613 laws (instructions) which no one could possibly keep all of them. We read as early as Exodus 35:1-2a, *And Moses gathered all the congregation of the children of Israel together, and said unto them, These are the words which the LORD hath commanded, that ye should do them. Six days shall work be done, but on the seventh day there shall be to you an holy day, a sabbath of rest to the LORD.*

On Pentecost in 2011, exactly two years later, the Lord revealed to me that I should implement it now, that He has not changed his mind about the day we should worship. I'm sure there will be some resentment by the Gentiles to worship on the Sabbath and by the Jews to accept and believe in the Brit Chadasha. He wants Jews and Gentiles to believe in the whole book rather than letting tradition dictate what you add to or take away from the truth of the Scriptures.

Acts 18:1 & 4–11 say,

After these things Paul departed from Athens, and came to Corinth. And he reasoned in the synagogue every sabbath, and persuaded the Jews and the Greeks. And when Silas and Timotheus were come from Macedonia, Paul was pressed in the spirit, and testified to the Jews that Jesus was Christ. And when they opposed themselves, and blasphemed, he shook his raiment, and said unto them, Your blood be upon your own heads; I am clean: from henceforth I will go unto the Gentiles. And he departed thence, and entered into a certain man's house, named Justus, one that worshipped God, whose house joined hard to the synagogue. And Crispus, the chief ruler of the synagogue, believed on the Lord with all his house; and many of the Corinthians hearing believed, and were baptized. Then spake the Lord to Paul in the night by a vision, Be not afraid, but speak, and hold not thy peace: For I am with thee, and no man shall set on thee to hurt thee: for I have much people in this city. And he continued there a year and six months, teaching the word of God among them.

If they got along back then, why can't we make it work today? The Lord said to Moses in Exodus 31:12–17,

And the LORD spake unto Moses, saying, Speak thou also onto the children of Israel, saying, Verily my sabbaths ye shall keep: for it is a sign between me and you throughout your generations; that ye may know that I am the LORD that doth sanctify you. Ye shall keep the sabbath therefore; for it is holy unto you: every one that defileth it shall surely be put to death: for whosoever doeth any work therein, that soul shall be cut off from among his people. Six days may work be done; but in the seventh is the sabbath of rest, holy to the LORD: whosoever doeth any work in the sabbath day, he shall surely be put to death. Wherefore the children of Israel shall keep the sabbath, to observe the sabbath throughout their generations, for a perpetual covenant. It is a sign between me and the children of Israel for ever: for in six days the LORD made heaven and earth, and on the seventh day he rested, and was refreshed.

He is ready for you to embrace the Holy Spirit, whom He sent to the Jews in Jerusalem on Pentecost two thousand years ago, as told in the Acts of the apostles in the Book of Acts, Chapters 2:1–25, 29–33, 36–39, and 4:11–12, confirmed in Joel 2:28-32a, and Psalm 16:8.

And when the day of Pentecost was fully come, they were all with one accord in one place. And suddenly there came a sound from heaven as of a rushing mighty wind, and it filled all the house (temple) where they were sitting. And there appeared unto them cloven tongues like as of fire, and it sat upon each of them. And they were all filled with the Holy Ghost, and began to speak with other tongues, as the Spirit gave them utterance. And there were dwelling at Jerusalem Jews, devout men, out of every nation under heaven. Now when this was noised abroad, the multitude came together and were confounded, because that every man heard them speak in his own language. And they were all amazed and marveled, saying one to another, Behold, are not all these which speak Galilaeans? And how we hear every man in our own tongue, wherein we were born? Parthians, and Medes, and Elamites, and the dwellers in Mesopotamia, and in Judaea, and Capadocia, in Pontus, and Asia, Phrygia, and Pamphylia, in Egypt, and in the parts of Libya about Cyrene, and strangers of Rome, Jews and proselytes, Cretes and Arabians, we do hear them speak in our tongues the wonderful works of God. And they were all amazed, and were in doubt, saying one to another, What meaneth this? Others mocking said, These men are full of new wine. But Peter, standing up with the eleven, lifted up his voice, and said unto them, Ye men of Judaea, and all ye that dwell at Jerusalem, be this known unto you, and harken to my words: For these are not drunken, as ye suppose, seeing it is but the third hour of the day. But this is that which was spoken by the prophet Joel; And it shall come to pass in the last days, saith God, I will pour out of my Spirit upon all flesh: and your sons and your daughters shall prophesy, and your young men shall see visions, and your old men shall dream dreams: And on my servants and on my handmaidens I will pour out in those days of my Spirit; and they shall prophesy: And I will shew wonders in heaven above, and signs in the earth beneath; blood, and fire, and vapour of smoke: The sun shall be turned into darkness, and the moon into blood, before that great and notable day of the Lord come: And it shall come to pass, that whosoever shall call on the name of the Lord shall be saved. (Joel 2:28-32a). Ye men of Israel, hear these words; Jesus of Nazareth, a man approved of God among you by miracles and wonders and signs, which God did by him in the midst of you, as ye yourselves also know: him, being delivered by the determinate counsel and foreknowledge of God, ye have taken, and by wicked hands have crucified and slain: Whom God hath raised up, having loosed the pains of death: because it was not possible that he should be holden of it. For David speaking concerning him, I foresaw the Lord always before my face, for he is on my right hand, that I should not be moved. (Psalm 16:8).

Men and brethren, let me freely speak unto you of the patriarch David, that he is both dead and buried, and his sepulchre is with us unto this day. Therefore being a prophet, and knowing that God had sworn with an oath to him, that of the fruit of his loins, according to the flesh, he would raise up Christ to sit on his throne; he seeing this before spake of the resurrection of Christ, that his soul was not left in hell, neither his flesh did see corruption.

This Jesus hath God raised up, whereof we all are witnesses. Therefore being by the right hand of God exalted, and having received of the Father the promise of the Holy Ghost, he hath shed forth this, which ye now see and hear. Therefore let all the house of Israel know assuredly, that God hath made that same Jesus, whom ye have crucified, both Lord and Christ. Now when they heard this, they were pricked in their heart, and said unto Peter and to the rest of the apostles, Men and brethren, what shall we do? Then Peter said unto them, Repent, and be baptized every one of you in the name of Jesus Christ for the remission of sins, and ye shall receive the gift of the Holy Ghost. For the promise is unto you, and to your children, and to all that are afar off, even as many as the Lord our God shall call. This is the stone which was set at nought of you builders, which is become the head of the corner. Neither is there salvation in any other: for there is none other name under heaven given among men, whereby we must be saved.

God also required that three feasts be kept; they are His feasts. *And the LORD spake unto Moses, saying, Speak unto the children of Israel, and say unto them, Concerning the feasts of the LORD, which ye shall proclaim to be holy convocations, even these are my feasts, which ye shall proclaim in their seasons* (Leviticus 23:1–2 and 4b).

1. Passover—Pesach—speaks of redemption. Messiah would be the Passover lamb, sacrificed for us. *Neither is there salvation in any other: for there is none other name under heaven given among men, whereby we must be saved* (Acts 4:12).

Fifty days later we celebrated Pentecost.

2. Pentecost—Shavuot—speaks of gathering. Messiah would send the Holy Spirit to gather both Jews and Gentiles into one body.

And when the day of Pentecost was fully come, they were all in one accord in one place. And suddenly there came a sound from heaven as of a rushing mighty wind, and it filled all the house where they were sitting. And there appeared unto them cloven tongues like as of fire, and it sat upon each one of them. And they were all filled with the Holy Ghost, and began to speak with other tongues, as the Spirit gave them utterance. And there were dwelling at Jerusalem Jews, devout men, out of every nation under heaven. Now when this was noised abroad, the multitude came together, and were confounded, because that every man heard them speak in his own language. And they were all amazed and marveled, saying one to another, Behold, are not all these which speak Galileans? And how hear we every man in our own tongue, wherein we were born? (Acts 2:1–8). This is what your Messiah did for you two thousand years ago.

> 3. Feast of Tabernacles—Sukkoth—points to the day the Messiah tabernacles among men as well as the day in the future when the Messiah will set up the messianic kingdom to once again tabernacle among men. Leviticus 23: 33-34, 41-44,

And the LORD spake unto Moses, saying, Speak to the children of Israel, saying, The fifteenth day of this seventh month shall be the feast of tabernacles for seven days unto the LORD. And ye shall keep it a feast unto the LORD seven days in the year. It shall be a statute for ever in your generations: ye shall celebrate it in the seventh month. Ye shall dwell in booths seven days; all that are Israelites born shall dwell in booths: That your generations may know that I made the children of Israel do dwell in booths, when I brought them out of the land of Egypt: I am the LORD your God. And Moses declared unto the children of Israel the feasts of the LORD

To my surprise, I also learned that the Messiah was not born on Christmas Day, the date chosen by Constantine and Pope Julius l. He was born on the Feast of Tabernacles. Let's follow the biblical logic. In the days of Herod, King of Judea, there was a Jewish priest named Zacharias who belonged to the Abia division. The service of the priests was scheduled for the last two weeks of the fourth month of the Jewish religious calendar, 15–29 Tammuz, June–July. Zacharias was serving in the second Jewish temple in Jerusalem when he was chosen to enter the holy place to burn incense outside the Holy of Holies. In order to prove the birth date of Yeshua, I need to convince you that it all started with John. I will copy the whole chapter of Luke 1:1-80,

There was in the days of Herod, the king of Judea, a certain priest named Zacharias, of the course of Abia and his wife was of the daughters of

Aaron, and her name was Elisabeth. And they were both righteous before God, walking in all the commandments and ordinances of the Lord blameless. And they had no child, because that Elisabeth was barren, and they both were now well stricken in years. And it came to pass, that while he executed the priest's office, his lot was to burn incense when he went into the temple of the Lord. And the whole multitudes of the people were praying without at the time of incense. And there appeared unto him an angel of the Lord standing on the right side of the altar of incense. And when Zacharias saw him, he was troubled, and fear fell upon him. But the angel said unto him, Fear not, Zacharias: for thy prayer is heard; and thy wife Elisabeth shall bear thee a son, and thou shalt call his name John. And thou shalt have joy and gladness; and many shall rejoice in his birth. For he shall be great in the sight of the Lord, and shall drink neither wine nor strong drink; and he shall be filled with the Holy Ghost, even from his mother's womb. And many of the children of Israel shall he turn to the Lord their God. And he shall go before him in the spirit and power of Elias, to turn the hearts of the fathers to the children, and the disobedient to the wisdom of the just; to make ready a people prepared for the Lord. And Zacharias said unto the angel,Whereby shall I know this? for I am an old man, and my wife well stricken in years. And the angel answering said unto him, I am Gabriel that stand in the presence of God; and am sent to speak unto thee and to shew thee these glad tidings. And, behold, thou shalt be dumb, and not able to speak, until the day that these things shall be performed, because thou believest not my words, which shall be fulfilled in their season. And the people waited for Zacharias, and marveled that he tarried so long in the temple. And when he came out, he could not speak unto them; and they perceived that he had seen a vision in the temple: for he beckoned unto hem, and remained speechless. And it came to pass, that, as soon as the days of his ministration were accomplished, he departed to his own house. And after those days his wife Elisabeth conceived and hid herself five months, saying, Thus hath the Lord dealt with me in the days wherein he looked on me, to take away my reproach among men. And in the sixth month the angel Gabriel was sent from God unto a city of Galilee, named Nazareth, to a virgin espoused to a man whose name was Joseph, of the house of David; and the virgin's name was Mary. And the angel came in unto her, and said, Hail, thou that art highly favoured, the Lord is with thee: blessed art thou among women. And when she saw him, *she was troubled at his saying, and cast in her mind what manner of salutation this should be. And the angel said unto her, Fear not, Mary: for thou hast found favour with God. And, behold, thou shalt conceive in thy womb, and bring forth a son, and shalt call his name JESUS. He shall be great, and shall be called the Son of the Highest: and the Lord God shall give unto him the throne of his father David: And he shall reign over the house of Jacob for ever; and of his kingdom there shall be no end. Then said Mary unto the angel, How shall this be, seeing I know not a man? And the angel answered and said unto her, The Holy Ghost shall come upon thee, and the power of the Highest shall overshadow thee: therefore also that holy thing which shall be born of thee shall be called the Son of God. And, behold, thy cousin Elisabeth, she hath also conceived a son in her old age: and this is the sixth month with her, who was called barren. For with God nothing shall be impossible. And Mary said, Behold the handmaid of the Lord; be it unto me according to thy word. And the angel departed from her. And Mary arose in those days, and went into the hill country with haste, into a city of Juda; and entered into the house of Zacharias, and saluted Elisabeth. And it came to pass, that, when Elisabeth heard the salutation of Mary, the babe leaped in her womb; and Elisabeth was filled with the Holy Ghost: and she spake out with a loud voice, and said, Blessed art thou among women, and blessed is the fruit of thy womb. And whence is this to me that the mother of my Lord should come to me? For, lo, as soon as the voice of thy salutation sounded in mine ears, the babe leaped in my womb for joy. And blessed is she that believed: for there shall be a performance of those things which were told her from the Lord. And Mary said, my soul doth magnify the Lord, and my spirit hath rejoiced in God my Saviour. For he hath regarded the low estate of his handmaiden: for, behold, from henceforth all generations shall call me blessed. For he that is mighty hath done to me great things; and holy is his name. And his mercy is on them that fear him from generation to generation. He hath shewed strength with his arm; he hath scattered the proud in the imagination of their hearts. He hath put down the mighty from their seats, and exalted them of low degree. He hath filled the hungry with good things; and the rich he hath sent empty away. He hath holpen his servant Israel, in remembrance of his mercy; as he spake to our fathers, to Abraham, and to his seed for ever. And Mary abode with her about three months, and returned to her own house. Now Elisabeth's full time came that she should be delivered, and she brought forth a son. And her neighbors and her cousins heard how the Lord had shewed great mercy upon her; and they rejoiced with her. And it came to pass, that on the eight day came to circumcise the child; and they called him Zacharias, after the name of his father. And his mother answered and said, Not so; but he shall be called John. And they said unto her, There is none of thy kindred that is called by this name. And they made signs to his father, how he would have him called. And he asked for a writing table, and wrote, saying, his name is John. And they marveled all. And his mouth was opened immediately, and his tongue loosed, and he spake, and praised God. And fear came on all that dwelt round about them: and all these sayings were noised abroad throughout all the hill country of Judaea. And all they that heard them laid them up in their hearts, saying, What manner of child shall this be! And the hand of the Lord was with him. And his father Zacharias was filled with the Holy Ghost, and prophesied, saying, Blessed be the Lord God of Israel; for he hath visited and redeemed his people, and hath raised up an horn of salvation for us in the house of his servant David; as he spake by the mouth of his holy prophets, which have been since the world began: That we should be saved from our enemies, and from the hand of all that hate us; To perform the mercy promised to our fathers, and to remember his holy covenant; The oath which he sware to our father Abraham, that he would grant unto us, that we being delivered out of the hand of our enemies might serve him without fear, in holiness and righteousness before him, all the days of our life. And thou, child, shalt be called the prophet of the Highest: for thou shalt go before the face of the Lord to prepare his ways; to give knowledge of salvation unto his people by the remission of their sins, through the tender mercy of our God; whereby the dayspring from on high visited us, to give light to them that sit in darkness and in the shadow death, to guide our feet into the way of peace. And the child grew, and waxed strong in spirit, and was in the deserts till the day of his shewing to Israel.*

Some of these Scriptures are also written in the Tanakh. They are 1 Chronicles 24:10; Exodus 40:5; Malachi 4:5; Ezekiel 3:26 & 24:27; Genesis 21:2 & 30:23; Isaiah 7:14; Daniel 9:23; Judges 6:12; Psalm 71:19; Psalm 111:9; Exodus 20:6; Psalm 103:17; Isaiah 40:10; Psalm 107:9; Genesis 17:12; 1 Kings 1:48; and Psalm 32:17. The following events give the dates when Zacharias was in the temple:

- Zacharias was in the temple: Hebrew date 15–29 Tammuz; Gregorian date 21 June–6 July, 6 BC.

- The earliest John could have been conceived is on the first of Av, which is on or before July 7, 6 BC. He was born on Passover 15–21 Nisan, which is April 4–10, 5 BC.

- Yeshua was conceived Tevet—December, 6 BC.

- Yeshua was born during the feast of Tabernacles 15–21 Tishri, which was September 29–October 6, 5 BC.

- Simeon and Anna were in the temple when Joseph and Mary presented Yeshua on the fortieth day after His birth in late Cheshvan, which is early November.

- Now I copy the Scriptures that describe the birth of Yeshua from Luke Chapter 2:1-52,

And it came to pass in those days, that there went out a decree from Caesar Augustus, that all the world should be taxed. And this taxing was first made when Cyrenius was governor of Syria. And all went to be taxed, every one into his own city. And Joseph also went up from Galilee, out of the city of Nazareth, into Judaea, unto the city of David, which is called Bethlehem; because he was of the house and lineage of David: to be taxed with Mary his espoused wife, being great with child. And so it was, that, while they were there, the days were accomplished that she should be delivered. And she brought forth her firstborn son, and wrapped him in swaddling clothes, and laid him in a manger; because there was no room for them in the inn. And there were in the same country shepherds abiding in the field, keeping watch over their flock by night. And, lo, the angel of the Lord came upon them, and the glory of the Lord shone round about them: and they were sore afraid. And the angel said unto them, Fear not: for, behold, I bring you good tidings of great joy, which shall be to all people. For unto you is born this day in the city of David a Saviour, which is Christ the Lord. And this shall be a sign unto you; Ye shall find the babe wrapped in swaddling clothes, lying in a manger. And suddenly there was with the angel a multitude of the heavenly host praising God, and saying, Glory to God in the highest and on earth peace, good will toward men. And it came to pass, as the angels were gone away from them into heaven, the shepherds said one to another, Let us now go even unto Bethlehem, and see this thing which is come to pass, which the Lord hath made known unto us. And they came with haste, and found Mary, and Joseph, and the babe lying in a manger. And when they had seen it, they made known abroad the saying which was told them concerning this child. And all they that heard it wondered at those things which were told them by the shepherds. But Mary kept all these things, and pondered them in her heart. And the shepherds returned, glorifying and praising God for all the things that they had heard and seen, as it was told unto them. And when eight days were accomplished for the circumcising of the child, his name was called JESUS, which was so named of the angel before he was conceived in the womb. And when the days of her purification according to the law of Moses were accomplished, they brought him to Jerusalem, to present him to the Lord; as it is written in the law of the Lord, Every male that openeth the womb shall be called holy to the Lord; and to offer a sacrifice according to that which is said in the law of the Lord, A pair of turtledoves, or two young pigeons. And, behold, there was a man in Jerusalem, whose name was Simeon; and the same man was just and devout, waiting for the consolation of Israel: and the Holy Ghost was upon him. And it was revealed unto him by the Holy Ghost, that he should not see death, before he had seen the Lord's Christ. And he came by the Spirit into the temple: and when the parents brought the child Jesus, to do for him after the custom of the law, then took he him up in his arms, and blessed God, and said, Lord, now lettest thou thy servant depart in peace, according to thy word: For mine eyes have seen thy salvation, which thou hast prepared before the face of all people; a light to lighten the Gentiles, and the glory of thy people Israel. And Joseph and his mother marveled at those things which were spoken of him. And Simeon blessed them, and said unto Mary his mother, Behold this child is set for the fall and rising again of many in Israel; and for a sign which shall be spoken against; Yea, a sword shall pierce through thy own soul also, that the thoughts of many hearts may be revealed. And there was one Anna, a prophetess, the daughter of Phanuel, the tribe of Aser: she was of a great age, and had lived with an husband seven years from her virginity; And she was a widow of about fourscore and four years, which departed not from the temple, bur served God with fastings and prayers night and day. And she coming in that *instant gave thanks likewise unto the Lord, and spake of him to all them that looked for redemption in Jerusalem. And when they had performed all things according to the law of the Lord, they returned into Galilee, to their own city Nazareth. And the child grew and waxed strong in spirit, filled with wisdom: and the grace of God was upon him. Now his parents went to Jerusalem every year at the feast of the Passover. And when he was twelve years old, they went up to Jerusalem after the custom of the feast. And when they had fulfilled the days, as they returned, the child Jesus tarried behind in Jerusalem; and Joseph and his mother knew not of it. But they, supposing him to have been in the company, went a day's journey; and they sought him among their kinfolk and acquaintance. And when they found him not, they turned back again to Jerusalem, seeking him. And it came to pass, that after three days, they found him in the temple, sitting in the midst of the doctors, both hearing them, and asking them questions And all that heard him were astonished at his understanding and answers. And when they saw him, they were amazed: and his mother said unto him, Son, why hast thou thus dealt with us? behold, thy father and I have sought thee sorrowing. And he said unto them, How is it that ye sought me? wist ye not that I must be about my Father's business? And they understood not the saying which he spake unto them. And he went down with them, and came to Nazareth, and was subject to them: but his mother kept all these sayings in her heart. And Jesus increased in wisdom and stature, and in favour with God and man.*

The Scriptures relating to this chapter in the Tanakh are Micah 5:2; 1 Samuel 2:34; Leviticus 12:2–8; Numbers 3:13; Genesis 46:30; Isaiah 42:6 & 8:14; Psalm 42:10; Joshua 19:24; and Exodus 23:14–15.

Another plunder that was made in that Yeshua was not crucified on Good Friday. Various groups and denominations have been misleading their followers for many years. If we expect Yeshua to return soon, we must own up to the truth. The Holy Spirit gave me the inspiration on July 15, 2011, to clear up the confusion surrounding the day of His crucifixion. Most of Christendom observes Good Friday as the day Yeshua was crucified. It is a lie from the pit of hell. Some hold to the opinion that He was crucified on Thursday, others believe on Wednesday, which more people come to believe after they study the truth of the Scriptures for themselves.

During the last week of His ministry, Yeshua fulfilled this messianic prophecy. His triumphant entry into Jerusalem before His crucifixion fulfilled the prophecy of His being the Messiah in Zechariah 9:9, *Rejoice greatly, O daughter of Zion; shout, O daughter of Jerusalem: behold, thy King cometh unto thee: He is just, and having salvation: lowly, and riding upon an ass, and upon a colt the foal of an ass.* Matthew describes it in Chapter 21:1–14,

> *And when they drew nigh unto Jerusalem, and were come to Beth-pha-ge, unto the mount of Olives, then sent Jesus two disciples, Saying unto them, Go into the village over against you, and straightway ye shall find an ass tied, and a colt with her: loose them, and bring them unto me. And if any man say ought unto you, ye shall say, The Lord hath need of them; and straightway he will send them. All this was done, that it might be fulfilled which was spoken by the prophet, saying, Tell ye the daughter of Sion, Behold, thy King cometh unto thee, meek, and sitting upon an ass, and a colt the foal of an ass. And the disciples went, and did as Jesus commanded them. And brought the ass, and the colt, and put on them their clothes, and they set him thereon. And a very great multitude spread their garments in the way; others cut down branches from the trees and strawed them in the way. And the multitude that went before, and that followed, cried, saying, Hosanna to the son of David: Blessed is he that cometh in the name of the Lord; Hosanna in the highest. And when he was come into Jerusalem, all the city was moved, saying, Who is this? And the multitude said, this is Jesus the prophet of Nazareth of Galilee. And Jesus went into the temple of God, and cast out all them that sold and bought in the temple, and overthrew the tables of the moneychangers, and the seats of them that sold doves, and said unto them, It is written, My house shall be called the house of prayer; but ye have made it a den of thieves. And the blind and the lame came to him in the temple; and he healed them.*

Yeshua arrived in Jerusalem on the eve of Nisan 9 to fulfill His Father's will that He be the Lamb of God who would take away the sins of the world. Lambs chosen for Passover must be separated from their parents for seven days before the day of preparation. Yeshua was anointed for His death by Mary on Nisan 10. A sacrificial lamb must be anointed on this day—four days before Passover. In the year Yeshua was crucified, Nisan

10 was indicated to be a Saturday Sabbath. Four days later, on Wednesday, Yeshua was crucified. Yeshua not only must have fulfilled every specific prophecy, but also every example, or He could not have been the Messiah. John the Baptist pointed to Yeshua and declared in John 1:36, *And looking upon Jesus as he walked, he saith, Behold the Lamb of God!*

The lamb who was to take away the sins of the world must have been sacrificed on the day of preparation. If not, He would not have fulfilled the prophecies that identified Him as the Messiah. Yeshua had to fulfill every prophecy related to His first coming: to be born of a virgin, to be born in Bethlehem, to open the eyes of the blind, to make the deaf hear, to make the lame leap like deer, to be betrayed for thirty pieces of silver, to be beaten, to be cut off from the land of the living for the sins of others, and dozens of other prophecies foretold by the prophets. He came in "the fullness of the time." *But when the fullness of the time was come, God sent forth his Son, made of a woman, made under the law, to redeem them that were under the law, that we might receive the adoption of sons. And because ye are sons, God hath sent forth the Spirit of his Son into your hearts, crying, Abba, Father. Wherefore thou art no more a servant, but a son; and if a son, then an heir of God through Christ* (Galatians 4:4–7). The day and the hour He was nailed to the cross and raised from the grave was important.

Paul describes in 1 Corinthians 5:7, *Purge out therefore the old leaven, that ye may be a new lump, as ye are unleavened. For even Christ our Passover is sacrificed for us.*

The primary reason the vast majority of Christendom accepts Friday as the day of the crucifixion is that Yeshua was crucified on the day of preparation—the day before the Sabbath. Jewish Sabbath refers not only to the last day of the week (Saturday), but also to certain holy days or feast days. He was laid in the tomb just prior to the High Sabbath, not on the regular Saturday Sabbath.

We read in John 19:31–33,

The Jews therefore, because it was the preparation, that the bodies should not remain upon the cross on the Sabbath day, (for the Sabbath day was an high day) besought Pilate that their legs might be broken, and that they might be taken away. Then came the soldiers, and break the legs of the first, and of the other which was crucified with him. But when they came to Jesus, and saw that he was dead already, they break not his legs.

Yeshua was laid in the tomb minutes before the beginning of the High Sabbath at 6:00 p.m., the twelfth Hebrew hour. Thursday began a few minutes later.

If, as the majority of Christians believe, Yeshua was crucified on Friday, His body would have lain in the tomb for only twenty-four to twenty-six hours—one night and one day. It is evident from the Book of Esther, the Book of Jonah, and other Scriptures that when a time period is given as one day and one night, it is equal to twenty-four hours. Two days and two nights mean forty-eight hours; three days and three nights means seventy-two hours.

Thorough study of the Bible reveals that Yeshua's birth, crucifixion, and resurrection have been fraudulently reported. We should know and believe the truth before we can accept that at His return in the clouds He will catch us up in the Rapture.

Following is a day by day and hourly description of the process. The biblical evidence definitely places the crucifixion of Christ on a Wednesday. The Friday crucifixion is always justified on the ground that the Jews counted a part of a day as a full day, therefore enabling the three days and three nights to be encompassed in a Friday to a Sunday. However, the scriptures, when carefully examined, do not verify this tradition as it was stated here.

Nisan 14: Lord's Passover (Israel's Passover preparation day)

Tuesday, 6:00 p.m. (first watch): Yeshua observed Passover in the upper room with His apostles. (There was no lamb; Yeshua Himself was to be the lamb).

Tuesday, 9:00 p.m. (second watch): Yeshua was arrested and taken to Caiaphas to be judged.

Tuesday, 12:00 a.m. (third watch): Yeshua was judged and found guilty of blasphemy by the Sanhedrin.

Wednesday, 6:00 a.m. (first hour): Yeshua was taken to Pilate at the Antonia Fortress to be sentenced.

Wednesday, 9:00 a.m. (third hour): Yeshua was nailed to the cross.

Wednesday, 12:00 p.m.: Darkness fell over the earth until the ninth hour.

Wednesday, 3:00 p.m. (ninth hour): Yeshua died and gave up the ghost.

Nisan 15: Israel's Passover Day—First Day of Unleavened Bread

Wednesday, 6:00 p.m.: Yeshua's body was placed in the tomb.

Wednesday, 6:00 p.m. to Thursday, 6:00 p.m.: Yeshua's body was in the tomb for one night and one day (twenty-four hours).

Nisan 16: Second Day of Unleavened Bread

Thursday, 6:00 p.m. to Friday, 6:00 p.m.: Yeshua's body laid in the tomb for a second night and second day (forty-eight hours).

Nisan 17: Third Day of Unleavened Bread (Jewish Sabbath)

Friday, 6:00 p.m. to Saturday, 6:00 p.m.: Yeshua's body lay in the tomb for three day (seventy-two hours). *For as Jonas was three days and three nights in the whale's belly: so shall the Son of man be three days and three nights in the heart of the earth.* (Matthew 12:40). Yeshua declared in John 14:19b, *Because I live, ye shall live also.*

Many people fasten a mezuzah to their front door. Some even have them in additional rooms in their home. In 2009, I bought a pretty ceramic one, which had the Scriptures from the Torah rolled up inside (Ex. 13:2–17; Deut. 6:4–9 & 13–23). When I tried to nail mine on the doorpost of my front door with a very long nail without touching the mezuzah itself, it broke into three pieces. Since I'm "born again" I have accepted Yeshua in my heart. The Holy Spirit revealed to me later that day that I have the Scriptures written on my heart, as stated in Hebrews 8:10. As such, I don't need the reminder of a mezuzah or phylacteries that contain these Scriptures strapped to different places on my body, as many Jewish people do. It is the Holy Spirit's job to guide me daily and convict me from within if I sin. But I need to know Him first. Why go backwards again?

I read in 'Jewish Voice Connections' August 2011 where Marcela Goldstein wrote that the enemy hates all believers, but the ones he hates the most are Jewish believers, simply because he is trying to postpone the return of the Lord, and that will happen when the Jewish People claim 'Baruch Haba B'Shem Adonai' or 'blessed is He who comes in the name of the Lord.' Satan knows he is already defeated, but he tries to delay his definitive destruction, bringing a variety of delays, opposition, financial oppression, and diseases to our Jewish ministries.

When Daniel prophesied of the coming antichrist, he said, *Thus shall he do in the most strong holds with a strange god, whom he shall acknowledge and increase with glory: and he shall cause them to rule over many, and shall divide the land for a gain* (Daniel 11:39). This is not to take place until the antichrist has arrived. In the meantime, Jerusalem is not to be split.

I like to examine Israel's necessary dependence on God at different times. Only after all resources and confidence in their ability to help themselves had vanished did they turn to God, Who had been waiting all along. Are we not like that today?

Let me refresh your memory with a few examples. After Adam lost the title deed to Satan, the Messiah took it away from him and redeemed Israel by shedding His blood on the cross. Throughout history, Israel's survival was threatened numerous times and the only way they could overcome their difficulties was through the realization of their dependence on God's commitment. The United Nations was of no help. We will experience the same thing ourselves as a result of the push to divide Jerusalem. In time, all the countries of the world will forsake you. The only way out of your situation is through God Almighty. Let's read about how God has miraculously intervened in the past to ensure Israel's survival.

1. In the times of Abraham, Jacob, and Joseph, there was a great famine. With each famine, they were threatened with starvation. When Abraham first arrived in the land of Canaan, we read in Genesis 12:10, *and there was a famine in the land: and Abram went down into Egypt to sojourn there; for the famine was grievous in the land.* It was then that he told his wife to lie and say she was his sister. Next, Joseph the dreamer was sold to Ishmaelites as a slave. The Ishmaelites were on their way to Egypt to sell spices. In turn, they sold Joseph to Potiphar, an officer of pharaoh's guard in Egypt. What the brothers had meant for evil, God turned to good and protected them from starvation later. Joseph was promoted to second in command under the Pharaoh himself.

Then there passed by Midianites merchantmen; and they drew and lifted up Joseph out of the pit, and sold Joseph to the Ishmaelites for twenty pieces of silver; and they brought Joseph into Egypt. And when all the land of Egypt was famished, the people cried to Pharaoh for bread: and Pharaoh said unto all the Egyptians, Go unto Joseph; what he saith to you, do. And the famine was over all the face of the earth: and Joseph opened all the storehouses, and sold unto the Egyptian; and the famine waxed sore in the land of Egypt. And all countries came into Egypt to Joseph for to buy corn; because that the famine was so sore in all the lands. Now when Jacob saw that there was corn in Egypt, Jacob said unto his sons, Why do ye look one upon another? And he said, Behold, I have heard that there is corn in Egypt: get you down thither, and buy for us from thence; that we may live, and not die. And the sons of Israel came to buy corn among those that came: for the famine was in the land of Canaan. And Joseph said unto them, Fear not: for am I in the place of God? But as for you, ye thought evil against me; but God meant it unto good, to bring to pass, as it is this day, to save much people alive. (Genesis 37:28; 41:55–57; 42:1–2 and 5; 50:19–21).

2. Then it appeared as if there were no children being born to Abraham and Sarah. Yet his descendents, which God told him were to be as many as the stars of the heavens and the sand on the beach, seemed only a dream. Again, God comes to the rescue. It is beautifully described in Romans 4:18–21,

Who against hope believed in hope, that he might become the father of many nations, according to that which was spoken, So shall thy seed be. And being not weak in faith, he considered not his own body now dead, when he was about an hundred years old, neither yet the deadness of Sarah's womb: He staggered not at the promise of God through unbelief; but was strong in faith, giving glory to God; And being fully persuaded that, what he had promised, he was able also to perform.

3. This time, Pharaoh gave orders to the midwives to kill the Jewish baby boys at birth. Why? Did he think the baby girls would grow into women and someday marry these men? Or, even worse, become slaves so that within one generation, all Israelites would be extinguished? God must have put the right words into the midwives' mouths, as explained in Exodus 1:15–22,

*And the king of Egypt spake to the Hebrew midwives, of which the name of
the one was Shiphrah, and the name of the other Puah: And he said, When
ye do the office of a midwife to the Hebrew women, and see them upon the
stools; if it be a son, then ye shall kill him: but if it be a daughter, then
she shall live. But the midwives feared God, and did not as the king of
Egypt commanded them, but saved the men children alive. And the king of
Egypt called for the midwives, and said unto them, Why have ye done this
thing, and have saved the men children alive? And the midwives said unto
Pharaoh, Because the Hebrew women are not as the Egyptian women;
for they are lively, and are delivered ere the midwives come unto them.
Therefore God dealt well with the midwives: and the people multiplied,
and waxed very mighty. And it came to pass, because the midwives feared
God, that he made them houses. And Pharaoh charged all his people, saying, Every son that is born ye shall cast into the river, and every daughter
ye shall save alive.*

This was around the time of Moses' birth, so his fate was also at
stake. What a mighty man of God he turned out to be. Was God in on
his protection? You'd better believe it. He trusted him in the hands of
Pharaoh's own daughter.

*And the woman conceived, and bare a son: and when she saw him that
he was a goodly child, she hid him three months. And when she could not
longer hide him, she took for him an ark of bulrushes, and daubed it with
slime and with pitch, (waterproof) and put the child therein; and she laid
it in the flags by the river's brink. And his sister stood afar off, to wit what
would be done to him. And the daughter of Pharaoh came down to wash
herself at the river; and her maidens walked along by the river's side; and
when she saw the ark among the flags, she sent her maid to fetch it. And
when she had opened it, she saw the child: and, behold, the babe wept.
And she had compassion on him, and said, This is one of the Hebrews'
children. Then said his sister to Pharaoh's daughter, Shall I go and call
thee a nurse of the Hebrew women, that she may nurse the child for thee?
And Pharaoh's daughter said to her, Go. And the maid went and called
the child's mother. And Pharaoh's daughters said unto her, Take this child
away, and nurse it for me, and I will give thee thy wages. And the woman
took the child, and nursed it. And the child grew, and she brought him*

unto Pharaoh's daughter, and he became her son. And she called his name Moses: and she said, because I drew him out of the water. And it came to pass in those days, when Moses was grown, that he went out unto his brethren, and looked on their burdens (Exodus 2:2–11a).

4. Another time, God came to the rescue when Pharaoh and his army drowned in pursuit of the Israelites who had run away after they had been allowed to gather and worship in Exodus 14:5–7, 10, 13–17, 21–23, 26–31, and 15:1–2,

And it was told the king of Egypt that the people fled: and the heart of Pharaoh and of his servants was turned against the people, and they said, why have we done this, that we have let Israel go from serving us? And he made ready his chariot, and took his people with him: And he took six hundred chosen chariots, and all the chariots of Egypt, and captains over every one of them. And when Pharaoh drew nigh, the children of Israel lifted up their eyes, and, behold, the Egyptians marched after them; and they were sore afraid: and the children of Israel cried out unto the LORD. And Moses said unto the people, Fear ye not, stand still, and see the salvation of the LORD, which he will shew to you today: for the Egyptians whom ye have seen today, ye shall see them again no more for ever. The LORD shall fight for you, and ye shall hold your peace. And the LORD said unto Moses, Wherefore criest thou unto me? speak to the children of Israel, that they go forward: But lift thou up thy rod, and stretch out thine hand over the sea, and divide it: and the children of Israel shall go on dry ground through the midst of the sea. And I, behold, I will harden the hearts of the Egyptians, and they shall follow them: and I will get me honor upon Pharaoh, and upon all his host, upon his chariots, and upon his horsemen. And Moses stretched out his hand over the sea; and the LORD caused the sea to go back by a strong east wind all that night, and made the sea dry land, and the waters were divided. And the children of Israel went into the midst of the sea upon the dry ground: and the waters were a wall unto them on their right hand, and on their left. And the Egyptians pursued, and went in after them to the midst of the sea, even all Pharaoh's horses, his chariots, and his horsemen. And the LORD said unto Moses, Stretch out thine hand over the sea, that the waters may come again upon the Egyptians, upon their chariots, and upon their horsemen.

And Moses stretched forth his hand over the sea, and the sea returned to his strength when the morning appeared; and the Egyptians fled against it; and the LORD overthrew the Egyptians in the midst of the sea. And the waters returned, and covered the chariots, and the horsemen, and all the host of Pharaoh that came into the sea after them; there remained not so much as one of them. But the children of Israel walked upon dry land in the midst of the sea; and the waters were a wall unto them on their right hand and on their left. Thus the LORD saved Israel that day out of the hand of the Egyptians; and Israel saw the Egyptians dead upon the seashore. And Israel saw that great work which the LORD did upon the Egyptians: and the people feared the LORD, and believed the LORD, and his servant Moses. Then sang Moses and the children of Israel this song unto the LORD, for he hath triumphed gloriously: the horse and his rider hath he thrown into the sea. The LORD is my strength and song, and he is become my salvation: he is my God, and I will prepare him a habitation; my father's God, and I will exalt him.

I remember singing this song in some of our congregations several years ago. Is this not an awesome account of God's provision and deliverance of His people?

5. What should have been a trip of eleven days for all of them to reach the Promised Land took the Israelites forty years, because of their rebellion. All the children of Israel murmured against Moses and Aaron: and the whole congregation said unto them, Would God that we had died in the land of Egypt. Therefore God allowed part of the generation of the Israelites to die off, with the exception of Joshua and Caleb. Moses had previously sent ten spies to check out and possess the land, as God had called him to do. Only Joshua and Caleb returned with a good report, that they could conquer and overtake the inhabitants as described in Numbers 14:7–12a,

And they spake unto all the company of the children of Israel, saying, the land, which we passed through to search it, is an exceeding good land. If the LORD delights in us, then he will bring us into this land, and give it us: a land which floweth with milk and honey. Only rebel not ye against the LORD, neither fear ye the people of the land; for they are bread for us: their defense is departed from them, and the LORD is with us: fear them not. But all the congregation bade stone them with stones. And the glory of the LORD appeared in the tabernacle of the congregation before all the children of Israel. And the LORD said unto Moses, How long will this people provoke me? And how long will it be ere they believe me, for all the signs which I have shewed among them? I will smite them with the pestilence, and disinherit them.

Yet these entire years God took care of them. He fed them daily Manna, neither did their shoes nor their clothes wear out. They still developed a murmuring spirit and wanted to go back to Egypt.

6. Israel's survival was once again at stake when the Israelites forsook the Lord and followed other gods. Their idolatry and sin angered God greatly, but in His mercy He sent judges to deliver them, as seen in Judges 2:1-2 & 11-15,

And an angel of the LORD came up from Gilgal to Bochim, and said, I made you to go up out of Egypt, and have brought you unto the land which I sware unto your fathers; and I said, I will never break my covenant with you. And ye shall make no league with the inhabitants of this land; ye shall throw down their altars: but ye have not obeyed my voice: why have ye done this? And the children of Israel did evil in the sight of the LORD, and served Baalim: And they forsook the LORD God of their fathers, which brought them out of the land of Egypt, and followed other gods, of the gods of the people that were round about them, and bowed themselves unto them, and provoked the LORD to anger. And they forsook the LORD, and served Baal and Ashtaroth. And the anger of the LORD was hot against Israel, and he delivered them into the hands of spoilers that spoiled them, and he sold them into the hands of their enemies round about, so that they could not any longer stand before their enemies. Whithersoever they went out, the hand of the LORD was against them for evil, as the LORD had said, and as the LORD had sworn unto them: and they were greatly distressed.

7. In the eighth century BC only a miracle of God spared Judah from the destruction of the Assyrian invasion. Israel's ten

northern tribes had already been taken captive in 722 BC when they surrounded Jerusalem to conquer it. The Lord intervened through the devotion of King Hezekiah. The angel of the Lord delivered the Jewish people in one night with the killing of 185,000 Assyrians.

In the ninth year of Hoshea the king of Assyria took Samaria, and carried Israel away into Assyria, and placed them in Halah and in Habor by the river of Gozan, and in the cities of the Medes. For so it was, that the children of Israel had sinned against the LORD their God, which had brought them up out of the land of Egypt, from under the hand of Pharaoh king of Egypt, and had feared other gods. And walked in the statutes of the heathen, whom the LORD cast out from before the children of Israel, and of the kings of Israel, which they had made. And the children of Israel did secretly those things that were not right against the LORD their God, and they built them high places in all their cities, from the tower of the watchmen to the fenced city. And they set them up images and groves in every high hill, and under every green tree: And there they burnt incense in all the high places, as did the heathen whom the LORD carried away before them; and wrought wicked things to provoke the LORD to anger: For they served idols, whereof the LORD had said unto them, Ye shall not do this thing. Yet the LORD testified against Israel, and against Judah, by all the prophets, and by all the seers, saying, Turn ye from your evil ways, and keep my commandments and my statutes according to all the law which I commanded your fathers, and which I sent to you by my servants the prophets. Notwithstanding they would not hear, but hardened the necks, like to the neck of their fathers, that did not believe in the LORD their God. And they rejected his statutes, and his covenant that he made with their fathers, and his testimonies which he testified against them; and they followed vanity, and became vain, and went after the heathen that were round about them, concerning whom the LORD had charged them, that they should not do like them. And they left all the commandments of the LORD their God, and made them molten images, even two calves, and made a grove, and worshipped all the host of heaven, and served Baal. And they caused their sons and their daughters to pass through the fire, and used divination and enchantments, and sold themselves to the devil in the sight of the LORD, to provoke him to anger. Therefore the LORD was very angry with Israel, and removed them out of his sight: there was none left but the tribe of Judah only. Also Judah kept not the commandments of the LORD their God, but walked in the statutes of Israel, which they made. And the LORD rejected all the seed of Israel, and afflicted them, and delivered them into the hand of spoilers, until he had cast them out of his sight. (2 Kings 17:6–20).

8. Judah's rebellion against God and His prophets, who warned them time and again, is the result of the following Scriptures:

Moreover all the chief of the priests, and the people, transgressed very much after all the abominations of the heathen; and polluted the house of the LORD which he had hallowed in Jerusalem. And the LORD God of their fathers sent to them by his messengers, rising up betimes, and sending; because he had compassion on his people, and on his dwelling place: But they mocked the messengers of God, and despised his words, and misused his prophets, until the wrath of the LORD arose against his people, till there was no remedy. Therefore he brought upon them the king of the Chaldees, who slew their young men with the sword in the house of their sanctuary, and had no compassion upon young man or maiden, old man, or him that stooped for age: he gave them all into his hand. And all the vessels of the house of God, great and small, and the treasures of the house of the LORD, and the treasures of the king, and of his princes, all these he brought to Babylon. And they burnt the house of God, and brake down the wall of Jerusalem, and burnt all the palaces thereof with fire, and destroyed all the goodly vessels thereof. And them that had escaped from the sword carried he away to Babylon; where they were servants to him and his sons until the reign of the kingdom of Persia. (2 Chronicles 36:14–20).

9. Through Esther's brave intervention, directed by God, the Jewish people survived the threat of extinction once more. They remember her courageous act yearly at the feast of Purim. Haman was promoted to grand vizier by the king, and lower-ranking officials were ordered to pay homage to him. Mordecai, Esther's uncle, refused, which enraged Haman. He refused because he was a Benjamite and Haman was a descendant of Agag, the king of Amalek—Israel's bitter

enemy. In revenge, Haman plotted to exterminate the Jews and offered the king ten thousand talents—equivalent to 30 million shekels. (1 talent is 60 minas, 1 mina is 50 shekels. 60x50 is 3,000 shekels, ten thousand talents x 3,000 shekels is 30 million shekels) Ahasuerus, the Persian king, refused the bribe, but the order of annihilation was stamped by his signet ring. The decree was published by the couriers and the commandment was given in every province. The Jews fasted and there was great mourning among them. Esther decided to see the king on the third day of her fast. She was risking her life by visiting the king uninvited. She asked him and Haman to a banquet. Maybe you would like to read the whole book of Esther. Although Satan had already figured out the plot, and through Haman he would exterminate the Jews, God nixed his plan.

Then Mordecai commanded to answer Esther, Think not with thyself that thou shalt escape in the king's house, more than all the Jews. For if thou altogether holdest thy peace at this time, then shall there enlargement and deliverance arise to the Jews from another place; but thou and thy father's house shall be destroyed: and who knoweth whether thou art come to the kingdom for such a time as this? Then Esther bade them return Mordecai this answer, Go, gather together all the Jews that are present in Shushan, and fast ye for me, and neither eat nor drink three days, night or day: I also and my maidens will fast likewise; and so will I go in unto the king, which is not according to the law: and if I perish, I perish. So Mordecai went his way, and did according to all that Esther had commanded him. Now it came to pass on the third day, that Esther put on her royal apparel, and stood in the inner court of the king's house, over against the king's house: and the king sat upon his royal throne in the royal house, over against the gate of the house. Then said the king unto her, what wilt thou, queen Esther? and what is thy request? it shall be even given thee to the half of the kingdom. And Esther answered, If it seem good unto the king, let the king and Haman come this day unto the banquet that I have prepared for him. Yet all this availeth me nothing, so long as I see Mordecai the Jew sitting at the king's gate. Then said Zeresh his wife and all his friends unto him, Let a gallows be made of fifty cubits high, and tomorrow speak thou unto the king that Mordecai may be hanged thereon: then go thou in merrily with the king unto the banquet. And the thing pleased Haman; and he caused the gallows to be made. On that night could not the king sleep, and he commanded to bring the book of records of the chronicles; and they were read before the king. And it was found written, that Mordecai had told of Bigthana and Teresh, two of the king's chamberlains, the keepers of the door, who sought to lay hand on the king Ahasuerus. And the king said, What honor and dignity hath been done to Mordecai for this? Then said the king's servants that ministered unto him, There is nothing done for him. So Haman came in. And the king said unto him, what shall be done unto the man whom the king delighteth to honor? Now Haman thought in his heart, To whom would the king delight to do honor more than to myself? And Haman answered the king, For the man whom the king delighteth to honor. Let the royal apparel be brought which the king useth to wear, and the horse that the king rideth upon, and the crown royal which is set upon his head. Then took Haman the apparel and the horse, and arrayed Mordecai, and brought him on horseback through the street of the city, and proclaimed before him, Thus shall it be done unto the man whom the king delighteth to honor. And the king said again unto Esther on the second day at the banquet of wine, What is thy petition, Queen Esther? and it shall be granted thee: and what is thy request? And it shall be performed, even to the half of the kingdom. And Esther the queen answered and said, If I have found favor in thy sight, O king, and if it please the king, let my life be given me at my petition, and my people at my request: For we are sold, I and my people, to be destroyed, to be slain, and to perish. But if we had been sold for bondmen and bondwomen, I had held my tongue, although the enemy could not countervail the king's damage. Then the king Ahasuerus answered and said unto Esther the queen, who is he, and where is he, that durst presume in his heart to do so? And Esther said, the adversary and enemy is this wicked Haman. Then Haman was afraid before the king and the queen. And Harbonah, one of the chamberlains, said before the king, Behold also, the gallows fifty cubits high, which Haman had made for Mordecai, who had spoken good for the king, standeth in the house of Haman. Then the king said, Hang him thereon. So they hanged Haman on the gallows that he had prepared for Mordecai. Then was the king's wrath pacified. On that day did the king Ahasuerus give the house of Haman the Jew's enemy unto Esther the queen. And Mordecai came before the king; for Esther had told what he was unto her. And the king took off his ring, which he had taken from Haman, and gave it unto Mordecai. And Esther set Mordecai over the house of Haman. And Esther spake yet again before the king, and fell down at his feet, and besought him with tears to put away the mischief of Haman the Agagite, and his device that he had devised against the Jews. Then the king held out the golden scepter toward Esther. So Esther arose, and stood before the king, And said, If it please the king, and if I have found favor in his sight, and the thing seem right before the king, and I be pleasing in his eyes, let it be written to reverse the letters devised by Haman the son of Hammedatha the Agagite, which he wrote to destroy the Jews which are in all the king's provinces: For how can I endure to see the destruction of my kindred? Then the king Ahasuerus said unto Esther the queen and Mordecai the Jew, Behold, I have given Esther the house of Haman, and him they have hanged upon the gallows, because he laid his hand upon the Jews. (Esther 4:13–17; 5:1, 3–4, 13–14; 6:1–3, 6–8, 11; 7:2–6, 9 & 10; 8:1–7).

10. The Romans tried to destroy Israel from around 66 AD to 73 AD. Finally, in 70 AD, they burned Jerusalem to the ground under the leadership of the Roman general Titus. Again a remnant was spared. Yeshua Himself had prophesied it some forty years before, about a month before His crucifixion. He had already raised Jairus's daughter and the widow's son from Nain. When He raised Lazarus after being dead for four days, the Pharisees definitely wanted Yeshua killed. We read of the Roman occupation afterward. Yeshua said in Luke 21:20–24,

And when ye see Jerusalem compassed with armies, and then know that the desolation thereof is nigh. Then let them which are in Judea flee to the mountains; and let them which are in the midst of it depart out; and let not them that are in the countries enter thereunto. For these are the days of vengeance, that all things which are written may be fulfilled. But woes unto them that are with child, and to them that give suck, in those days! For there shall be great distress in the land, and wrath upon this people.

And they shall fall by the edge of the sword, and shall be led away captive into all nations: and Jerusalem shall be trodden down of the Gentiles, until the times of the Gentiles are fulfilled.

And in John 11:48: If we let him thus alone, all men will believe on him: and the Romanss hall come and take away both our place and nation.

11. Israel's survival was threatened throughout the Christian era, and it still is today. Christianity got a bad name because some who called themselves Christian are only religious people and fanatics. Throughout history, we have witnessed anti-Semitism. The most serious time of persecution was the Holocaust under Hitler's reign in Germany, when an estimated six million Jews were exterminated. Hitler misled many, as they sat by silently or even helped promote his evil plans. But there were also some who risked or lost their lives trying to hide Jews. The Jewish people endured a lot, many being cast from their homeland for many years, not to mention the awful memories Holocaust survivors still hold to this day.

Although I was able to show that I am an American citizen at the airport in Tel Aviv on my second trip to Israel, my German accent gave me away and my video camera was confiscated, including the videotape. My suitcases were searched and the gifts that I had purchased weren't wrapped back up properly, so a few pieces broke. Why? Because I had stayed with an Arab family or because I am German-born? I was returning from Ghana, West Africa, and stopped to visit my Arabic Christian friends outside of Bethlehem for a few days. It gave me a chance to see and film some biblical sites. I can understand now that the father-in-law of my friend was screaming as I taped the surrounding area from their balcony, with him standing below. He did not want any harm come to him because of me. I tried to inform my Arabic friends of the way I was being treated at the airport, but their phone connections were cut off.

You had to have been there among the locals during that time to understand both sides—that of the Arabs and the Jews. A reminder to any person traveling on their own: have the phone number of the American embassy with you so you can call for help if needed. The man who checked my luggage told me I could not take the video camera on the airplane with me. He would not allow me to board my flight. In fact, he told one of the flight attendants in my presence that I was not to board. I was flying to Germany to visit my ailing father and had contacted my sister to let her know what time I would arrive at the airport in Munich. I could not wait for another flight since she would be traveling from quite a distance away to pick me up, so I had to give in to his demands in order to make my connection. After my return to the USA, I wrote to the proper Israeli authorities several times to request the replacement of my video camera. I was told in a return letter that my case had been turned over to an insurance company. I received a second letter with the same response when I tried again. I am still waiting for them to make good on confiscating my property.

In reality, I should have been so upset that I would be unable to speak to the Jewish couple next to me on the airplane. Instead, I shared Scriptures from the Torah with them. They were from Hebron and were astounded at my knowledge of their country and the Torah. When we landed in Germany, I was kind enough to give them enough German marks so that they could get a taxi to their hotel. Instead of an eye for an eye, I practiced true Christianity by sharing with them what they were in need of.

In my earlier studies, I learned that in 1948, Israel was reborn as a nation and awarded its homeland by the British. You have to admit that it was an act of God. Britain was running short of acetone used to manufacture high explosives for torpedo boats. A Russian Jewish chemist, Dr. Cheim Weizmann who had lived in England for twenty years, invented the substitute for the much-needed explosive material. He offered it free of charge—asking in return that Palestine be freed from the oppression of the Turks and become a national homeland for the Jewish people. The Turks fled without one shot being fired.

I read a long time ago that in the course of its history, Jerusalem has been destroyed fourteen times. It bounced back every time. Why? First, God called Abraham from his homeland in Genesis 12:1–2, *Now the LORD had said unto Abram, Get thee out of thy country, and from thy kindred, and from thy father's house, unto the land that I will shew thee: and I will make of thee a great nation, and I will bless thee, and make thy name great; and thou shalt be a blessing.* Then God gave Abraham the land as a gift in Genesis 17:8, *And I will give unto thee and to thy seed after thee, the land wherein thou art a stranger, all the land of Canaan, for an everlasting possession; and I will be their God.* Anyone who wants to control Israel will have to fight God. Those who fight God should give up; there is no chance for victory. *As birds flying, so will the LORD of hosts defend Jerusalem; defending also he will deliver it; and passing over he will preserve it* (Isaiah 31:5). Is this why we call it the *Promised Land?* Even after being dispersed in 70 AD for more then 1900 years, the Jews returned. God told them in Ezekiel 36:24 *For I will take you from among the heathen, and gather you out of all countries, and will bring you into your own land.*

God gave us free will to choose our destiny. Instead, the people wanted their own way without God, just as many of us do. Yeshua Himself said in Luke 13:34, *O Jerusalem, Jerusalem, which killest the prophets, and stonest them that are sent unto thee; how often would I have gathered thy children together as a hen doth gather her brood under her wings, and ye would not!* We can get into all kinds of trouble by being disobedient. The Jewish people have been wandering the earth for many years, despised and homeless. They suffered great persecution but were never totally destroyed. From a human standpoint, it seemed they were doomed for extinction. It is said that the total number of Holocaust victims may be close to seven million. At least half a million Jews were killed in the Soviet Union during the six months leading up to December 1941.

I lived in Germany for the first twenty-five years of my life and can recall the war as a child. I became an American citizen in 1967, as soon as I was eligible. I feel an urgent need to ask all Jewish people for forgiveness for what Adolph Hitler—who was not even a German; he was born in Austria—or any other German inflicted upon you. I am truly sorry. The people under him had to obey his orders or they would be locked up or worse. My own uncle made a comment against the Nazi party in a *Gasthaus.* The next day, he was picked up and put behind bars. After the war, he walked for several weeks from the camp he had been held in to my folks' home, pushing a heavy wooden wheelbarrow containing his few belongings. All this time, he had had no idea where his wife and infant child were. My folks had taken them in. He didn't even know if they were alive.

There is little known about the estimated ten thousand Germans who were killed in Russia. When Hitler attacked Russia, he liberated those who were remaining. A friend of mine was only a young girl when she left with her mother and some others. Her elderly mother told me they had walked for days, fearful of being caught by Russian soldiers. They were only women and children, the men were all at war. The drive for power can turn people into animals, especially in wartime. That is why they all need to meet Yeshua as their Messiah.

Again, Hitler was not a German. He received his German citizenship in Braunschweig. To top it off, he was part Jewish on his mother's side. According to my investigation, he was recruited by Dietrich Eckhart, who was a Satanist. Eckhart was supposedly told by satan to find a vessel for the body of antichrist and assumed he had found him in Hitler. Once in power, Hitler started the Third Reich and all his SS men were indoctrinated. The swastika on their uniform was their insignia. The Bible warns us in several different Scriptures: *Now the Spirit speaketh expressly, that in the latter times some shall depart from the faith, giving heed to seducing spirits, and doctrines of devils; speaking lies in hypocrisy; having their conscience seared with a hot iron* (1 Timothy 4:1–2). Yeshua said in John 8:44, *ye are of your father the devil, and the lusts of your father ye will do. He was a murderer from the beginning, and abode not in the truth, because there is no truth in him. When he speaketh a lie, he speaketh of his own: for he is a liar, and the father of it.*

From whence come wars and fighting's among you? come they not hence, even of your lusts that war in your members? Submit yourselves therefore to God. Resist the devil, and he will flee from you (James 4:1 & 7). *From Revelation 9:21, Neither repented they of their murders, nor of their sorceries, nor of their fornication, nor of their thefts.*

12. Once more, during the impending great tribulation, Israel's survival will be greatly threatened. It is prophesied in the Word of God. But nothing can happen that God does not allow. God's grace is what protects many of His people in

spite of their past sins and rebellions. God is faithful and His love and forgiveness are not shown to us because we are worthy of it or deserve it, but based on His plan and mercy. Yeshua foretold in Matthew 24:6–9,

And ye shall hear of wars and rumors of wars: see that ye be not troubled: for all these things must come to pass, but the end is not yet. For nation shall rise against nation, and kingdom against kingdom: and there shall be famines, and pestilences, and earthquakes, in divers places. And these are the beginning of sorrows. Then shall they deliver you up to be afflicted, and shall kill you: and ye shall be hated of all nations for my name's sake.

Are we not getting close to the time? The end mentioned is not the end of the world, it is the end of this age. But deliverance to all Israel is coming only through the Messiah Himself. Paul tells us of Yeshua's great deliverance in Romans 11:25–27,

For I would not, brethren that ye should be ignorant of this mystery, lest ye should be wise in your own conceits; that blindness in part is happened to Israel, until the fullness of the Gentiles be come in. And so all Israel shall be saved: as it is written, There shall come out of Sion the Deliverer, and shall turn away ungodliness from Jacob: For this is my covenant unto them, when I shall take away their sins.

Old Testament prophets proclaimed it in the Tanakh: *To appoint unto them that mourn in Zion, to give unto them beauty for ashes, the oil of joy for mourning, the garment of praise for the spirit of heaviness; that they might be called trees of righteousness, the planting of the LORD, that he might be glorified* (Isaiah 61:3). It is worth repeating that the Messiah will put His law in their minds and write it on their hearts, as described in Jeremiah 31:31–33,

Behold, the days come, saith the LORD, that I will make a new covenant with the house of Israel, and with the house of Judah, not according to the covenant that I made with their fathers in the day that I took them by the hand to bring them out of the land of Egypt; which my covenant they brake, although I was an husband unto them, saith the LORD: But this shall be the covenant that I will make with the house of Israel; After those days, saith the LORD, I will put my law in their inward parts, and write it in their hearts; and will be their God, and they shall be my people.

After those days, He says, He will make a covenant with the house of Israel, which is the Brit Chadasha. He will put His law in their inward parts by writing it on their hearts. Since it was prophesied as a future happening, that He will be their God and they will be His people, a born-again experience of the Jews was forthcoming which can happen anytime, as soon as you allow it. Paul wrote in Philippians 2:9–13,

Wherefore God also hath highly exalted him, and given him a name which is above every name: that at the name of Jesus every knee should bow, of things in heaven, and things in earth, and things under the earth; and that every tongue should confess that Jesus Christ is Lord, to the glory of God the Father. Wherefore, my beloved, as ye have always obeyed, not as in my presence only but now much more in my absence, work out your own salvation with fear and trembling. For it is God which worketh in you both to will and to do his good pleasure. Amos 9:15, And I will plant them upon their land, and they shall no more be pulled up out of their land which I have given them, saith the LORD thy God.

Why allow the experience of the seven years of tribulation to become a reality? Why don't you ask the Messiah into your heart so that you, too, can be caught up with the believers in Yeshua when He appears in the clouds to rapture us? Many in the past have claimed to be Yeshua—your Messiah. Why don't you ask God Himself if He had a son? He will give you the truth. We read in 2 Peter 3:9, *The Lord is not slack concerning his promise, as some men count slackness; but is longsuffering to usward, not willing that any should perish, but that all should come to repentance.*

A quarter of the Bible is devoted to prophecy, most of which has already been fulfilled. Eighty percent of the Bible deals with the Jews, telling of your past, present, and future. God has your future recorded and you can't run away from it. Why then is it so hard to obey Him? Have you ever asked yourself why we know so much about the history of the Jewish people, but not much about any other race or people? All thirty-nine books of the Tanakh were written by Jews, and only two of the twenty-six books of the Brit Chadasha was not written by a Jew—the Book of Luke and the Book of Acts

Many of you know that the musical instruments, garments, and utensils for the next temple have already been produced for several years in Jerusalem. They will be used when the third temple is built and blood sacrifice is restored, but it will be destroyed again after the antichrist has desecrated it. It must all come to pass because it was prophesied many years ago and is recorded in the Scriptures.

Those of you who accept Yeshua as your Messiah and are born again are called Messianic or completed Jews and don't need to wait for blood sacrifices. Yeshua shed His blood for our sins once and for all. We read in Hebrews 10:3–4 and 9:11–22,

But in those sacrifices there is a remembrance again made of sins every year. For it is not possible that the blood of bulls and of goats should take away sins. But Christ being come an high priest of good things to come, by a greater and more perfect tabernacle, not made with hands, that is to say, not of this building; neither by the blood of goats and calves, but by his own blood he entered in once into the holy place, having obtained eternal redemption for us. For if the blood of bulls and goats, and the ashes of an heifer sprinkling the unclean, sanctifies to the purifying of the flesh: How much more shall the blood of Christ, Who through the eternal Spirit offered himself without spot to God, purge your conscience from dead works to serve the living God? And for this cause he is the mediator of the New Testament (covenant), that by means of death, for the redemption of the transgressions that were under the first testament (covenant), they which are called might receive the promise of eternal Inheritance. For where a testament is, there must also of necessity be the death of the testator. For a testament is of force after men are dead: otherwise it is of no strength at all while the testator lives. Whereupon neither the first testament was dedicated without blood. For when Moses had spoken every precept to all the people according to the law, he took the blood of calves and of goats, with water, and scarlet wool, and hyssop, and sprinkled both the book, and all the people, saying, This is the blood of the testament (covenant) which God has enjoined upon you. Moreover he sprinkled with blood both the tabernacle, and all the vessels of the ministry. And almost all things are by the law purged with blood; and without shedding of blood is no remission.

At the beginning of July 1997, I watched an unusual program on Christian television. A cattle rancher from Texas who was raising red heifers gave a telephone interview. He said that a rabbi from Israel had inspected and approved four of them, which had been reproducing. In the beginning of the following year, he should have been able to deliver a multitude of pregnant red heifers to Israel. The one accepted, which they thought was the right one, turned out to have three white hairs, which made it not kosher and therefore unacceptable.

According to rabbinical standards, the animal used in the purification process is the only sacrifice for which the animal has to be a special color. The process must be performed outside the camp rather than at the altar. It is the only sacrifice that requires that the ashes be kept. The ashes are sprinkled in water to be used to purify priests before they can minister. The temple artifacts and the temple itself must also be readied.

Two thousand years ago, the last red heifer had to be perfect. He was judged for color, disposition, and quality. This will be the tenth one since Eleazar, which is believed to be the last one, and will introduce the Messiah according to rabbinical belief. I have heard it said that Israel never looked for the red heifer. Someone always provided one and at times, that someone was a Gentile.

The Temple Institute in Jerusalem announced on April 8th 2002 that less than a month before a red heifer was born in Israel. The rabbis who inspected her on the farm found her to be kosher and were satisfied that this heifer could indeed be a candidate to be used in the process of purification described in the book of Numbers. It was said, that it is an important development towards the rebuilding of the Holy Temple.

Here is the biblical account of the red heifer:

And the LORD spake unto Moses and unto Aaron, saying, This is the ordinance of the law which the LORD hath commanded, saying, Speak unto the children of Israel, that they bring thee a red heifer without spot, wherein is no blemish, and upon which never came yoke: And ye shall give her unto Eleazar the priest, that he may bring her forth without the camp, and one shall slay her before his face: And Eleazar the priest shall take of her blood with his finger, and sprinkle of her blood directly before the tabernacle of the congregation seven times: And one shall burn the heifer, in his sight; her skin, and her flesh, and her blood, with her dung, shall she burn: And the priest shall take cedar wood, and hyssop, and scarlet, and cast it into the midst of the burning of the heifer. Then the priest shall wash his clothes, and he shall bathe his flesh in water, and afterward he shall come to the camp, and the priest shall be unclean until the even. And he that burneth her shall wash his clothes in water, and bathe his flesh in water, and shall be unclean until the even. And a man that is clean shall gather up the ashes of the heifer, and lay them up without the camp in a clean place, and it shall be kept for the congregation of the children of Israel for a water of separation: it is a purification for sin. And he that gathereth the ashes of the heifer shall wash his clothes, and be unclean until the even: and it shall be unto the children of Israel, and unto the stranger that sojourneth among them, for a statute forever. (Numbers 19:1–10).

No heifers were sacrificed after the destruction of the temple in 70 AD. The ordinance of the red heifer has played a significant role in Jewish tradition. It must be killed when it is three years old according to Genesis 15:9a, *And he said unto him, Take me an heifer of three years old.* If the ashes cleanse outwardly, then the flesh and blood of Yeshua cleanses your conscience inwardly. I am curious as to how you have your sins forgiven now while you are waiting for the tribulation temple to be built?

The Expositor's Study Bible by Jimmy Swaggart explains in Numbers 19:9–10, that this was only a symbol of the real purification that would come with the death of Yeshua on the cross. In the symbol, the ashes would be mixed with water and then applied to that which was polluted. The Word *forever* pertained to the entirety of the time of the law. When Yeshua came, this was fulfilled and was no longer needed because His blood cleanses from all sin. It is reaffirmed in 1 John 1:7, *But if we walk in the light, as he is in the light, we have fellowship one with another, and the blood of Jesus Christ his Son cleanseth us from all sin.*

According to my studies, the blue dye needed in the making of the temple garments comes from the ink of a certain snail which had vanished for over thirteen hundred years and only several years ago appeared again on beaches. It is a certain blue called 'Techelet' in Hebrew which is much like royal blue, used in the making of temple garments. The name of the snail which produces this ink is called 'Chilazon'.

You will find in the Tanakh that a Rabbi came upon some hidden prophecies that were not discovered until a few years ago. God is giving us His secrets at His appointed time. There is no doubt Who He is and that the Tanakh is valid. We are instructed in Psalm 122:6, *pray for the peace of Jerusalem: they shall prosper that love thee.* Although people take a number of different positions in interpreting the future of Israel, the only truth is straight from the Word of God. Through the Jews, Messianic blessings came to mankind. The apostle Paul talks about his brethren according to the flesh in Romans 9:4–9,

Who are Israelites; to whom pertaineth the adoption, and the glory, and the covenants, and the giving of the law, and the service of God, and the promises; whose are the fathers, and of whom as concerning the flesh Christ came, who is over all, God blessed for ever. Amen. Not as though the word of God hath taken no effect. For they are not all Israel, which are of Israel: neither, because they are the seed of Abraham, are they all children: but in Isaac shall thy seed be called. That is, they which are the children of the flesh, these are not the children of God: but the children of the promise are counted for the seed. For this is the word of promise, at this time will I come, and Sarah shall have a son.

God also has a plan for Ishmael's descendants, which He will bless. This is also recorded in the Tanakh. If you read not only this book volume two, but also volume three when it is published, you will discover that God revealed to me in 1986 to bring you all together, which I will describe in Isaiah 19:16-25. Oh, what an awesome God! It began when He called Abraham away from his home who was not a Jew, but he was obedient to what God had planned for him and his descendants.

God made the covenant with Abram, later called Abraham, and called him out of his home country in Genesis 12:1–3, *Now the LORD had said unto Abram, Get thee out of thy country, and from thy kindred, and from thy father's house, unto a land that I will shew thee: And I will make of thee a great nation, and I will bless thee, and make thy name great; and thou shalt be a blessing: and I will bless them that bless thee, and curse him that curseth thee: and in thee shall all families of the earth be blessed.* "Families" in Hebrew is *mishpachah* (pronounced meesh-pah-chah). It means a family of people, a type, a class, or a tribe. It can be an immediate family, or as broad as a whole nation. In the foregoing Scripture, God called them all the families of the earth. The law described was given by Moses. Paul continues in Romans 1:16–17 and 10:1, *For I am not ashamed of the gospel of Christ: for it is the power of God unto salvation to every one that believeth; to the Jew first, and also to the Greek. (Gentile) For therein is the righteousness of God revealed from faith to faith: as it is written, The just shall live by faith. Brethren, my heart's desire and prayer to God for Israel is that they might be saved.*

Years ago, I heard a Jewish Rabbi say on Christian television, that a Jew does not think that he needs to be saved. Furthermore that the Brit Chadasha is a fabrication and he doesn't like goyim (Gentiles). Yet in increasing numbers, Jews are coming to know their Messiah. The Holy Spirit is opening their spiritual eyes and drawing them in. Many finally realize that they can receive their Messiah and still remain a Jew!

Corinthians 2:14-16 explains, *But the natural man receiveth not the things of the Spirit of God: for they are foolishness unto him: neither can he know them, because they are spiritually discerned. But he that is spiritual judgeth all things, yet he himself is judged of no man. For who hath known the mind of the Lord, that he may instruct him? But we have the mind of Christ.* Confirmed in Job 15:8 *Hast thou heard the secret of God? And dost thou restrain wisdom to thyself?*

We read that Nicodemus was searching for the truth in John 3:1-21, *There was a man of the Pharisees, named Nicodemus, a ruler of the Jews: The same came to Jesus by night, and said unto him, Rabbi, we know that thou art a teacher come from God: for no man can do these miracles that thou doest, except God be with him. Jesus answered and said unto him, Verily, verily, I say unto thee, Except a man be born again, he cannot see the kingdom of God. Nicodemus said unto him, How can a man be born when he is old? Can he enter the second time into his mother's womb, and be born? Jesus answered, Verily, verily, I say unto thee, Except a man be born of water and of the Spirit, he cannot enter into the kingdom of God. That which is born of the flesh is flesh; and that which is born of the Spirit is spirit. Marvel not that I said unto thee, Ye must be born again. The wind bloweth where it listeth, and thou hearest the sound thereof, but canst not tell whence it cometh, and whither it goeth: so is every one that is born of the Spirit. Nicodemus answered and said unto him, How can these things be? Jesus answered and said unto him, Art thou a master of Israel, and knowest not these things? Verily, verily, I say unto thee, We speak that we do know, and testify that we have seen; and ye receive not our witness. If I have told you earthly things, and ye believe not, how shall ye believe, if I tell you of heavenly things? And no man has ascended up to heaven, but he that came down from heaven, even the Son of man which is in heaven. And as Moses lifted up the serpent in the wilderness, even so must the Son of man be lifted up: That whosoever believeth in him should not perish, but have eternal life. For God so loved the world, that he gave his only begotten Son, that whosoever believeth in him, should not perish, but have everlasting life. For God sent not his Son into the world to condemn the world; but that the world through him might be saved. He that believeth on him is not condemned: but he that believeth not is condemned already, because he hath not believed in the name of the only begotten Son of God. And this is the condemnation, that light is come into the world, and men loved darkness rather then light, because their deeds were evil. For every one that doeth evil hateth the light, neither cometh to the light, lest his deeds should be reproved. But he that doeth truth cometh to the light, that his deeds might be made manifest, that they are wrought in God.*

I heard from a Jewish friend who had just recently returned from a visit to Israel that a lot of Jews have accepted their Messiah and many are in the process of doing so.

Yeshua Himself was Jewish. It is a historical fact that they laid Him in a tomb after they crucified Him on the cross. He rose after three days. Afterward, He ascended to heaven and sent us the Holy Spirit, who lives in us forever. Psalm 33:12 says, *Blessed is the nation whose God is the LORD; and the people whom he hath chosen for his own inheritance.* Followed by 2 Chronicles 6:6, *But I have chosen Jerusalem, that my Name might be there; and have chosen David to be over my people Israel.*

My dear people, God is talking about you. If you could only grasp it, Yeshua was the founder of Christianity and we are His followers. Does that seem strange to you? Is that why you live in denial? Many of you have been indoctrinated into believing that the Brit Chadasha, which has you still waiting for your Messiah, is fabricated. Some of your teachers need to admit that they are wrong in never accepting the Brit Chadasha themselves. Yeshua made this new covenant with them and therefore they should have been able to teach it to you. But many of you still choose to live only in the law that Moses taught. Following are a few Scriptures from the Tanakh that substantiate the truth. Yeshua was prophesied many hundreds of years ago by your Jewish prophets before he was ever born.

742 BC: *Therefore the Lord himself shall give you a sign. Behold a virgin shall conceive, and bear a son, and shall call his name Immanuel* (Isaiah 7:14).

710 BC: *But thou, Bethlehem Ephratah, though thou be little among the thousands of Judah, yet out of thee shall he come forth unto me that is to be ruler of Israel, whose goings forth have been of old, from everlasting* (Micah 5:2).

Yet have I set my king upon my holy hill of Zion (Psalm 2:6).

For dogs have compassed me: the assembly of the wicked have enclosed me: they pierced my hands and my feet (Psalm 22:16).

700 BC: *Who hath ascended up into heaven, or descended? Who hath gathered the wind in his fist? Who hath bound the waters in a garment? Who hath established all the ends of the earth? What is his name, and what is his son's name, if thou canst tell? Every word of God is pure: he is a shield unto them that put their trust in him* (Proverbs 30:4–5).

712 BC: *Surely he hath borne our griefs, and carried our sorrows: yet we did esteem him stricken, smitten of God, and afflicted* (Isaiah 53:4).

698 BC: *And the Redeemer shall come to Zion, and unto them that turn from transgression in Jacob, saith the LORD* (Isaiah 59:20).

519 BC: *Sing and rejoice, O daughter of Zion: for, lo, I come, and I will dwell in the midst of thee, saith the Lord* (Zechariah 2:10).

Who do you think these Scriptures talk about if not of Yeshua your Messiah?

It is said that Yeshua's second coming is mentioned 380 times in the Scriptures. I did not count them myself and hope this number is correct, but even if it were only mentioned ten times, and if you believe in God and the Tanakh, you have no choice but to accept and practice the truth. The keeping of rituals won't save you. Yeshua said in Matthew 9:13b, *For I am not come to call the Righteous, but sinners to Repentance.*

A Jewish man who is ministering to the Jewish people told me recently that there are many Jewish beliefs, from liberal to orthodox. However, most Jews today are secular and do not go to synagogue. Do you even know and understand what all is written in your Tanakh?

A short time ago, I communicated with a Rabbi from New York via e-mail. I asked him why many Jewish people do not accept the Brit Chadasha, which was written by Jews. I was shocked by his answer. He replied, "The Brit Chadasha (the New Covenant or New Testament) is in its very name and concept a repudiation of the Jewish people's 'Brit'—the covenant made between the children of Israel and God at Mt. Sinai. It would ludicrous for a Jew who still is committed to the original covenant to accept a second Brit that states that his Brit is no longer valid. To ask why Jews do not accept a book written by other Jews would be like asking why England became upset when British subjects wrote a declaration of independence. Clearly the British subjects who wrote the Declaration of Independence were British subjects rejecting British sovereignty. The Jews who wrote the Brit Chadasha were rejecting the "sovereignty" of the Torah. So of course Jews reject it—even if was written by other misguided Jews. I hope this clarifies things for you."

His explanation of the Brit Chadasha bothered me, and I quoted him numerous Scriptures. I told him our exchange should give both of us a lot to think about and explore. I would have liked to have heard from him again with a different verdict, but this ended our correspondence. He, like many others evidently do not understand their Scriptures they read and teach. I will send him a copy of the book when it is printed and hope that the Holy Spirit will remove the veil. Are you afraid to call Him Abba Father? You don't even call Him by His name; instead, you call Him *HaShem,* which means "The name." Did you distend yourself from Him so far, that you have to address Him in the third person? We read in Zechariah 13:9, *And I will bring the third part through the fire, and will refine them as silver is refined, and will try them as gold is tried: they shall call on my name, and I will hear them: I will say, It is my people: and they shall say, The LORD is my God.*

Christians wait for the Second Coming of Yeshua, Jews await their Messiah for the first time, the Buddhists the fifth Buddha, the Hindus wait for Krishna, Muslims and Iranians for the 12th Imam Mahdi, their Messiah out of Iran. Muslims are told not to touch or read the Scriptures, they consider it blasphemy. If they do, the truth is, Holy Spirit will draw them. Yeshua is letting us know in Matthew 24:5 & 24, *For many shall come in my name, saying, I am Christ; and shall deceive many. For there shall arise false Christs, and false prophets, and shall shew great signs and wonders; insomuch that, if it were possible, they shall deceive the very elect.* A friend of mine sent me an e-mail in May: Subject, "Iran claims discovery of ancient 'Gospel' will prove Islam and destroy Christianity." The Shia Muslim leaders of Iran are trying desperately to stamp out the explosive growth of Christianity inside Iran and the Muslim world. They are killing pastors ... and declaring that the Twelfth Imam – their so-called 'messiah' – is going to be revealed soon. Now the mullahs are claiming they have a document that will destroy Christianity. One of them is claiming that a version of the Gospel of Barnabas, found in 2000, will prove that Islam is the final and righteous religion and the revelation will cause the collapse worldwide of Christianity. Why are Muslims by the thousand converting to Christianity? In Chapter 41 of the Barnabas Gospel, is the statement; "God has hidden himself as Archangel Michael ran them (Adam and Eve) out of heaven, (and) when Adam turned, he noticed that at top of the gateway to heaven, it was written 'La elah ela Allah, Mohamad rasool Allah,'" meaning Allah is the only God and Mohammad his prophet. The good news is that millions of Muslims around the world are waking up to the falsehood of Islam and are discovering that Yeshua is, in fact the Way, the Truth and the Life and that no one comes to the Father and enters heaven except through Yeshua (John 14:6).

The latest deception here is, that certain 'so called Christian' churches merged with Muslims, calling their new belief Crislam. How deceptive. Their promoters introducing the emerging 'ONE WORLD RELIGION.' They believe that they are worshipping the same God, which is absolutely not true. They worship Allah a moon god, which the average Muslim does not even know, that the crescent is their moon god symbol. History tells us that Islam is a modern version, traced back by scholars to the ancient fertility religion of the moon god of Arabia, who were pagans. They need to die as martyrs in order to be assured of paradise. They refuse to belief in the Trinity. Our God paid for our sins with His life by shedding His blood on the cross. By accepting Him we are assured of heaven and have eternal life. How can you, spiritually speaking, afford to fellowship with Muslims? Were do you think they will lead you? We read in Amos 3:3, *Can two walk together, except they be agreed?* This is why we need to know the truth in order to discern for ourselves and keep from being deceived. The Bible tells us clearly in 2 Thessalonians 2:3, *Let no man deceive you by any means: for that day shall not come, except their come a falling away first, and that man of sin be revealed, the man of perdition.* Many years ago Muslims had control over Spain and lost it, but they are not giving up. At this present time Spain's population is 40% Muslim. What do you think their goal is - even with you?

When I was raised in Germany as a Catholic we went to church on Saturday to confess our sins to the priest. He then, supposedly as God's representative asked us to pray a few Hail Mary's and forgave us our sins, so that we could take Communion the next morning during the church service. The following week, we most likely were back to confess the same sins again. It was all the work of the flesh – head knowledge. Did God have to bring me to the USA so I could get born again fourteen years later at age thirty-nine? Is the next Scripture also fitting for me? Jeremiah 1:5, *Before I formed thee in the belly, I knew thee; and before thou comest forth out of the womb I sanctified thee. And I ordained thee a prophet unto the nations.* I remember after I was born again I was able to quote Scriptures that I had never read before. Later God blessed me with the gift of being an international evangelist. I have a registered ministry with the State of Washington since 1985 which allows me also to marry and bury people. At age seventy four I'm still going strong. This time He has me write it in a book for the Jewish people, to give the whole nation of Israel the opportunity to receive Him as their Messiah. Had I stayed in Germany this would of never happened. In fact sometime in 2009 the Holy Spirit revealed to me that in time to come, someone will offer me an honorary doctor title. This will have to be God's doing.

This is how it is with most of you, you only have head knowledge. The supernatural is foreign to you, to have this born again experience and allow the Holy Spirit to direct your life. Try it. I guarantee you, you will never be the same. Ask God the Father if He has a Son called Yeshua. I'm positive that He will answer you. Yeshua is quoted as saying in Matthew 5:17, *Think not that I am come to destroy the law, or the prophets: I am not come to destroy, but to fulfill.*

If I'm going to establish the body of Christ—Yeshua—as it was prophesied over me more than twenty-five years ago, the Holy Spirit has to do a mighty work to confirm it to all the rebellious ones. I'm obeying what the Lord asks me to do, the rest is up to Him to convince and convict them. Shortly after I accepted Him into my heart - before I only had Him in my head, - one day at the altar I said, "Lord, use me." I have been in training now for about thirty-five years, never knowing what my next assignment will be. I started ministering one on one, afterwards I held small meetings. From 1985 to 1987 I shared my testimony in different churches in two of our states. In time the Lord promoted me to international evangelist. I ministered healing and preached in Ghana, West Africa on my three trips there. I remember accompanying a lady to the hospital where I laid my hands on two different ladies as I prayed with them for healing. One had a stomach problem and was in great pain. They sent her home shortly afterwards. The other one was an old lady. Her daughter told me that she was a fetish priestess who came to the hospital to die. She too was sent home the next day after I prayed with her to be delivered of the demons and led her to receive Yeshua as her Lord. I told the daughter to find a Bible believing church. I warned her of the pastor's reaction since this was her hometown. The employees of the hotel were I stayed came knocking on my door as early as 7am before they had to report for work, to have me pray for their needs. My taxi driver became my regular driver. Every other day he drove me to different places. One evening we went to one of the hotel cook's home, where I ministered to him, his wife and their young boys about seven and nine years old. Daily at breakfast I made it a point to talk to him and wrote him some Scriptures down which he took home to his son to read and explain, because he and his wife were both illiterate. I also ministered on two of my trips each in Egypt and Israel. At home locally I minister to whatever need arises and where the Holy Spirit leads me. I prayed for an older mans hearing to be restored in a neighboring town. After he could hear he refused to put his hearing aids away, he said that they cost to much. A ten year old girls sight was restored after I laid my hands on her and prayed for healing. She wore very thick glasses. Afterwards she read from the Bible fluent like an adult. A friend of mine told me about her newly married neighbor with a drug problem. I invited him to church one day. While we were listening to the preaching he told me afterwards, that something lifted itself from within his body and went out through his head. He was delivered and set free, never desiring any more drugs. I describe them in my last book. A few months ago I prayed for a lady from Viet Nam for deliverance from Buddhism and prayed with her to receive Yeshua and baptizing her in the YMCA swimming pool were she is a member. This is the fourth Christian book that I wrote.

On September 22, 2010, TBN, a Christian television station, was broadcasting statistics of church growth around the world. Two former Muslims from Egypt announced that already five years ago sixteen thousand Muslims leave their faith every day and receive Yeshua as their Savior. He appears to them in dreams and visions and even shows Himself on mirrors.

The largest Muslim nation is Indonesia, with a population in excess of 235 million.

Pakistan is the second largest with over 187 million, of which 95-98% are Muslims. They are divided into two major sects: the majority of them practice Sunni Islam, while the Shia's are the minority who make up an estimated 5-20%.

Egypt's population is 85 million, of which are 80-90% Sunni Muslims, Christians count for 15–18 millions . World wide there are 2.1 billion Muslims.

In the July magazine of 'The Philadelphia Trumpet' Mohamed Mursi, the Muslim Brotherhood presidential candidate stated the following: "Yes, Jerusalem is our goal. We shall pray in Jerusalem, or die as martyrs on its threshold." The article continued: "The caliphate – the capital of the United States of the Arabs – will be Jerusalem, God willing."

A Jewish friend sent me the following e-mail on June 29th that on June 24th ... a member of the Muslim Brotherhood, Mohamed Morsi, became president-elect of Egypt. ...

We watched it here on television, where his presidency was announced from the Tahrir Square in Cairo, where he won the election by a narrow 51% margin.

Iran's population is just under 79 Million, of which are 89% Shia and 9% Sunni.

The Iraqi current population is over 31 million, of which are 60-65% Shia Muslims and 32-37% Sunni Muslims. 3% are Christians.

The population of India is 1.22 billion with 900 million Hindus. China has 350 million Buddhists.

The population of Afghanistan is around 30 million.

The count of the Israeli population since the beginning of 2012 is 7,836,000 of which are 75.3% Jewish, amounting to about 5,901,000. 20.5% are Arabs of 1,610,000. 4.2 % are others, counting 325,000, of which are 7,500 Christians.

Jews make up 1 percent of the world's population, yet 176 Nobel Price winners have been Jews. I have the names of the recipients for Literature, World Peace, Chemistry, Economics, Medicine and Physics from 1901 till 2008 but I could not find anyone to give me permission to print them.

A friend of mine received this disturbing e-mail on January 16th 2012. This is part of it:

'Fatah's Top Religious Authority Calls for Genocide of Jews.' Last week, the principal Palestinian Authority religious leader, the Mufti.... Islamic goal....

"The Hour (for Resurrection) will not come until you fight the Jews.

The Jew will hide behind stones or trees.

Then the stones or trees will call:

Oh Muslim, servant of Allah, there is a Jew behind me, come and kill him."

Is this not reason enough to accept your Messiah in order to have protection.

We read in Psalm 91:8 — 12, *Only with thine eyes shalt thou behold and see the reward of the wicked. Because thou hast made the LORD, which is my refuge, even the most High, thy habitation; There shall no evil befall thee, neither shall any plague come nigh thy dwelling. For he shall give his angels charge over thee, to keep thee in all thy ways. They shall bear thee up in their hands, lest thou dash thy foot against a stone.*

In December 2010, a secular Muslim Iranian television station called Tapesh, which is the largest Farsi-speaking network in the world, began broadcasting Christian healing services during prime time each Friday evening. I'm sure that in time, out of curiosity, Muslims will want to find out who brings those miracles to pass. In Los Angeles alone are 1.5 million Farsi speaking people. God called an Iranian pastor here to minister on TBN Nejat TV, whose program reaches four times daily fifty to seventy million people in the Middle East. The Iranian government anounced, that in one city fifty thousand people came to know Yeshua. This pastor said, if they say fifty it is most likely fivehundred thousand.

Psalm 46:10 tells us, *Be still, and know that I am God: I will be exalted among the heathen, I will be exalted in the earth.*

Let me inject some Scriptures here about Abraham and the Law of Moses.

He therefore that ministered to you the Spirit, and worketh miracles among you, doeth he it by the works of the law, or by the hearing of faith? Even as Abraham believed God, and it was accounted to him for righteousness. Know ye therefore, that they, which are of faith, the same are the children of Abraham. And the scripture, foreseeing that God would justify the heathen through faith, preached before the gospel unto Abraham, saying, In thee shall all nations be blessed. So then they which be of faith are blessed with faithful Abraham. For as many as are of the works of the law are under the curse: for it is written, Cursed is every one that continueth not in all things which are written in the book of the law to do them. But that no man is justified by the law in the sight of God, it is evident: for, The just shall live by faith. And the law is not of faith: but, the man that doeth them shall live in them. Christ hath redeemed us from the curse of the law, being made a curse for us: for it is written, Cursed is every one that hangeth on a tree: That the blessing of Abraham might come on the Gentiles through Jesus Christ; that we might receive the promise of the Spirit through faith. Brethren, I speak after the manner of men; though it be but a man's covenant, yet if it be confirmed, no man disannulleth, or addeth thereto. Now to Abraham and his seed were the promises made. He saith not, and to seeds, as of many; but as of one, and to thy seed, which is Christ. And this I say, that the covenant, that was confirmed before of God in Christ, the law, which was four hundred and thirty years after, can not disannul, that it should make the promise of none effect. For if the inheritance be of the law, it is no more of promise: but God gave it to Abraham by promise. Wherefore then serveth the law? It was added because of transgressions, till the seed should come to whom the promise was made; and it was ordained by angels in the hand of a mediator. Now a mediator is not a mediator of one, but God is one. Is the law then against the promises of God? God forbid: for if there had been a law given which could have given life, verily righteousness should have been by the law. But the scripture hath concluded all under sin that the promise by faith of Jesus Christ might be given to them that believe. But before faith came, we were kept under the law, shut up unto the faith, which should afterwards be revealed. Wherefore the law was our schoolmaster to bring us to Christ, that we might be justified by faith. But after that faith is come, we are no longer under a schoolmaster. For ye are all the children of God by faith in Christ Jesus. For as many of you as have been baptized into Christ have put on Christ. There is neither Jew nor Greek, there is neither bond nor free, there is neither male nor female: for ye are all one in Christ Jesus. And if ye be Christ's, then are ye Abraham's seed, and heirs according to the promise (Galatians 3:5–29).

God intended that the law lead His people to Yeshua. These foregoing Scriptures tell that we are sons of God and heirs to the promise through faith in Yeshua. God provides our sonship through Yeshua. Abba is an intimate Aramaic word for *father*, as described in Galatians 4:3–7,

Even so we, when we were children, were in bondage under the elements of the world: But when the fullness of the time was come, God sent forth His Son, made of a woman, made under the law, to redeem them that were under the law, that we might receive the adoption of sons. And because ye are sons, God hath sent forth the Spirit of his Son into your hearts,

crying, Abba, Father. Wherefore thou art no more a servant, but a son; and
if a son, then an heir of God through Christ.

Would it not be better to admit that you are wrong once you have
been told the truth, instead of sending many straight to hell by denying that without salvation in Yeshua, you cannot see God? Satan has
a hold on you. He wants you to keep him company in hell. We read
many Messianic prophecies, which is history written in advance like
in Deuteronomy 18:18, *I will raise them up a Prophet from among their*
brethren, like unto thee, and will put my words in his mouth; and he shall
speak unto them all that I shall command him.

This prophet that God raised up was Yeshua. Let these next
Scriptures sink in and ponder them as you read of the promise of the
coming Messiah in Isaiah 9:6–7,

For unto us (the Jews) a child is born, unto us a Son is given: and the
government shall be upon his shoulder: and his name shall be called
Wonderful, Counselor, The mighty God, The everlasting Father, The Prince
of Peace. Of the increase of his government and peace there shall be no
end, upon the throne of David, and upon his kingdom, to order it, and to
establish it with judgment and with justice from henceforth even forever.
The zeal of the LORD of hosts will perform this.

The ancient prophets were very specific when they wrote about
Israel's coming deliverer. In fact, 332 prophetic Scriptures in the
Tanakh tell of the first coming of Yeshua. Allow me to give a partial
listing of portrayals of Yeshua from the Tanakh, which were fulfilled
by Yeshua in the Brit Chadasha. There are at least twenty in the book
of Psalms alone. It is my prayer that your spiritual eyes will open
and your mind will understand God's awesome truth. I would like to
show you that Yeshua, the Messiah was already here and will return
a second time. He is mentioned in every chapter in the Scriptures,
including the Torah, which is a shadow of the salvation message. The
Torah points us to Yeshua, who is God in the flesh. He came to reconcile His creation to Himself and to show us how to live by His example. He came to restore what Adam lost when Eve listened to Satan in
the Garden of Eden where they ate from the tree of forbidden fruit.

In Genesis chapter 3, Yeshua came as the second Adam to reclaim the title deed to the earth, which Adam lost to Satan. In return, Yeshua died for our sins, which originated with Adam and Eve. Around five hundred years before he was crucified, buried, and resurrected, the crucifixion of the Messiah was foretold in Zechariah 13:6, *And one shall say unto him, What are these wounds in thine hands? Then he shall answer, Those with which I was wounded in the house of my friends.*

Can you deny the truth of your Messiah's coming after comparing these ninety-two prophecies that I describe from the Tanakh? And Yeshua's fulfillment? They should facilitate your understanding.

Genesis 17:19: He is the seed of Isaac. Romans 9:7; Hebrews 11:18

Genesis 22:18; 26:4: He is a blessing to the Gentiles. Galatians 3:8,16; Hebrews 6:14

Deuteronomy 21:13: He will be cursed on the tree. Galatians 3:13

Deuteronomy 18:15, 18–19: He was a prophet. John 6:14; 7:40; Acts 3:22–23

2 Samuel 7:12–13, 16, 25–26: He established the throne of David forever. Matthew 19:28; 21:4; 25:31

Job 19:25–27: He is the promised redeemer. John 5:28–29; Galatians 4:4; Ephesians 7:11, 14

Psalm 2:7: He is the son of God. Matthew 3:17

Psalm 8:6: He is ruler of all. Hebrew 2:8

Psalm 16:10: He rises from death. Matthew 28:7

Psalm 22:16: His hands and feet pierced. John 20:27

Psalm 22:18: Lots are cast for His clothes. Matthew 27:35–36

Psalm 34:20: His bones are unbroken. John 19:32–33 & 36

Psalm 35:11: He is accused by false witnesses. Mark 14:57

Psalm 35:19: He was hated without cause. John 15:25

Psalm 40:7–8: He delights in God's will. Hebrew 10:7

Psalm 41:9: He was betrayed by a friend. Luke 22:47

Psalm 45:6: He is the eternal king. Hebrews 1:8

Psalm 68:18: He ascended to heaven. Acts 1:9–11

Psalm 69:9: He was zealous for God's house. John 2:17

Psalm 69:21: He was given vinegar and gall. Matthew 27:34

Psalm 109:4: He prays for His enemies. Luke 23:34

Psalm 109:8: His betrayer was replaced. Acts 1:20
Psalm 110:1: He rules over His enemies. Matthew 22:44
Psalm 110:4: He is a priest forever. Hebrews 5:6
Psalm 118:22: He is the chief cornerstone. Matthew 21:4
Psalm 118:26: He comes in the name of the Lord. Matthew 21:9
Proverbs 30:4: He was declared to be the son of God. Matthew 3:17; Mark 14:61–62; Luke 1:35; John 3:13; 9:35–38; 11:21; Romans 1:2–4
Isaiah 2:2–4: He was repentance for the nations. Luke 24:47
Isaiah 6:9–10: He hardened their hearts. Matthew 13:14–15; John 12:39–40; Acts 28:25–27; Romans 10:6–9; 2 Peter 1:17
Isaiah 7:14: He was born of a virgin. Matthew 1:22–23
Isaiah 8:14–15: He was a rock of offense. Romans 9:33; 1 Peter 2:8
Isaiah 9:6–7: He was God with us. Matthew 1:21, 23; Luke 1:32–33; John 8:58; 10:30; 14:19; 2 Corinthians 5:19; Colossians 2:9
Isaiah 9:12: He was the light out of darkness. Matthew 4:14–16; Luke 2:32
Isaiah 11:1–10: He was full of wisdom and power. Matthew 3:16; John 3:34; Romans 15:12; Hebrew 1:9
Isaiah 16:4–5: He was reigning in mercy. Luke 1:31–33
Isaiah 22:21–25: He is a nail in a sure place. Revelation 3:7
Isaiah 28:16: He was a stone in Zion. Romans 9:33; 1 Peter 2:6
Isaiah 29:18–19: He made the deaf hear, the blind see. Matthew 5:3; 11:5; John 9:39
Isaiah 32:1–4: He is king of kings and lord of lords. Revelation 19:16; 20:6
Isaiah 33:22: He is the son of the highest. Luke 1:32; 1 Timothy 1:17; 6:15
Isaiah 40:3–5: His way was prepared. Matthew 3:3; Mark 1:3; Luke 3:4–5; John 1:23
Isaiah 40:10–11: He, the shepherd, dies for His sheep. John 10:11; 1 Peter 2:24–25
Isaiah 42:1–16: He was a meek servant. Matthew 12:17–21; Luke 2:32
Isaiah 49:6–12: He was a light to the Gentiles. Acts 13:47; 2 Corinthians 6:2

Isaiah 50:6: He was scourged and spat upon. Matthew 26:67; 27:26 & 30; Mark 14:65; 15:15,19; Luke 22:63–65; John 19:11

Isaiah 52:13; 53:1–12: He was rejected by His people. Matthew 8:17, 27:1–2, 12–14

Isaiah 52:13; 53:1–12: He suffered vicariously. Mark 15:3–4, 27–28; Luke 23:1–25

Isaiah 52:13; 53:1–12: He was silent when accused. Luke 23:32–34; John 1:29; 11:49–52

Isaiah 52:13; 53:1–12: He was crucified with transgressors. John 12:37–38; Acts 8:28–35

Isaiah 52:13; 53:1–12: He was buried with the rich. Acts 10:43; 13:38–39; 1 Corinthians15:3; Ephesians 1:7; 1 Peter 2:21–25; 1 John 1:7 & 9

Isaiah 55:4–5: He called nations that knew him not. John 18:37; Romans 9:25–26; Revelation 1:5

Isaiah 59:16–20: He was the deliverer out of Zion. Romans 11:26–27

Isaiah 60:1–3: He allowed the Gentiles to walk in the light. Luke 2:32

Isaiah 61:1–3: He was anointed to preach liberty. Luke 4:17–19; Acts 10:38

Isaiah 62:11: He promised salvation to the Jews. Thy king cometh. Matthew 21:5

Isaiah 63:1–3: He was a vesture dipped in blood. Revelation 19:13

Isaiah 63:8–9: He was afflicted with the afflicted. Matthew 25:34–40

Isaiah 65:9: He promised his elect an inheritance. Romans 11:5, 7; Hebrews 7:14; Revelation 5:5

Isaiah 65:17–25: He will create new heavens and a new earth. 2nd Peter 3:13; Revelation 21:1

Jeremiah 23:5–6: He is the lord our righteousness. John 2:19–21; Romans 1:3–4; Ephesians 2:20–21; 1 Peter 2:5

Jeremiah 30:9: He is born a king. John 18:37; Revelation 1:5

Jeremiah 31:15: Massacre of infants. Matthew 2:17–18

Jeremiah 31:22: He was conceived by the Holy Spirit. Matthew 1:20; Luke 1:35

Jeremiah 31:31–34: He made a new covenant. Matthew 26:27–29; Mark 14:22–24; Luke 22:15–20; 1 Corinthians 11:25; Hebrews 8:8–12; 10:15–17; 12:24; 13:20

Jeremiah 33:15–17: He will be a spiritual house. John 2:19–21; Ephesians 2:20; 1 Peter 2:5

Ezekiel 21:26–27: He exalts the humble. Luke 1:52

Ezekiel 34: 23–24: He is the good shepherd. John 10:11

Daniel 2:34–35: He is the stone cut without hands. Acts 4:10–12

Daniel 2:44–45: His triumphant kingdom is forever. Luke 1:33; 1 Corinthians 15:24; Revelation 11:15

Daniel 7:13–14: His is an everlasting dominion. Matthew 24:30; 25:31; 26:64; Mark 14:61–62; Acts 1:9–11; Revelation 1:7

Daniel 7:27: His is a kingdom for the saints. Luke 1:33; 1 Corinthians 15:24; Revelation 11:15

Daniel 9:24–27: The time of his birth foretold. Matthew 24:15–21; 27:30; Luke 3:1

Hosea 3:5: Restoration of Israel. John 18:37; Romans 11:25–27

Hosea 11:1: The flight into Egypt. Matthew 2:15

Joel 2:28–32: His promise of the Holy Spirit. Acts 2:17–21; Romans 10:13

Amos 8:9: The sun will darken. Matthew 24:29; Acts 2:20; Revelation 6:12

Amos 9:11–12: He will restore the tabernacle. Acts 15:16–18

Micah 2:12–13: He will gather Israel. John 10:14, 26

Micah 4:1–8: His kingdom will be established. Luke 1:33

Micah 5:1–5: He will be born in Bethlehem. Matthew 2:1; Luke 2:4, 10–11

Habakkuk 2:14: The earth will be filled with the knowledge of the glory of the Lord. Romans 11:26; Revelation 21:23–26

Zechariah 2:10–13: He is the lamb on the throne. Revelation 5:13; 6:9; 21:24; 22:1–5

Zechariah 3:8: He, the branch, will have a holy priesthood. John 2:19–21; Ephesians 2:20–21; 1 Peter 2:5

Zechariah 6:12–13: He is a heavenly high priest. Hebrew 4:4; 8:1–2

Zechariah 9:9–10: He comes as king on a colt, bringing salvation. Matthew 21:4–5; Mark 11:9–10; Luke 20:38; John 12:13–15

Zechariah 11:12–13: He will be sold for thirty pieces of silver.
Matthew 26:14–15; 27:9–10: The money will buy the potter's field.
Zechariah 12:10: His body will be pierced. John 19:34 & 37
Zechariah 13:1, 6–7: He, the shepherd, will be smitten. Matthew 26:31
John 16:32: His sheep will be scattered.
Malachi 3:1: He will be preceded by a forerunner. Matthew 11:10; Luke 7:27
Malachi 3:3: He will purge our sins. Hebrews 1:3
Malachi 4:2–3: He will be the light of the world. Luke 1:78; John 1:9; 12:46; 2 Peter 1:19; Revelation 2:28; 19:11–16; 22:16
Malachi 4:5–6: He will send us Elijah. Matthew 11:14; 17:10–12

On June 5, 1997, American evangelical believers began Christian television programming with Jewish and Arabic subtitles on the Israeli Amos satellite to about fifteen countries in the Middle East (two hundred million people). I don't know if it is still on the air after all these years. These programs were intended to help people understand God's love and truth. We read in Psalm 2:8, *Ask of me, and I shall give thee the heathen for thine inheritance, and the uttermost parts of the earth for thy possession.*

1997 was also the thirtieth anniversary of the six-day war in 1967 between Israel, Syria, Jordan, and Egypt. In only a few days, Israel won over its aggressor, even though it was greatly outnumbered. Egypt's leader at the time, Abdul Nasser, had planned an attack on Israel. Somehow, it was postponed for a few days. While the Egyptian military were all at breakfast, Israel attacked and won the war in six days. Almost forty-five years have passed since then.

What I am about to describe is nothing short of a miracle. I watched it a few times on Christian television before I sent for the DVD *"Against All Odds"*.
If you have ever questioned the existence of our miraculous God, after reading this account, you should be convinced. David, a young tank commander, described his experience of the war up on the Golan

Heights on the northern border between Israel and Syria to a Jewish journalist from America who accepted Yeshua while on this assignment. The movie producer shared David's story on Christian television. The soldiers were crawling on their bellies, trying to detonate with their bayonets a minefield that had been booby-trapped by Syria. To their amazement, a strong gust of wind blew twenty-five to thirty inches of the dirt away, exposing the buried mines, allowing the soldiers to walk through the field without getting blown to pieces. Afterwards he had a work related accident which severed his spine. He laid seven years in the hospital, paralyzed from the waist down, unable to move his legs. One day he watched the *700 Club,* an American Christian television program, where he thought he was going to see dancing girls. Instead the host spoke about a healing. It was exactly the kind he needed and received it. The feeling came back into his legs. God healed him. The doctors called it a medical miracle. The people in the kibbutz disowned him when he shared Yeshua with them. He and his wife were going to be homeless unless he recanted.

An American ministry led by the Holy Spirit who had heard of his ordeal invited him to attend their Bible school in Texas. He accepted and became an ordained minister in Lynnwood, Washington. I have seen him several times host our local Christian program were she shared his testimony. He became the Messianic minister in Lynnwood of the Roots congregation many years ago. I have talked to his wife several times on the phone and per e-mail. What an awesome God we serve! David went to be with the Lord the end of June. I asked Sheila for permission to mention it in my book, which she gave me permission to do.

U.S. Secretary of State Henry Kissinger (himself an Austrian Jew) turned down then Israeli Prime Minister Golda Maier's request for arms to defend her country in the 1973 war. He is reported to have said to her: "Let the Israelis bleed a little." They could not survive the attacks for many more days. In her desperation, Maier called then-president Richard Nixon on his private phone at three o'clock one morning and said, "Mr. President, if you don't help us, the Jewish people will never survive."

He told her that he could almost hear his mother's voice. When he was a little boy, she would read him stories of the heroes from the

Tanakh. One afternoon, while he sat on her lap, she said, "Richard, someday you're going to be in a position where you can help save the Jewish people. And when that day comes, you must do everything in your power." He said that in that moment, as he recalled his mother's prophetic utterance, he realized for perhaps the first time in his presidency why he became president of the United States. He kept his word and Golda got whatever she asked for—every weapon, every vehicle, every piece of equipment, and all the ammunition to operate them. A virtual arsenal was airlifted overnight to Israel's frontlines.

It was the largest airlift of armaments since World War ll. Many military experts credited this decision as the essential element that saved Israel from destruction. The reality is that President Nixon (a Gentile) prevented Israel from losing the war, and for his actions he had to face a powerful Secretary of State who would turn against him. He had accepted the threat to his own presidency to save Israel in its hour of need. Before it was over, the Yom Kippur war of 1973 ended in one of the most incredible turnaround victories ever recorded in military history—all because of what a godly mother had instilled in her little boy and in the time of desperate need he obeyed. We say, Jehovah Jireh, my provider.

In the near future, the Jewish people will realize that their only friends are the Christians who believe in Yeshua. He called on me to open the spiritual eyes of many different religious groups so that they may choose to enter or reject the gates of heaven. He is the one you are still waiting for. There is much confusion as to whether He was already here because of manmade doctrines. Read Acts 11:25–26, *Then departed Barnabas to Tarsus, for to seek Saul: And when he had found him, he brought him unto Antioch. And it came to pass, that the whole year they assembled themselves with the church, and taught much people. And the (Jewish) disciples were called Christians first in Antioch.* What do you say to that? These Jewish disciples who were trained by Yeshua were called Christians. It began as a Jewish belief. The early believers translated the Hebrew *mashiach* into the Greek *christos,* which also means "anointed one." It was later translated into English as *Christ.* He was anointed by the Father to be our heavy yoke breaker and burden remover—if we let Him!

Can't you see that He wants to set you free from all sin, sickness, and disease? Believers are followers of Yeshua, no matter whether they are Jew or Gentile. If God healed them under the law, how much more healing can He do now that we are under grace after the death of Yeshua and His resurrection? The prayer of faith shall heal the sick, not the prayer of religion. We read in Acts 10:38, *How God anointed Jesus of Nazareth with the Holy Ghost and with power: who went about doing good, and healing all that were oppressed of the devil; for God was with Him.*

I, too, was raised to be religious. I speak from experience. I know I would not have been allowed to enter heaven with what little head knowledge I had. But now I have a relationship with Yeshua, and know the truth, which I would not trade for anything. We read in Acts 4:12, *Neither is there salvation in any other: for there is none other name under heaven given among men, whereby we must be saved.* Let me explain what the Scriptures say about Israel's rejection in Romans 11:5–12,

Even so then at this present time also there is a remnant according to the election of grace. And if by grace, then is it no more of works: otherwise grace is no more grace. But if it be of works, then is it no more grace: otherwise work is no more work. What then? Israel hath not obtained that which he seeketh for; but the election hath obtained it, and the rest were blinded. According as it is written, God hath given them the spirit of slumber, eyes that they should not see, and ears that they should not hear: unto this day. And David saith, Let their table be made a snare, and a trap, and a stumblingblock, and a recompense unto them. Let their eyes be darkened, that they may not see, and bow down their back alway. I say then, Have they stumbled that they should fall? God forbid: but rather through their fall salvation is come to the Gentiles, for to provoke them to jealousy. Now if the fall of them be the riches of the Gentiles; how much more their fullness?

When Yeshua touches His feet on the Mount of Olives at His second coming and shows you the nail prints in His hands and feet, you will have proof that He was here once before. His second and final return to earth is when He will rule the world from Jerusalem.

Why wait any longer when you can experience His forgiveness of your sins now? Remember the ceremony in the Torah. The high priest used to go once a year into the Holy of Holies with the blood of an animal to have your sins forgiven for another year. Since there is no blood sacrifice now, the only way is through faith in Yeshua, who made a new and everlasting covenant with us by His death on the cross.

We who believe in Yeshua as our Savior are still awaiting the prophetic fulfillment of the rapture—the believers' journey home and the awakening of the Torah saints, as described in 1 Thessalonians 4:13–18,

> But I would not have you to be ignorant, brethren, concerning them which are asleep, that ye sorrow not, even as others which have no hope. For if we believe that Jesus died and rose again, even so them also which sleep in Jesus will God bring with Him. For this we say unto you by the Word of the Lord, that we which are alive and remain unto the coming of the Lord shall not prevent them which are asleep. For the Lord himself shall descend from heaven with a shout, with the voice of the archangel, and with the trump of God: and the dead in Christ shall rise first. Then we, which are alive and remain, shall be caught up together with them in the clouds, to meet the Lord in the air, and so shall we ever be with the Lord. Wherefore comfort one another with these words.

In the meantime, while we are waiting to be raptured before the tribulation starts and the appearance of the Antichrist, which is called pre-trib we like to share God's saving grace with as many people as we can. You, too, can be among those that will be celebrating the marriage supper of the lamb during the seven years with Yeshua before the terrible tribulation takes place on earth. Some people believe in the mid- or post rapture. It means that we won't get raptured until the middle of the seven year tribulation, while others insist that it won't take place until the end of the seven year tribulation. This is Satan's doings, causing all this confusion. I don't believe that God allows us to be confused, I rather believe that it is Satan's trickery. If you can not buy or sell without the mark of the beast, what are you going to eat during these three-and-a-half or seven years? Worse yet, how do you get around in your car without gas to get food? It is spelled out in Daniel 7:23, *Thus he said, the fourth beast shall be the fourth kingdom upon earth, which shall be diverse from all kingdoms, and shall devour the whole earth. And shall tread it down, and break it in pieces.* (World government of the Antichrist) Followed by Revelation 13:16 & 17, *And he causeth all, both small and great, rich and poor, free and bound, to receive the mark in their right hand, or in their foreheads: And that no man might buy or sell, save he that had the mark, or the name of the beast, or the number of his name.*

This is why we need to be ready at all times, because Yeshua could rapture us at any moment. He tells us in Mark 13:30-33, *Verily I say unto you, that this generation shall not pass, till all these things be done. Heaven and earth shall pass away: but my words shall not pass away. But of that day and that hour knoweth no man, no, not the angels which are in heaven, neither the Son, but the Father. Take ye heed, watch and pray: for ye know not when the time is.*

We read that God made the Abrahamic covenant with Abraham in Genesis 15: 7-10 & 17-18, *And he said unto him, I am the LORD that brought thee out of Ur of the Chaldees, to give thee this land to inherit it. And he said, Lord GOD, whereby shall I know that I shall inherit it. And he said unto him, Take me an heifer of three years old, and a she goat of three years old, and a ram of three years old, and a turtledove, and a young pigeon. And he took unto him all these, and divided them in the midst, and laid each piece one against another: but the birds divided he not. And it came to pass, that, when the sun went down, and it was dark, behold a smoking furnace, and a burning lamp that passed between those pieces. In the same day the LORD made a covenant with Abram, saying, Unto thy seed have I given this land, from the river of Egypt unto the great river, the river Euphrates.*

This prophetic Scripture describes the Antichrist in Daniel 9:27, *And he shall confirm the covenant with many for one week: and in the midst of the week he shall cause the sacrifice and the oblation to cease, and for the overspreading of abominations he shall make it desolate, even until the consummation, and that determined shall be poured upon the desolate.*

The apostle Paul wrote in 2 Thessalonians 2:3-4, *Let no man deceive you by any means: for that day shall not come, except there come a falling away first, and that man of sin be revealed, the son of perdition; who opposeth and exalteth himself above all that is called God, or that is* worshipped; so that he as God sitteth in the temple of God, shewing himself that he is God.

Here is an excerpt of what John saw in a vision while he was in the spirit.

After this I beheld, and lo, a great multitude, which no man could number, of all nations, and kindred's, and people and tongues, stood before the throne, and before the Lamb, clothed with white robes, and palms in their hands; And cried with a loud voice, saying, Salvation to our God which sitteth upon the throne, and unto the Lamb. And all the angels stood round about the throne, and about the elders and the four beasts, and fell before the throne on their faces, and worshiped God, Saying, Amen: Blessing, and glory, and wisdom, and thanksgiving, and honor, and power, and might, be unto our God for ever and ever, Amen. And one of the elders answered, saying unto me, What are these which are arrayed in white robes? and whence came they? And I said unto him, Sir, thou knowest. And he said to me, These are they which came out of great tribulation, and have washed their robes, and made them white in the blood of the Lamb. Therefore are they before the throne of God, and serve him day and night in his temple: and he that sitteth on the throne shall dwell among them. They shall hunger no more, neither thirst any more, neither shall the sun light on them, nor any heat. For the Lamb which is in the midst of the throne shall feed them, and shall lead them unto living fountains of waters: and God shall wipe away all tears from their eyes. (Revelation 7:9–17).

You can read in the book of Revelation about all the pain and sorrows the tribulation will bring. Men want to die, but they can't. What a catastrophe it will be. About twenty-five hundred years earlier it was already prophesied in Zechariah 14:12, *And this shall be the plague wherewith the LORD will smite all the people that have fought against Jerusalem; Their flesh shall consume away while they stand upon their feet, and their eyes shall consume away in their holes, and their tongue shall consume away in their mouth.*

All this can be avoided if you believe in the following Scriptures. When we receive Yeshua as our Savior and make Him Lord we receive the Holy Spirit who then lives in us described in 1 Corinthians 3:16-17, *Know ye not that ye are the temple of God, and that the Spirit of God dwelleth in you? If any man defile the temple of God, him shall God destroy;*

for the temple of God is holy, which temple ye are. The antichrist can not come on the scene as long as the Christians (church) are not raptured. Our presence on earth prevent him from appearing, described in 2 Thessalonians 2:6-8, *And now ye know what withholdeth that he might be revealed in his time. For the mystery of iniquity doth already work: only he who now letteth will let, until he (church) be taken out of the way. And then shall that Wicked be revealed, whom the Lord shall consume with the spirit of his mouth, and shall destroy with the brightness of his coming.*

Yet Israel will welcome the antichrist with open arms. He will promise them seven years of peace and perform signs and wonders. When the Jewish people finally realize that they have been betrayed by the antichrist, who will sit in the temple to be worshiped as God during the last half of the tribulation (forty-two months), the believing Jewish remnant will flee to Petra, where they will be protected. Petra lies about 180 miles south of Amman in Jordan. It is the place where Esau's descendants lived. Today, Petra is visited by many who travel to the Holy Land. It will be Israel's hiding place from the wrath of the antichrist. Why will God send them there? Petra belongs to Jordan, a mainly Islamic country. I will back it up with Scriptures shortly.

In the spring of 1998, the Lord prompted me to mail a registered letter to King Hussein of Jordan, while he was still alive, telling him of his upcoming responsibility. It actually was a prophetic message. When Yeshua returns from heaven with His saints just prior to the battle of Armageddon, He will save the remnant of Israel by revealing Himself to them in Petra.

We read about antichrist in Revelation 13:5–9,

And there was given unto him a mouth speaking great things and blasphemies; and power was given unto him to continue forty and two months. And he opened his mouth in blasphemy against God, to blaspheme his name, and his tabernacle, and them that dwell in heaven. And it was given unto him to make war with the saints, and to overcome them: and power was given him over all kindred's, and tongues, and nations. And all that dwell upon the earth shall worship him, whose names are not written in the book of life of the Lamb slain from the foundation of the world. If any man have an ear, let him hear.

At this time, power will be given to the antichrist over the unbelievers and hypocrites. You see, the true believers have been raptured and are praising God in heaven. The many who will remain on earth will realize that their religious beliefs kept them out of heaven, since their own opinions and false interpretations of the Scriptures are not God's Word. The only way to join those who are already raptured and in heaven is to be martyred for becoming a believer in Yeshua. You might want to consider changing your mind and become a pre trib believer. How else will you survive the tribulation?

God has a message for Moab and Petra to allow the 144,000 Jews and their converts to safely escape the trap of the antichrist in Isaiah 16:3—4, *execute judgment; make thy shadow as the night in the midst of the noonday; hide the outcasts; betray not him that wandereth. Let mine outcast dwell with thee, Moab; be thou a covert to them from the face of the spoiler: for the extortioner is at an end, the spoiler ceaseth, the oppressors are consumed out of the land.* Another description of the Jewish remnants fleeing the city of Jerusalem for the wilderness area of Petra is given in the book of Revelation 12:6, *And the woman fled into the wilderness, where she had a place prepared of God, that they should feed her there a thousand two hundred and threescore days.*

The woman is symbolic of Israel, who will flee into the wilderness of Petra for 1,260 days or three and a half years. The symbol of the bird in the following Scripture is a promise to the Jews from God. *And to the woman were given two wings of a great eagle, that she might fly into the wilderness, into her place, where she is nourished for a time, and times, and half a time, from the face of the serpent* (Revelation 12:14). Psalm 91:4, *He shall cover thee with his feathers, and under his wings shalt thou trust; his truth shall be thy shield and buckler.* This time, however, when pushed in the corner, the Jewish remnants will accept God's offer. Yet About two thousand years ago, Yeshua wept over Jerusalem and in His own words said in Matthew 23:37, *O Jerusalem, Jerusalem, thou that killest the prophets, and stonest them which are sent unto thee, how often would I have gathered her chickens under her wings, and ye would not.*

But God commandeth his love toward us, in that, while we were yet sinners, Christ died for us (Romans 5:8). *For I am not ashamed of the gospel of Christ: for it is the power of God unto salvation to every one that believeth; for the Jew first, and also to the Greek* (Romans 1:16).

Following are some powerful Scriptures. Please give them serious thought as you read them. *But Esaias is very bold, and saith, I was found of them that sought me not; I was made manifest unto them that asked not after me. But to Israel he saith, All day long I have stretched forth my hands to a disobedient and gainsaying people* (Romans 10:20–21). *Neither is there salvation in any other: for there is none other name under heaven given among men, whereby we must be saved* (Acts 4:12).

And we know that all things work together for good to them that love God, to them who are the called according to his purpose. For none of us liveth to himself and no man dieth to himself. For whether we live, we live unto the Lord; and whether we die, we die unto the Lord: whether we live therefore, or die, we are the Lord's. For to this end Christ both died, and rose, and revived, that he might be Lord both of the dead and living. But why dost thou judge thy brother? or why dost thou set at naught thy brother? For we shall all stand before the judgment seat of Christ. For it is written, As I live, saith the Lord, every knee shall bow to me, and every tongue shall confess to God. So then every one of us shall give account of himself to God. Let us not therefore judge one another any more: but judge this rather, that no man put a stumblingblock or an occasion to fall in his brother's way. For the kingdom of God is not meat and drink; but righteousness, and peace, and joy in the Holy Ghost. For he that in these things serveth Christ is acceptable to God, and approved of men. Let us therefore follow after the things which make for peace, and things wherewith one may edify another (Romans 8:28; 14:7–13, 17–19).

Since you don't believe in the Brit Chadasha, l confirm it with your prophet Isaiah 29:10-14,

For the LORD hath poured out upon you the spirit of deep sleep, and hath closed your eyes: the prophets and your rulers, the seers hath he covered. And the vision of all is become unto you as the words of a book that is sealed, which men deliver to one that is learned, saying, Read this, I pray thee: and he saith, I cannot; for it is sealed. Wherefore the Lord said, Forasmuch as this people draw near me with their mouth, and with their lips do honor me, but have removed their heart far from me, and their fear toward me is taught by the precept of men: Therefore, behold, I will proceed to do a marvelous work among this people, even a marvelous work and a wonder: for the wisdom of their wise men shall perish, and the understanding of their prudent men shall be hid.

Even in the Torah way back in Deuteronomy 29:1–6,

These are the words of the covenant, which the LORD commanded Moses to make with the children of Israel in the land of Moab, beside the covenant which he made with them in Horeb. And Moses called unto all Israel, and said unto them, Ye have seen all that the Lord did before your eyes in the land of Egypt unto Pharaoh, and unto all his servants, and unto all his land; The great temptations which thine eyes have seen, the signs, and those great miracles: Yet the LORD hath not given you an heart to perceive, and eyes to see, and ears to hear, unto this day. And I have led you forty years in the wilderness: your clothes are not waxen old upon you, and thy shoe is not waxen old upon thy foot. Ye have not eaten bread, neither have ye drunk wine or strong drink: that ye might know that I am the LORD your God.

Normally one cannot survive, yet God fed them manna, gave them water to drink, and let their shoes and clothes grow with them, so that they did not wear out. They did not need a doctor or medicine. Is that not miraculous, God took care of them all the way. As a baby grew, so also its shoes and the clothe on its body for forty years. Yet they still complained and murmured, so God let part of them die off because they were not thankful.

As we read different Scripture verses, we discover that the people of Israel are uniquely known as God's people, which no human force is able to change. His eternal faithfulness to them and His wondrous works on their behalf are described in Psalm 105:1–45,

Oh, give thanks unto the LORD; call upon his name: make known his deeds among the people. Sing unto him, sing psalms unto him: talk ye of all his wondrous works. Glory ye in his holy name: let the heart of them rejoice that seek the LORD. Seek the LORD, and his strength: seek his face

evermore. Remember his marvelous works that he hath done; his wonders, and the judgments of his mouth; O ye seed of Abraham his servant, ye children of Jacob his chosen. he is the LORD our God: his judgments are in all the earth. he hath remembered his covenant forever, the word which he commanded to a thousand generations. Which covenant he made with Abraham, and his oath unto Isaac; And confirmed the same unto Jacob for a law, and to Israel for an everlasting covenant: Saying, Unto thee will I give the land of Canaan, the lot of your inheritance: When they were but a few men in number; yea, very few, and strangers in it. When they went from one nation to another, from one kingdom to another people; he suffered no man to do them wrong: yea, he reproved kings for their sakes; Saying, Touch not mine anointed, and do my prophets no harm. Moreover he called for a famine upon the land: he brake the whole staff of bread. he sent a man before them, even Joseph, who was sold for a servant: Whose feet they hurt with fetters: he was laid in iron: Until the time that his word came: the word of the LORD tried him. The king sent and loosed him; even the ruler of the people, and let him go free. He made him lord of his house and ruler of all his substance: To bind his princes at his pleasure; and teach his senators wisdom. Israel also came into Egypt; and Jacob sojourned in the land of Ham. And increased his people greatly; and made them stronger than their enemies. He turned their heart to hate his people, to deal subtly with his servants. He sent Moses his servant; and Aaron whom he had chosen. They shewed his signs among them, and wonders in the land of Ham. He sent darkness, and made it dark; and they rebelled not against his Word. He turned their waters into blood, and slew their fish. Their land brought forth frogs in abundance, in the chambers of their kings. He spake, and there came divers sorts of flies, and lice in all their coasts. He gave them hail for rain, and flaming fire in their land. He smote their vines also and their fig trees; and brake the trees of the coasts. He spake, and the locusts came, and caterpillars, and that without number, and did eat up all the herbs in their land, and devoured the fruit of their ground. He smote also all the firstborn in their land, the chief of all their strength. He brought them forth also with silver and gold: and there was not one feeble person among their tribes. Egypt was glad when they departed: for the fear of them fell upon them. He spread a cloud for a covering; and fire to give light in the night. The people asked, and he brought quails, and satisfied them with the bread of heaven. He opened the rock, and the waters gushed out; they ran in the dry places like a river. For he remembered his holy promise, and Abraham his servant. And he brought forth his people with joy and his chosen with gladness: And gave them the lands of the heathen: and they inherited the labor of the people; that they might observe his statutes, and keep his laws. Praise ye the LORD.

If He did all that for His people, could it be possible that through Yeshua, He now wants to be your everything? We read in Ephesians 2:10 & 16–22 and Galatians 2:20,

For we are his workmanship, created in Christ Jesus unto good works, which God hath before ordained that we should walk in them. And that he might reconcile both unto God in one body by the cross, having slain the enmity thereby: And came and preached peace to you, which were afar off, and to them that were nigh. For through him we both have access by one Spirit unto the Father. Now therefore ye are no more strangers and foreigners, but fellow citizens with the saints, and of the household of God. And are built upon the foundation of the apostles and prophets, Jesus Christ himself being the chief corner stone; In whom all the building fitly framed together groweth unto an holy temple in the Lord: In whom ye also are builded together for an habitation of God through the Spirit. I am crucified with Christ: nevertheless I live; yet not I, but Christ liveth in me: and the life which I now live in the flesh, I live by the faith of the Son of God, who loved me, and gave himself for me.

Paul writes again in Romans 10:1–17,

Brethren, my heart's desire and prayer to God for Israel is that they might be saved. For I bear them record that they have a zeal of God, but not according to knowledge. For they being ignorant of God's righteousness, and going about to establish their own righteousness, have not submitted themselves unto the righteousness of God. For Christ is the end of the law for righteousness to every one that believeth. For Moses described the righteousness which is of the law, that the man which doeth those things shall live by them. But the righteousness, which is of faith, speaketh on this wise, Say not in thine heart, Who shall ascend into heaven? (That is, to bring Christ down from above) Or, Who shall descend into the deep?

(That is, to bring up Christ again from the dead) But what said it? The word is nigh thee, even in thy mouth, and in thy heart: that is, the word of faith, which we preach; That if thou shalt confess with thy mouth the Lord Jesus, and shalt believe in thine heart that God hath raised him from the dead, thou shalt be saved. For with the heart man believeth unto righteousness; and with the mouth confession is made unto salvation. For the scripture saith, Whosoever believeth on him shall not be ashamed. For there is no difference between the Jew and the Greek: for the same Lord over all is rich unto all that call upon him. For whosoever shall call upon the name of the Lord shall be saved. How then shall they call on him in whom they have not believed? and how shall they believe in him of whom they have not heard? and how shall they hear without a preacher? And how shall they preach, except they be sent? as it is written, How beautiful are the feet of them that preach the gospel of peace, and bring glad tidings of good things! But they have not all obeyed the gospel. For Esaias saith, Lord, who hath believed our report? So then faith cometh by hearing, and hearing by the word of God.

What about Romans 11:25–34,

For I would not, brethren, that ye should be ignorant of this mystery, lest ye should be wise in your own conceits; that blindness in part is happened to Israel, until the fullness of the Gentiles be come in. And so all Israel shall be saved: as it is written, There shall come out of Sion the Deliverer, and shall turn away ungodliness from Jacob: For this is my covenant unto them, when I shall take away their sins. For as ye in times past have not believed God, yet have now obtained mercy through their unbelief: Even so have these also now not believed, that through your mercy they also may obtain mercy. For God hath concluded them all in unbelief, that he might have mercy upon all. For who hath known the mind of the Lord? or who hath been his counselor? Yes, all Israel will be saved! Revelation 1:7, *Behold, he cometh with clouds; and every eye shall see him, and they also which pierced him: and all kindred's of the earth shall wail because of him. Even so, Amen.*

Once a persecutor of the believers in Yeshua, Paul wrote to the Corinthian church in 2 Corinthians 3:2–18,

Ye are our epistle written in our hearts, known and read of all men: Forasmuch as ye are manifestly declared to be the epistle of Christ ministered by us, written not with ink, but with the Spirit of the living God; not in tables of stone, but in fleshly tables of the heart. And such trust have we through Christ to God-ward: Not that we are sufficient of ourselves to think any thing as of ourselves; but our sufficiency is of God; Who also hath made us able ministers of the new testament; not of the letter, but of the spirit: for the letter killeth, but the spirit giveth life. But if the ministration of death, written and engraven in stones, was glorious, so that the children of Israel could not stedfastly behold the face of Moses for the glory of his countenance; which glory was to be done away: How shall not the ministration of the spirit be rather glorious? For if the ministration of condemnation be glory, much more doth the ministration of righteousness exceed in glory. For even that which was made glorious had no glory in this respect, by reason of the glory that excelleth. For if that which is done away was glorious, much more that which remaineth is glorious. Seeing then that we have such hope, we use great plainness of speech: And not as Moses, which put a veil over his face, that the children of Israel could not stedfastly look at the end of that which is abolished: But their minds were blinded: for until this day remaineth the same veil untaken away in the reading of the old testament; which veil is done away in Christ. But even unto this day, when Moses is read, the veil is upon their heart. Nevertheless when it shall turn to the Lord, the veil shall be taken away. Now the Lord is that Spirit: and where the Spirit of the Lord is, there is liberty. But we all, with open face beholding as in a glass the glory of the Lord, are changed into the same image from glory to glory, even as by the Spirit of the Lord.

There are hidden revelations in the Hebrew Scriptures. Each letter is a word in Hebrew.

- Genesis and Exodus

Every fiftieth letter spells "law" (The Torah).

- Leviticus

Every eighth letter spells "Jehovah" (seven letters x seven letters x seven letters...)

- Numbers and Deuteronomy

Every fiftieth letter spells "law" backward.
Law—Yeshua—Wal

- Yeshua is the center of the law.

The book of Deuteronomy in Hebrew tells the story of the Holocaust, with the names of Hitler, Eichmann, and several concentration camps. In another book, there is reference to the Gulf War, with the name Schwarzkopf and a count of the number of missiles that would fall on Tel Aviv.

There are many more up-to-date occurrences; we only have to search for them. The genealogy from Adam to Noah, Genesis 5 (Plan of Salvation):

Hebrew	English
Adam	Man
Seth	Appointed
Enoch	Mortal
Kenan	Sorrow
Mahalalel	The Blessed God
Jared	Shall come down
Enoch	Teaching
Methuseh	His death shall bring
Lamech	The Despairing
Noah	Rest

Here is the meaning of the English words: Man (is) appointed mortal sorrow (but) the blessed God shall come down, teaching (that) His death shall bring rest to the despairing.

Encoded in the book of Isaiah 53:8-10 at evenly spaced intervals are the words, "Yeshua is My Name"— the story of the crucifixion.

You may know that Jewish synagogues throughout the world follow the same Torah reading, beginning at Rosh Hashanna and continuing throughout the year.

On the day Genesis 15 was being read, where God confirms to Abraham the covenant of the land to His descendants, a certain incident occurred.

In verse 17, it reads, *And it came to pass, that, when the sun went down, and it was dark, behold a smoking furnace, and a burning lamp that passed between those pieces.*

In Hebrew, it reads as follows: *decreed GOD into Rabin evil fire fire. An evil fire (twice) into Rabin God decreed.*

On the day this passage was being read throughout the Jewish world, Prime Minister Yitzhak Rabin was assassinated! It is even more remarkable since the passage deals with God's covenant of the land to Israel, written three thousand years ago. Prime Minister Rabin was viewed by a majority of Israel's population as having betrayed their God-given right to the land in the so-called "peace process."

I remember reading about it. In the year 5757 in the Jewish calendar, which was our 1997, the words "for you" were found encoded with the meaning that it was not for us to be known any sooner. Political events are described in the year they took place with the names of the participants from whatever country they originated.

Explanation is later given in your own coded Hebrew text, identifiable now by revelation from God. Several researchers studied them for years. There is no doubt remaining that it is truly God's word. There are many more coded messages described and many books written about the subject.

What does one do with this peculiar observation? Is this just a coincidence? The Rabbis are fond of pointing out that *coincidence* is not a kosher word! I have heard it said that coincidence is when God remains anonymous. There are no accidents in God's kingdom. Is it a hidden prophecy then? The Maastricht Agreement of 1920, the Camp David Agreement, and the Oslo Agreement, signed on the White House lawn, are all manmade and all in violation of God's covenant of the land to Israel. God uses the foolish to confound the wise. Why was some of this coded information not discovered and known to us many years ago? Are we getting closer to the end of this age?

God included many hidden coded messages in the text of the Tanakh, such as *Yeshua* in Hebrew—translated into Greek as *Iosous* and later into English as *Jesus* from Genesis all the way to Malachi. Check in your Hebrew text and you will discover that it reads, "Yeshua is my name." He is opening your spiritual eyes to the truth so that there will be no question in your mind. You will have to admit that the

Holy Spirit inspired all the Scriptures. We read in Philippians 4:13, *I can do all things through Christ which strengtheneth me.* Remember, without God, you cannot win, and with God you cannot lose.

In the Tanakh, God spoke through His prophets; in the Brit Chadasha, He speaks to us directly through the Holy Spirit. Before Yeshua ascended to heaven, He told His followers in John 14:25–26, *These things have I spoken unto you, being yet present with you. But the Comforter, which is the Holy Ghost, whom the Father will send in my name, he shall teach you all things, and bring all things to your remembrance, whatsoever I have said unto you.*

This is my commandment, That ye love one another, as I have loved you. Greater love hath no man than this, that a man lay down his life for his friends. Ye are my friends, if ye do whatsoever I command you. Henceforth I call you not servants; for the servant knoweth not what his lord doeth: but I have called you friends; for all things that I have heard of my Father I have made known unto you (John 15:12–15).

A fitting prophecy was given to me. I have stayed up many nights in order to study and write this book. The prophetess begins, "Father, we thank you for your daughter. I heard the Lord saying, that you have worked, for the night is coming when man's work will be done." The prophetess continues, "He gives me for you. *Ye are of God, little children, and have overcome them: because greater is he that is in you, than he that is in the world* (1 John 4:4). I see you have many things thrown at you. I see you kind of putting your arm up. Things have been thrown at you, like tin cans and everything. I see you, like Stephen, 'saying, Father, forgive them, for they know not what they do. You have prayed, 'Yeshua, make me like You.' Yeshua is saying that you didn't know to be made like Him then you go through the same things He went through. He went through rejection, He went through false accusations, but yet because He is greater in you, than he in the world, you're able to say, as Stephen said and as Yeshua said, Father, forgive them, for they know not what they do. He gives me 2 Timothy 2:15, *Study to shew thyself approved unto God, a workman that needeth not to be ashamed, rightly dividing the word of truth.* I see you with a basket over your arm, feeding the people with the Word of God. You are very selective. You're looking around in your basket for the right word for the right person. Yeshua wants you to know that it is a blessing to the people that you do not just feed them all the same things. You have prayed and asked Yeshua. He says, 'Daughter, I can trust you to feed my people that what they need, that which will affect them.' He says, 'Many prophecies have been said about you and you have wondered whether they will come to pass and when. Now is the time. Now is the time that you will see many of these words come to pass.' He gives me 1 Timothy 1:18, *This charge I commit unto thee, son Timothy, according to the prophecies which went before on thee, that thou by them mightest war a good warfare.* We thank you for revealing to your daughter these prophetic words, whether they are on tape, written down, or hidden in her heart. Lord, from many different sources for many years, I have seen some of them coming to light. Lord, I just pray that you give your daughter strength and everything she needs. The finances and the strength to go where you want her to go and do what you want her to do. Thank you, Lord. Hallelujah, Amen."

The basket most likely means the Scriptures from which I write and speak to different denominations and groups. Muslims need to hear different Scriptures than Jews, and so on. The Lord can trust me, as He revealed to her. I have studied many hours in order to feed His people that which affects them—the proper Scriptures. It seems to me that many will be affected as they turn from their religious doctrine and become His people. God's people! I am ready to fulfill what the Holy Spirit revealed to me and what has been prophesied over me for years. I am pregnant with my calling from God and ready to deliver, which includes the birthing of your understanding about your Messiah.

In a different meeting at my home, the prophetess prophesied that I would lead many souls to Yeshua and into the baptism in the Holy Spirit. The apostle Paul writes in 1 Corinthians 2:7–8, *For we speak the wisdom of God in mystery, even the hidden wisdom, which God ordained before the world unto our glory: Which none of the princes of this world knew: for had they known it, they would not have crucified the Lord of glory.* Merriam-Webster's Collegiate Dictionary describes mystery as "a religious truth that one can know only by revelation and cannot fully understand." In other words, it can't be taught. It is a divine revelation from the Holy Spirit. First, you must be born again, and then filled with the Holy Spirit. It is not something understood with the mind; it is beyond human understanding. You have to experience it.

We read that God spoke directly to certain people in the Tanakh, as in Genesis 12:1, *Get thee out of your country...unto a land that I will show you.* Or as the burning bush in Exodus 3:4. Through his prophets in the Tanakh, visions were seen in Ezekiel 8:4, 11:24, through dreams in Daniel 2:3, and angels in Zechariah 1:9, *But now God will speak to us through His son, who is the Word made flesh.* And in Genesis 1:1, *In the beginning God created the heaven and the earth.*

Genesis 1:26a tells us, *And God said, Let Us make man in Our image, after Our likeness.* The Hebrew name for God is Elohim, which means plurality with unity. God the Father, His Son Yeshua, and the Holy Spirit were from the very beginning active in the creation of man.

Each is called God.

Father—2 Thessalonians 2:16, *And may our Master Y'shua the Mashiyach himself, and Elohim our Father, who has loved us, and given us everlasting consolation and a good hope through his grace* (Aramaic English New Testament).

Yeshua—Philippians 2:5–6, *Let this mind be in you, which was also in Christ Jesus: Who, being in the form of God, thought it not robbery to be equal with God.* Colossians 1:15, *Who is the image of the invisible God, the firstborn of every creature.*

Holy Spirit—John 4:24, *God is Spirit: and they that worship him must worship him in spirit and in truth.*

Each is called Lord.

Father—Luke 10:21, *In that hour Jesus rejoiced in spirit, and said, I thank thee, O Father, Lord of heaven and earth, that thou hast hid these things from the wise and prudent, and hast revealed them unto babes: even so, Father; for so it seemed good in thy sight.*

Yeshua—Acts 2:36, *Truly, therefore, let all the house of Israel know that Elohim has made this Y'shua the Mashiyach whom you executed on a stake both Master YHWH and Mashiyach* (Aramaic English New Testament).

Both of these above Scriptures are taken from the Aramaic English New Testament. Copyright 2008. Used by permission of Netzari Press.

Holy Spirit—2 Corinthians 3:17, *Now the Lord is that Spirit: and where the Spirit of the Lord is, there is liberty.*

Each endures forever.

Father—Isaiah 9:6, *For unto us a child is born, unto us a son is given: and the government shall be upon his shoulder: and his name shall be called Wonderful, Counselor, The mighty God, The everlasting Father, The Prince of Peace.* And Revelation 1:6, *And hath made us kings and priests unto God and his Father; to him be glory and dominion for ever and ever. Amen.*

Yeshua—1 John 5:20, *We know that the Son of God is come, and hath given us an understanding, that we may know him that is true, and we are in him that is true, even in his Son Jesus Christ. This is the true God, and eternal life.*

Holy Spirit—Hebrews 9:14, *How much more shall the blood of Christ, who through the eternal Spirit offered himself without spot to God, purge your conscience from dead works to serve the living God?*

CHAPTER 2

Yeshua is Our High Priest

Many of the following Scriptures should be familiar to you since they have already been quoted in the Tanakh. For instance, Isaiah 42:1–8,

Behold my servant, whom I uphold; mine elect, in whom my soul delighteth; I have put my spirit upon him: (which is Yeshua's anointing) he shall bring forth judgment to the Gentiles. He shall not cry, nor lift up, nor cause his voice to be heard in the street. A bruised reed shall he not break, and the smoking flax shall he not quench: he shall bring forth judgment unto truth. He shall not fail nor be discouraged, till he have set judgment in the earth: and the isles shall wait for his law. Thus saith God the LORD, he that created the heavens, and stretched them out; he that spread forth the earth, and that which cometh out of it; he that giveth breath unto the people upon it, and spirit to them that walk therein: I the LORD have called thee in righteousness, and will hold thine hand, and will keep thee, and give thee for a covenant of the people, for a light to the Gentiles; to open the blind eyes, to bring out the prisoners from the prison, and them that sit in darkness out of the prison house. I am the LORD: that is my name: and my glory will I not give to another, neither my praise to graven images.

On May 31, 1997, the Holy Spirit instructed me to introduce you to the whole book of Hebrews. I had no idea at that time how God was having me put this book together, but I obeyed. It has been a learning process for thirty five years, with Him revealing step-by-step what He wants me to tell you.

When Yeshua made His public entrance into Jerusalem, the Jewish leaders rejected Him because their understanding of Him was religious instead of spiritual, as quoted in Psalm 118:19–22, *Open to me the gates of righteousness: I will go into them, and I will praise the LORD: This gate of the LORD, into which the righteous shall enter. I will praise thee: for thou hast heard me, and art become my salvation. The stone which the builders refused is become the head stone of the corner.* This cornerstone is none other than Yeshua Himself.

We read in Isaiah 65:1a, *I am sought of them that asked not for me; I am found of them that sought me not.*

You will learn from these 13 chapters of the Epistle to the Hebrews that under Moses, the Israelites lived under the law. Now, in the New Testament, the Brit Chadasha, they live under grace. Yeshua is your High Priest. Starting with Hebrews 1:1 to 13:25,

GOD, who in sundry (various) times and in divers (various) manners spake in time past unto the fathers by the prophets, Hath in these last days spoken unto us by his Son, whom he hath appointed heir of all things, by whom also he made the worlds; Who being the brightness of his glory, and the express image of his person, and upholding all things by the word of his power, when he had by himself purged our sins, sat down on the right hand of the Majesty on high; being made so much better than the angels, also he hath by inheritance obtained a more excellent name than they. For unto which of the angels said he at any time, Thou art my Son, this day have I begotten thee? And again, I will be to him a Father, and he shall be to me a Son? And again, when he bringeth in the first-begotten into the world, he saith, And let all the angels of God worship him. And of the angels he saith, Who maketh his angels spirits, and his ministers a flame of fire. But unto the Son he saith, Thy throne, O God, is for ever and ever: a scepter of righteousness is the scepter of thy kingdom. Thou hast loved righteousness, and hated iniquity; therefore God, even thy God, hath anointed thee with the oil of gladness above thy fellows. And, Thou, Lord, in the beginning hast laid the foundation of the earth; and the heavens are the works of thine hands: They shall perish; but thou remainest; and they all shall wax old as doth a garment; And as a vesture shalt thou fold them up, and they shall be changed: but thou art the same, and thy years shall not fail. But to which of the angels said he at any time, Sit on my right hand, until I make thine enemies thy footstool? Are they not all ministering spirits, sent forth to minister for them who shall be heirs of salvation?

Therefore we ought to give the more earnest heed to the things which we have heard, lest at any time we should let them slip. For if the word spoken by angels was steadfast, and every transgression and disobedience received a just recompense of reward; How shall we escape, if we neglect so great salvation; which at the first began to be spoken by the Lord, and was confirmed unto us by them that heard him; God also bearing them witness, both with signs and wonders, and with divers miracles, and gifts of the Holy Ghost, according to his own will? For unto the angels hath he not put in subjection the world to come, whereof we speak. But one in a certain place testified, saying, What is man, that thou art mindful of him? or the son of man, that thou visitest him? Thou madest him a little lower than the angels; thou crownest him with glory and honor, and didst set him over the works of thy hands; thou hast put all things in subjection under his feet. For in that he put all in subjection under him, he left nothing that is not put under him. But now we see not yet all things put under him. But we see Yeshua, who was made a little lower than the angels for the suffering of death, crowned with glory and honor; that he by the grace of God should taste death for every man. For it became him, for whom are all things, and by whom are all things, in bringing many sons unto glory, to make the captain of their salvation perfect through sufferings. For both he that sanctifieth and they who are sanctified are all of one; for which cause he is not ashamed to call them brethren. Saying I will declare thy name unto my brethren, in the midst of the church will I sing praise unto thee. And again, I will put my trust in him. And again, Behold I and the children which God hath given me. Forasmuch then as the children are partakers of flesh and blood, he also himself likewise took part of the same; that through death he might destroy him that had the power of *death, that is, the devil; And deliver them who through fear of death were all their lifetime subject to bondage. For verily he took not on him the nature of angels; but he took on him the seed of Abraham. Wherefore in all things it behooved him to be made like unto his brethren, that he might be a merciful and faithful high priest in things pertaining to God, to make reconciliation for the sins of the people. For in that he himself hath suffered being tempted, he is able to succor them that are tempted.*

Wherefore, holy brethren, partakers of the heavenly calling, consider the Apostle and High Priest of our profession, Yeshua; who was faithful to him that appointed him, as also Moses was faithful in all his house. For this man was counted worthy of more glory than Moses, inasmuch as he who hath builded the house hath more honor than the house. For every house is builded by some man; but he that built all things is God. And Moses verily was faithful in all his house, as a servant, for a testimony of those things which were to be spoken after; But Yeshua as a son over his own house; whose house are we, if we hold fast the confidence and the rejoicing of the hope firm unto the end.

Wherefore as the Holy Ghost saith, Today if ye will hear his voice, harden not your hearts, as in the provocation, in the day of temptation in the wilderness: When your fathers tempted me, proved me, and saw my works forty years. Wherefore I was grieved with that generation, and said, They do alway err in their heart; and they have not known my ways. So I sware in my wrath, They shall not enter into my rest. Take heed, brethren, lest there be in any of you an evil heart of unbelief, in departing from the living God. But exhort one another daily while it is called To-day; lest any of you be hardened through the deceitfulness of sin. For we are made partakers of Yeshua, if we hold the beginning of our confidence steadfast unto the end; While it is said, Today if ye will hear his voice, harden not your hearts, as in the provocation. For some, when they had heard, did provoke howbeit not all that came out of Egypt by Moses. But with whom was he grieved forty years? Was it not with them that had sinned, whose carcasses fell in the wilderness? And to whom sware he that they should not enter into his rest, but to them that believed not? So we see that they could not enter in because of unbelief.

Let us therefore fear, lest, a promise being left us of entering into his rest, any of you should seem to come short of it. For unto us was the gospel preached, as well as unto them; but the word preached did not profit them, not being mixed with faith in them that heard it. For we which have believed do enter into rest, as he said, As I have sworn in my wrath, if they shall enter into my rest; although the works were finished from the foundation of the world. For he spake in a certain place of the seventh day on this wise, And God did rest the seventh day from all his works. And in this place again, If they shall enter into my rest. Seeing therefore it remaineth that some must enter therein, and they to whom it was first preached entered not in because of unbelief: Again, he limiteth a certain day, saying in David, To-day after so long a time; as it is said, To-day if ye will hear his voice, harden not your hearts. For if Jesus had given them rest, then would he not afterward have spoken of another day. There remaineth therefore a rest to the people of God. For he that is entered into his rest, he also hath ceased from his own works, as God did from his. Let us labor therefore to enter into that rest, lest any man fall after the same example of unbelief. For the word of God is quick, and powerful, and sharper than any two-edged sword piercing even to the dividing asunder of soul and spirit, and of the joints and marrow, and is a discerner of the thoughts and intents of the heart. Neither is there any creature that is not manifest in his sight; but all things are naked and opened unto the eyes of him with whom we have to do. Seeing then that we have a great high priest, that is passed into the heavens, Yeshua the Son of God, let us hold fast our profession. For we have not an high priest which cannot be touched with the feeling of our infirmities; but was in all points tempted like as we are, yet without sin. Let us therefore come boldly unto the throne of grace that we may obtain mercy, and find grace to help in time of need.

For every high priest taken from among men is ordained for men in things pertaining to God, that he may offer both gifts and sacrifices for sins: Who can have compassion on the ignorant, and on them that are out of the way; for that he himself also is compassed with infirmity. And by reason hereof he ought, as for the people, so also for himself, to offer for sins. And no man taketh this honor unto himself, but he that is called of God, as was Aaron. So also Christ glorified not himself to be made an high priest; but he that said unto him, Thou art my Son, to-day have I begotten thee. And he saith also in another place, Thou art a priest forever after the order of Melchisedec. Who in the days of his flesh, when he had offered up prayers and supplications with strong crying and tears unto him that was able to save him from death, and was heard in that he feared; Though he were a Son, yet learned he obedience by the things which he suffered; And being made perfect, he became the author of eternal salvation unto all them that obey him; Called of God an high priest after the order of Melchisedec. Of whom we have many things to say, and hard to be uttered, seeing ye are dull of hearing. For when for the time ye ought to be teachers, ye have need that one teach you again which be the first principles of the oracles of God; and are become such as have need of milk, and not of strong meat. For every one that useth milk is unskillful in the word of righteousness; for he is a babe. But strong meat belongeth to them that are of full age, even those who by reason of use have their senses exercised to discern both good and evil.

Therefore, leaving the principles of the doctrine of Yeshua, let us go on unto perfection; not laying again the foundation of repentance from dead works, and of faith toward God, of the doctrine of baptisms, and of laying on of hands, and of resurrection of the dead, and of eternal judgment. And this will we do, if God permit. For it is impossible for those who were once enlightened, and have tasted of the heavenly gift, and were made partakers of the Holy Ghost, and have tasted the good word of God, and the powers of the world to come, if they shall fall away, to renew them again unto repentance, seeing they crucify to themselves the Son of God afresh, and put him to an open shame. For the earth which drinketh in the rain that cometh oft upon it, and bringeth forth herbs meet for them by whom it is dressed, receiveth blessing from God: But that which beareth thorns and briers is rejected, and is nigh unto cursing; whose end is to be burned. But, beloved, we are persuaded better things of you, and things that accompany salvation, though we thus speak. For God is not unrighteous to forget your work and labor of love, which ye have shewed toward his name, in that ye have ministered to the saints, and do minister. And we desire that every one of you do shew the same diligence to the full assurance of hope unto the end: That ye be not slothful, but followers of them who through faith and patience inherit the promises. For when God made promise to Abraham, because he could swear by no greater, he sware by himself, Saying, Surely blessing I will bless thee, and multiplying I will multiply thee. And so, after he had patiently endured, he obtained the promise. For men verily swear by the greater: and an oath for confirmation is to them an end of all strife. Wherein God, willing more abundantly to shew unto the heirs of promise the immutability of his counsel, confirmed it by an oath: That by two immutable things, in which it was impossible for God to lie, we might have a strong consolation, who have fled for refuge to lay hold upon the hope set before us: Which hope we have as an anchor of the soul, both sure and stedfast, and which entereth into that within the veil; Whither the forerunner is for us entered, even Yeshua, made an high priest for ever after the order of Melchisedec.

For this Melchisedec, king of Salem, priest of the most high God, who met Abraham returning from the slaughter of the kings, and blessed him; To whom also Abraham gave a tenth part of all; first being by interpretation King of righteousness, and after that also King of Salem, which is, King of peace; Without father, without mother, without descent, having neither beginning of days, nor end of life; but made like unto the Son of God; abideth a priest continually. Now consider how great this man was, unto whom even the patriarch Abraham gave the tenth of the spoils. And verily they that are of the sons of Levi, who receive the office of the priesthood, have commandment to take tithes of the people according to the law, that is, of their brethren, thought they come out of the loins of Abraham: But he whose descent is not counted from them received tithes of Abraham, and blessed him that had the promises. And without all contradiction the less is blessed of the better. And here men that die receive tithes; but there he receiveth them, of whom it is witnessed that he liveth. And as I may so say Levi also, who receiveth tithes paid tithes in Abraham. For he was yet in the loins of his father, when Melchisedec met him. If therefore perfection were by the Levitical priesthood, (for under it the people received the law,) what further need was there that another priest should rise after the order of Melchisedec, and not be called after the order of Aaron? For the priesthood being changed, there is made of necessity a change also of the law. For he of whom these things are spoken pertaineth to another tribe, of which no man gave attendance at the altar. For it is evident that our Lord sprang out of Juda; of which tribe Moses spake nothing concerning priesthood. And it is yet far more evident: for that after the similitude of Melchisedec there ariseth another priest, who is made, not after the law of a carnal commandment, but after the power of an endless life. For he testifieth, Thou are a priest forever after the order of Melchisedec. For there is verily a disannulling of the commandment going before for the weakness and unprofitableness thereof. For the law made nothing perfect, but the bringing in of a better hope did; by the which we draw nigh unto God. And inasmuch as not without an oath he was made priest; (For those priests were made without an oath; but this with an oath by him that said unto him, The Lord sware and will not repent, Thou art a priest for ever after the order of Melchisedec:) By so much was Yeshua made a surety of a better testament. And they truly were many priests, because they were not suffered to continue by reason of death: But this man, because he continueth ever, hath an unchangeable priesthood. Wherefore he is able also to save them to the uttermost that come unto God by him, seeing he ever liveth to make intercession for them. For such an high priest became us, who is holy, harmless, undefiled, separate from sinners, and made higher than the heavens; Who needeth not daily, as those high priests, to offer up sacrifice, first for his own sins, and then for the people's: for this he did once, when he offered up himself. For the law maketh men high priests which have infirmity; but the word of the oath, which was since the law, maketh the Son, who is consecrated for evermore.

Now of the things which we have spoken this is the sum: We have such an high priest, who is set on the right hand of the throne of the Majesty in the heavens; a minister of the sanctuary, and of the true tabernacle, which the Lord pitched, and not man. For every high priest is ordained to offer gifts and sacrifices: wherefore it is of necessity that this man have somewhat also to offer. For if he were on earth, he should not be a priest, seeing that there are priests that offer gifts according to the law: Who serve unto the example and shadow of heavenly things, as Moses was admonished of God when he was about to make the tabernacle: for, See, saith he, that thou make all things according to the pattern shewed to thee in the mount. But now hath he obtained a more excellent ministry, by how much also he is the mediator of a better covenant, which was established upon better promises. For if that first covenant had been faultless, then should no place have been sought for the second. For finding fault with them, he saith, Behold, the days come, saith the Lord, when I will make a new covenant with the house of Israel and with the house of Judah: Not according to the covenant that I made with their fathers in the day when I took them by the hand to lead them out of the land of Egypt; because they continued not in my covenant, and I regarded them not, saith the Lord. For this is the covenant that I will make with the house of Israel after those days, saith the Lord; I will put my laws into their mind, and write them in their hearts: and I will be to them a God, and they shall be to me a people: And they shall not teach every man his neighbor, and every man his brother, saying, Know the Lord: for all shall know me, from the least to the greatest. For I will be merciful to their unrighteousness, and their sins and their iniquities will I remember no more. (confirmation is given in Jeremiah 31:31-34) In that he saith, A new covenant, he hath made the first old. Now that which decayeth and waxeth old is ready to vanish away.

Then verily the first covenant had also ordinances of divine service, and a worldly sanctuary. For there was a tabernacle made; the first, wherein was the candlestick, and the table, and the shewbread; which is called the sanctuary. And after the second veil, the tabernacle which is called the Holiest of all; which had the golden censer, and the ark of the covenant overlaid round about with gold, wherein was the golden pot that had manna, and Aaron's rod that budded, and the tables of the covenant; And over it the cherubims of glory shadowing the mercyseat; of which we cannot now speak particularly. Now when these things were thus ordained, the priest went always into the first tabernacle, accomplishing the service of God. But into the second went the high priest alone once every year, not without blood, which he offered for himself, and for the errors of the people: The Holy Ghost this signifying, that the way into the holiest of all was not yet made manifest, while as the first tabernacle was yet standing: Which was a figure for the time then present, in which were offered both gifts and sacrifices, that could not make him that did the service perfect, as pertaining to the conscience; Which stood only in meats and drinks, and divers washings, and carnal ordinances, imposed on them until the time of reformation. But Christ being come an high priest of good things to come, by a greater and more perfect tabernacle, not made with hands, that is to say, not of this building; Neither by the blood of goats and calves, but by his own blood he entered in once into the holy place, having obtained eternal redemption for us.

For if the blood of bulls and of goats, and the ashes of an heifer sprinkling the unclean, sanctifieth to the purifying of the flesh: How much more shall the blood of Yeshua, who through the eternal Spirit offered himself without spot to God, purge your conscience from dead works to serve the living God? And for this cause he is the mediator of the new testament, that by means of death, for the redemption of the transgressions that were under the first testament, they which are called might receive the promise of eternal inheritance. For where a testament is, there must also of necessity be the death of the testator. For a testament is of force after men are dead; otherwise it is of no strength at all while the testator liveth. Whereupon neither the first testament was dedicated without blood. For when Moses had spoken every precept to all the people according to the law, he took the blood of calves and of goats, with water, and scarlet wool, and hyssop, and sprinkled both the book, and all the people. Saying, This is the blood of the testament which God hath enjoined unto you. Moreover he sprinkled with blood both the tabernacle, and all the vessels of the ministry. And almost all things are by the law purged with blood; and without shedding of blood is no remission. It was therefore necessary that the patterns of things in the heavens should be purified with these; but the heavenly things themselves with better sacrifices than these. For Yeshua is not entered into the holy places made with hands, which are the figures of the true; but into heaven itself, now to appear in the presence of God for us: Nor yet that he should offer himself often, as the high priest entereth into the holy place every year with blood of others; For then must he often have suffered since the foundation of the world: but now once in the end of the world hath he appeared to put away sin by the sacrifice of himself. And as it is appointed unto men once to die, but after this the judgment. So Christ (Yeshua) was once offered to bear the sins of many, and unto them that look for Him shall He appear the second time without sin unto salvation.

For the law having a shadow of good things to come and not the very image of the things, can never with those sacrifices which they offered year by year continually make the comers thereunto perfect. For then would they

YESHUA IS OUR HIGH PRIEST

not have ceased to be offered? because that the worshippers once purged should have had no more conscience of sins. But in those sacrifices there is a remembrance again made of sins every year. For it is not possible that the blood of bulls and of goats should take away sins. Wherefore when he comet into the world, he saith, Sacrifice and offering thou wouldest not, but a body hast thou prepared me: In burnt offerings and sacrifices for sin thou hast had no pleasure. Then said I, Lo, I come (in the volume of the book it is written of me,) to do thy will, O God. Above when he said, Sacrifice and offering and burnt offerings and offering for sin thou wouldest not, neither hadst pleasure therein; which are offered by the law; Then said he, Lo, I come to do thy will, O God. He taketh away the first, that he may establish the second. By the which will we are sanctified through the offering of the body of Yeshua once for all. And every priest standeth daily ministering and offering oftentimes the same sacrifices, which can never take away sins. For by one offering he hath perfected forever them that are sanctified. Whereof the Holy Ghost also is a witness to us: for after that he had said before. This is the covenant that I will make with them after those days, saith the Lord, I will put my laws into their hearts, and in their minds will I write them; and their sins and iniquities will I remember no more. Now where remission of these is, there is no more offering for sin. Having therefore, brethren, boldness to enter into the holiest by the blood of Yeshua, by a new and living way, which he hath consecrated for us, through the veil, that is to say, his flesh; And having an high priest over the house of God; let us draw near with a true heart in full assurance of faith having our hearts sprinkled from an evil conscience, and our bodies washed with pure water. Let us hold fast the profession of our faith without wavering; (for he is faithful that promised;) And let us consider one another to provoke unto love and to good works: Not forsaking the assembling of ourselves together, as the manner of some is; but exhorting one another: and so much the more, as ye see the day approaching. For if we sin willfully after that we have received the knowledge of the truth, there remaineth no more sacrifice for sins. But a certain fearful looking for of judgment and fiery indignation, which shall devour the adversaries. He that despised Moses' law dies without mercy under two or three witnesses. Of how much sorer punishment, suppose ye, shall he be thought worthy, who hath trodden under foot the Son of God, and hath counted the blood of the covenant, wherewith he was sanctified, an unholy thing, and hath done despite unto the Spirit of grace? For we know him that hath said, Vengeance belongeth unto me, I will recompense, saith the Lord. And again, The Lord shall judge his people. It is a fearful thing to fall into the hands of the living God. But call to remembrance the former days, in which, after ye were illuminated, ye endured a great fight of afflictions; Partly, whilst ye were made a gazing stock both by reproaches and afflictions; and partly, whilst ye became companions of them that were so used. For ye had compassion of me in my bonds, and took joyfully the spoiling of your goods, knowing in yourselves that ye have in heaven a better and an enduring substance. Cast not away therefore your confidence, which hath great recompense of reward. For ye have need of patience, that, after ye have done the will of God, ye might receive the promise. For yet a little while, and he that shall come will come, and will not tarry. Now the just shall live by faith: but if any man draw back, my soul shall have no pleasure in him. But we are not of them who draw back unto perdition; but of them that believe to the saving of the soul.

Now faith is the substance of things hoped for, the evidence of things not seen. For by it the elders obtained a good report. Through faith we understand that the worlds were framed by the word of God, so that things which are seen were not made of things which do appear; By faith Able offered unto God a more excellent sacrifice than Cain, by which he obtained witness that he was righteous, God testifying of his gifts; and by it he being dead yet speaket. By faith Enoch was translated that he should not see death; and was not found, because God had translated him; for before his translation he had this testimony, that he pleased God. But without faith it is impossible to please him; for he that comet to God must believe that he is a rewarder of them that diligently seek him. By faith Noah, being warned of God of things not seen as yet, moved with fear, prepared an ark to the saving of his house; by the which he condemned the world, and became heir of the righteousness which is by faith. By faith Abraham, when he was called to go out into a place which he should after receive for an inheritance, obeyed; and he went out, not knowing whither he went. By faith he sojourned in the land of promise, as in a strange country, dwelling in tabernacles with Isaac and Jacob, the heirs with him of the same promise: For he looked for a city which hath foundations, whose builder and maker is God. Through faith also Sara herself received strength to conceive seed, and was delivered of a child when she was past age, because she judged him faithful who had promised. Therefore sprang there even of one, and him as good as dead, so many as the stars of the sky in multitude, and as the sand which is by the sea shore innumerable. These all died in faith, not having received the promises, but having seen them afar off, and were persuaded of them, and embraced them, and confessed that they were strangers and pilgrims on the earth. For they that say such things declare plainly that they seek a country. And truly, if they had been mindful of that country from whence they came out, they might have had opportunity to have returned. But now they desire a better country, that is, an heavenly: wherefore God is not ashamed to be called their God: for he hath prepared for them a city. By faith Abraham, when he was tried, offered up Isaac: and he that had received the promises offered up his only begotten son. Of whom it was said; That in Isaac shall thy seed be called. Accounting that God was able to raise him up, even from the dead; from whence also he received him in a figure. By faith Isaac blessed Jacob and Esau concerning things to come. By faith Jacob, when he was a dying, blessed both the sons of Joseph; and worshipped, leaning upon the top of his staff. By faith Joseph, when he died, made mention of the departing of the children of Israel; and gave commandment concerning his bones. By faith Moses, when he was born, was hid three months of his parents, because they saw he was a proper child; and they were not afraid of the king's commandment. By faith Moses, when he was come to years, refused to be called the son of Pharaoh's daughter. Choosing rather to suffer affliction with the people of God, than to enjoy the pleasures of sin for a season. Esteeming the reproach of Christ (Yeshua) greater riches than the treasures in Egypt; for he had respect unto the recompense of the reward. By faith he forsook Egypt, not fearing the wrath of the king: for he endured, as seeing him who is invisible. Through faith he kept the passover, and the sprinkling of blood, lest he that destroyed the firstborn should touch them. By faith they passed through the Red Sea as by dry land: which the Egyptians as saying to do were drowned. By faith the walls of Jericho fell down, after they were compassed about seven days. By faith the harlot Rahab perished not with them that believed not, when she had received the spies with peace. And what shall I more say? for the time would fail me to tell of Gideon, and of Barak, and of Samson, and of Jephthae: of David also, and Samuel, and of the prophets. Who through fait subdued kingdoms, *wrought righteousness, obtained promises, stopped the mouth of lions, quenched the violence of fire, escaped the edge of the sword, out of weakness were made strong, waxed valiant in fight, turned to flight the armies of the aliens. Women received their dead raised to life again: and others were tortured, not accepting deliverance; that they might obtain a better resurrection. And others had trail of cruel mockings and scourgings, yea, moreover of bonds and imprisonment. They were stoned, they were sawn asunder, were tempted, were slain with the sword: they wandered about in sheepskins and goatskins; being destitute, afflicted, tormented. (Of whom the world was not worthy) they wandered in deserts, and in mountains, and in dens and caves of the earth. And these all, having obtained a good report through faith, received not the promise: God having provided some better thing for us, that they without us should not be made perfect.*

Wherefore seeing we also are compassed about with so great a cloud of witnesses, let us lay aside every weight, and the sin which doth so easily beset us, and let us run with patience the race that is set before us, Looking unto Jesus (Yeshua) the author and finisher of our faith; who for the joy that was set before him endured the cross, despising the shame, and is set down at the right hand of the throne of God. For consider him that endured such contradiction of sinners against himself, lest ye be wearied and faint in your minds. Ye have not yet resisted unto blood, striving against sin. And ye have forgotten the exhortation which speaketh unto you as unto children, my son, despise not thou the chastening of the Lord, nor, faint when thou art rebuked of him. For whom the Lord loveth he chasteneth, and scourgeth every son whom he receiveth. If ye endure chastening, God dealeth with you as with sons; for what son is he whom the father chasteneth not? But if ye be without chastisement, whereof all are partakers, then are ye bastards, and not sons. Furthermore we have had fathers of our flesh, which corrected us, and we gave them reverence: shall we not much rather be in subjection unto the Father of spirits, and live? For they verily for a few days chastened us after there own pleasure; but he for our profit, that we might be partakers of his holiness. Now no chastening for the present seemeth to be joyous, but grievous: nevertheless afterward it yieldeth the peaceable fruit of righteousness unto them which are exercised thereby. Wherefore lift up your hands which hang down, and the feeble knees; And make straight paths for your feet, lest that which is lame be turned out of the way; but let it rather be healed. Follow peace with all men, and holiness, without which no man shall see the Lord. Looking diligently lest any man fail of the grace of God; lest any root of bitterness springing up trouble you, and thereby many be defiled; Lest there be any fornicator, or profane person, as Esau, who for one morsel of meat sold his birthright. For ye know how that afterward, when he would have inherited the blessing, he was rejected: for he found no place of repentance, though he sought it carefully with tears unto the mount that might be touched, and that burned with fire, nor unto blackness, and darkness, and tempest. And the sound of a trumpet, and the voice of words; which voice they that heard entreated that the word should not be spoken to them any more: (For they could not endure that which was commanded, And if so much as a beast touch the mountain, it shall be stoned, or thrust through with a dart: And so terrible was the sight, that Moses said, I exceedingly fear and quake:) But ye are come unto mount Sion, and unto the city of the living God, the heavenly Jerusalem, and to an innumerable company of angels, To the general assembly and church of the firstborn, which are written in heaven, and to God the Judge of all, and to the spirits of just men made perfect, And to Jesus (Yeshua) the mediator of the new covenant, and to the blood of sprinkling, that speaketh better things than that of Abel. See that ye refuse not him that speaketh. For if they escaped not who refused him that spake on earth, much more shall not we escape, if we turn away from him that speaketh from heaven: Whose voice then shook the earth: but now he hath promised, saying, Yet once more I shake not the earth only, but also heaven. And this word, Yet once more, signified the removing of those things that are shaken, as of things that are made, that those things which cannot be shaken may remain. Wherefore we receiving a kingdom which cannot be moved, let us have grace, whereby we may serve God acceptably with reverence and godly fear: For our God is a consuming fire.

Let brotherly love continue. Be not forgetful to entertain strangers: for thereby some have entertained angels unawares. Remember them that are in bonds, as bound with them; and them which suffer adversity, as being yourselves also in the body. Marriage is honourable in all, and the bed undefiled: but whoremongers and adulterers God will judge. Let your conversation be without coveteousness; and be content with such things as ye have: for he hath said, I will never leave thee, nor *forsake thee. So that we may boldly say, The Lord is my helper, and I will not fear what man shall do unto me. Remember them, which have the rule over you, who have spoken unto you the word of God: whose faith follow, considering the end of their conversation. Jesus Christ (Yeshua) the same yesterday, and today, and forever. Be not carried about with divers and strange doctrines. For it is a good thing that the heart be established with grace; not with meats, which have not profited them that have been occupied therein. We have an altar, whereof they have no right to eat which serve the tabernacle. For the body of those beasts, whose blood is brought into the sanctuary by the high priest for sin, are burned without the camp. Wherefore Jesus said also, that he might sanctify the people with his own blood, suffered without the gate. Let us go forth therefore unto him without the camp, bearing his reproach. For here have we no continuing city, but we seek one to come. By him therefore let us offer the sacrifice of praise to God continually, that is, the fruit of our lips giving thanks to his name. But to do good and to communicate forget not: for with such sacrifices God is well pleased. Obey them that have the rule over you, and submit yourselves: for they watch over your souls, as they that must give account, that they may do it with joy, and not with grief: for that is unprofitable for you. Pray for us: for we trust we have a good conscience, in all things willing to live honestly. But I beseech you the rather to do this, that I may be restored to you the sooner. Now the God of peace, that brought again from the dead our Lord Jesus, (Yeshua) that great shepherd of the sheep through the blood of the everlasting covenant make you perfect in every good work to do his will, working in you that which is well-pleasing in his sight, through Jesus Christ; (Yeshua) to whom be glory for ever and ever. Amen. And I beseech you, brethren suffer the word of exhortation: for I have written a letter unto you in few words. Know ye that our brother Timothy is set at liberty; with whom, if he come shortly, I will see you. Salute all them that have the rule over you, and all the saints. They of Italy salute you. Grace be with you all. Amen.*

Now that the truth is presented, that Yeshua is your High Priest, will you practice what God told you? The Torah alone is proof enough that you cannot deny that Yeshua—the Anointed One—is your

Messiah, who was prophesied in the Scriptures by the psalmists and prophets. Yeshua is speaking about Himself, recorded in Isaiah 61:1, *"The spirit of the Lord GOD is upon me; because the LORD has anointed me to preach..."* He was born of a Jewish mother and lived the life of a Jew under the law of Moses. He died a Jew and is coming again as a Jew to rule the whole world from Jerusalem. He is the King of the Jews. Let me sum it up for you.

He came from the human family of Adam, as described in Genesis 3:15.

He came from the race line of Shem, as described in Genesis 9:25–27.

He came from the patriarch line of Abraham, as described in Genesis 18:18.

He came from the true heir line of Isaac, as described in Genesis 21:12.

He came from the national line of Jacob, as described in Genesis 28:3–4.

He came from the tribal line of Judah, as described in Genesis 49:10.

He came from the kingly line of David, as described in Psalm 132:11.

Eight hundred languages and dialects around the world in an estimated sixty thousand books were written about Him. He held a good share of the world's population in awe for about two thousand years. You have to agree that He is the most influential Jew the world has ever known. In fact, His accomplishments were so enormous that people changed the calendar to BC and AD—before Christ and "Anna Domini"—Latin for "Year of the Lord." The Bible is the best-selling book in history. He, too, studied the Hebrew Scriptures in the Tanakh.

I would like to give you a few more very important Scriptures in Luke 4:15-22,

And he taught in their synagogues, being glorified of all. And he came to Nazareth, where he had been brought up: and, as his custom was, he went into the synagogue on the Sabbath day, and stood up for to read. And there was delivered unto him the book of Esaias. And when he had opened the

book, he found the place where it was written, The Spirit of the Lord is upon me, because he hath anointed me to preach the gospel to the poor; he hath sent me to heal the brokenhearted, to preach deliverance to the captives, and recovering of sight to the blind, to set at liberty them that are bruised, to preach the acceptable year of the Lord. And he closed the book, and he gave it again to the minister, and sat down. And the eyes of all them that were in the synagogue were fastened on him. And he began to say unto them, This day is this scripture fulfilled in your ears. And all bare him witness, and wondered at the gracious words which proceeded out of his mouth. And they said, Is not this Joseph's son? This confirms to you that they believed Him!

There are 467 prophecies mentioned in the Scriptures, all of which point to one man. His name is Yeshua, your Messiah. In Isaiah 53, it is described that He will suffer humiliation, physical harm, and death in a violent manner. But at the end, He will come as a conquering King to destroy the enemies of Israel and set up the Messianic kingdom of peace and prosperity. He is your Savior and the giver of life.

Many wars in the past and present have been fought to annihilate the Jews. It is a spiritual matter that goes all the way back to the two half-brothers Isaac and Ishmael. This is not an assumption; it is a fact. Satan, the prideful angel, then called Lucifer, who was in charge of the worship in heaven, was kicked out. We read it in Isaiah 14:12–17, *How art thou fallen from heaven, O Lucifer, son of the morning! how art thou cut down to the ground, which didst weaken the nations! For thou hast said in thine heart, I will ascend into heaven, I will exalt my throne above the stars of God: I will sit also upon the mount of the congregation, in the sides of the north: I will ascend above the heights of the clouds; I will be like the most high. Yet thou shalt be brought down to hell, to the sides of the pit. They that see thee shall narrowly look upon thee, and consider thee, saying, Is this the man that made the earth to tremble, that did shake kingdoms; That made the world as a wilderness, and destroyed the cities thereof; that opened not the house of his prisoners?*

This devilish, demonic spirit can enter into a person and try to control him or her and bring ruin. It usually starts with lack of forgiveness, jealousy, and envy. In the end, God's Holy Spirit will prevail if we ask for His help and the person is willing to be delivered from the demon. But a born again Christian can not be demon possessed, oppressed yes, but not possessed. In the case of the Jews, God will destroy the armies that try to come against Israel. John wrote about Yeshua in John 7:43, *So there was a division among the people because of him.*

I wrote this chapter with great compassion, dear Jewish people. It was a privilege to have missed many hours of sleep during the preparation of this book. It is my pleasure to let you know how much God really loves you. As I was busy writing, one day the Lord made me understand that my sacrifice was not in vain because it became urgent that I finish the book.

Throughout your hardships, scattered throughout many nations and not having a home land for 1900 years you preserved your race. Even your Hebrew language was restored to you in 1982 as many returned from foreign lands. God already told you in 630 BC by Zephaniah chapter 3:9, *For then will I turn to the people a pure language, that they may all call upon the name of the LORD, to serve him with one consent.*

I remember the exodus of the Ethiopian Jews, who were arriving by planeloads. Later, I heard on Christian television that the blood donated by the black Jews was not welcomed in Israel. It is said that when the queen of Sheba from Ethiopia came to visit Solomon, she stayed quite a while and went home pregnant. Orthodox belief has it that the mother must be Jewish in order to be called a Jew. You will also read that Moses's wife was a black lady and that his own sister contracted leprosy by complaining about her.

The Bible points out in Acts 17:24–26,

God that made the world and all things therein, seeing that he is Lord of heaven and earth, dwelleth not in temples made with hands; neither is worshipped with men's hands, as though he needed any thing, seeing he giveth to all life, and breath, and all things; and hath made of one blood all nations of men for to dwell on all the face of the earth, and hath deter-mined the times before appointed, and the bounds of their habitation.

If God created them to look like that, who are we to look down on any person and count ourselves superior? You, of all people, who have experienced so much persecution, surely know. Yes, it is God's will that the Jews will return to their homeland. God will one day delight in His people and they will rejoice and experience that for which they have longed and suffered for. The prophet described it as best he could around 700 BC, more than twenty-five hundred years ago. He did not know about airplanes then. *Who are these that fly as a* cloud, *and as the doves to their windows? Surely the isles shall wait for me, and the ships of Tarshish first, to bring thy sons from far* (Isaiah 60:8–9a). I know several American Christian ministries that paid to have a number of Jews brought out of Russia in the past twenty-five years. A short time ago, I heard it announced on Christian television that every fourth person in Israel speaks Russian. A Swiss man who had a burden for the Jewish people became partners with an American, who told me himself that they brought several loads out via a large ship. The first one arrived in 1991. Last I heard, a few years ago, the count was up to fifty-five and still continuing. We read of the re-gathering of Israel in Zechariah 2:6–7, *Ho, ho, come forth, and flee from the land of the north, saith the LORD: for I have spread you abroad as the four winds of the heavens, saith the LORD. Deliver thyself, O Zion, that dwellest with the daughter of Babylon.* In the next verse, 8b, God describes you: *Who touches you, touches the apple of my eye.* Yes, the Jews will return home to Israel from the four corners of the world. Even the ones who live in the United States need to go home one day before the next prophecy comes to pass.

Zephaniah prophesied in chapter 3:8,

Therefore wait ye upon me, saith the LORD, until the day that I rise up to the prey: for my determination is to gather the nations, that I may assemble the kingdoms, to pour upon them mine indignation, even all my fierce anger: for all the earth shall be devoured with the fire of my jealousy.

Although there are many atheists among you today, you have kept your religion and where possible your language in tact. God bless you for prevailing.

Let me remind you once more what our loving and merciful God told Abraham in Genesis 17:7–8, 19 & 21b,

And I will establish my covenant between me and thee and thy seed after thee in their generations for an everlasting covenant, to be a God unto thee, and to thy seed after thee. And I will give unto thee, and thy seed after thee, the land wherein thou art a stranger, all the land of Canaan, for an everlasting possession; and I will be their God. And God said, Sarah thy wife shall bear thee a son indeed; and thou shalt call his name Isaac: and I will establish my covenant with him for an everlasting covenant, and with his seed after him. Which Sarah shall bear unto thee at this set time in the next year.

Will you allow what you are reading in this book to sink in and accept Him as your God and know Him as your Messiah?

The apostle Paul wrote in 2 Corinthians 3:2, 5–6, 12–18,

Ye are our epistle written in our hearts, known and read of all men. Not that we are sufficient of ourselves to think any thing as of ourselves; but our sufficiency is of God; Who also hath made us able ministers of the new testament; not of the letter, but of the spirit: for the letter killeth, but the spirit giveth live. Seeing then that we have such hope, we use great plainness of speech: And not as Moses, which put a veil over his face, that the children of Israel could not stedfastly look to the end of that which is abolished: But their minds were blinded: for until this day remaineth the same veil untaken in the reading of the old testament; which veil is done away in Christ. (Yeshua) But even unto this day, when Moses is read, the veil is upon their heart. Nevertheless when it shall turn to the Lord, the veil shall be taken away. Now the Lord is that Spirit: and where the Spirit of the Lord is, there is liberty. But we all, with open face beholding as in a glass the glory of the Lord, are changed into the same image from glory to glory, even as by the Spirit of the Lord.

In this book, God wants to expand your understanding of who you are in Him and what He really is to you, if you allow it.

Read Ephesians 2:15–18 & 4:13,

Having abolished in his flesh the enmity, even the Law of Commandments contained in Ordinances; for to make in himself of twain, (of Jews and Gentiles) one new man, so making peace and that he might reconcile both unto God in one body by the Cross, having slain the enmity thereby: and came and preached peace to you who were afar off, and to them who were nigh. For through him (Yeshua) we both (Jews and Gentiles) have access by one Spirit unto the Father. Till we all come in the unity of Faith, and of the knowledge of the Son of God, unto a perfect man, unto the measure of the stature of the fullness of Christ.

Early in the morning of May 21, 2007, the Holy Spirit revealed to me that Israel's enemy will be closing in on you, but you will get another chance. I have already cited several examples, including Esther, who, in the nick of time, saved the country from being annihilated by Haman. Is God sending me to warn you and point the urgent situation out to you? If you apply the principles mentioned in this book, Israel's revival is imminent.

Let me describe some of your past history, summarized in this rather lengthy Psalm 78:1–72,

Give ear, O my people, to my law: incline your ears to the words of my mouth. I will open my mouth in a parable: I will utter dark sayings of old:Which we have heard and known, and our fathers have told us. We will not hide them from their children, showing to the generation to come the praises of the LORD, and his strength, and his wonderful works that he hath done. For he established a testimony in Jacob, and appointed a law in Israel, which he commanded our fathers, that they should make them known to their children:That the generation to come might know them, even the children which should be born; who should arise and declare them to their children:That they might set their hope in God, and not forget the works of God, but keep his commandments: And might not be as their fathers, a stubborn and rebellious generation; a generation that set not their heart aright, and whose spirit was not steadfast with God. The children of Ephraim, being armed, and carrying bows, turned back in the day of battle. They kept not the covenant of God, and refused to walk in his law; And forgot his works, and his wonders that he had shewed them. Marvelous things did he in the sight of their fathers, in the land of Egypt, in the field of Zoan. He divided the sea, and caused them to pass through; and he made the waters to stand as an heap. In the daytime also he led them with a cloud, and all the night with a light of fire. He clave the rocks in the wilderness, and gave them drink as out of the great depths. He brought streams also out of the rock, and caused waters to run down like rivers. And they sinned yet more against him by provoking the most High in the wilderness. And they tempted God in their heart by asking meat for their lust. Yea, they spake against God; they said, Can God furnish a table in the wilderness? Behold, he smote the rock that the waters gushed out, and the streams overflowed; can he give bread also? Can he provide flesh for his people? Therefore the LORD heard this, and was wroth: so a fire was kindled against Jacob, and anger also came up against Israel; Because they believed not in God, and trusted not in his salvation: Though he had commanded the clouds from above, and opened the doors of heaven, and had rained down manna upon them to eat, and had given them of the corn of heaven. Man did eat angels' food: He sent them meat to the full. He caused an east wind to blow in the heaven: and by his power he brought in the south wind. He rained flesh also upon them as dust, and feathered fowls like as the sand of the sea: and let it fall in the midst of their camp, round about their habitations. So they did eat, and were well filled: for he gave them their own desire; they were not estranged from their lust. But while their meat was yet in their mouth, the wrath of God came upon them, and slew the fattest of them, and smote down the chosen men of Israel. For all this they sinned still, and believed not for his wondrous works. Therefore their days did he consume in vanity, and their years in trouble. When he slew them, then they sought him: and they returned and inquired early after God. And they remembered that God was their rock, and the high God their redeemer. Nevertheless they did flatter him with their mouth, and they lied unto him with their tongues. For their heart was not right with him, neither were they steadfast in his covenant. But he, being full of compassion, forgave their iniquity, and destroyed them not: yea, many a time turned he his anger away, and did not stir up all his wrath. For he remembered that they were but flesh; a wind that passeth away, and cometh not again. How oft did they provoke him in the wilderness, and grieve him in the desert! Yea, they turned back and tempted God, and limited the Holy One of Israel. They remembered not his hand, nor the day when he delivered them from the enemy. How he had wrought his signs in Egypt, and his wonders in the field of Zoan: And had turned their rivers into blood; and their floods, that they could not drink. He sent divers sorts of flies among them, which devoured them; and frogs, which destroyed them. He gave also their increase unto the caterpillar, and their labour unto the locust. He destroyed their vines with hail, and their sycamore trees with frost. He gave up their cattle also to the hail, and their flocks to hot thunderbolts. He cast upon them the fierceness of his anger, wrath, and indignation, and trouble, by sending evil angels among them. He made a way to his anger; he spared not their soul from death, but gave their life over to the pestilence; And smote all the firstborn in Egypt; the chief of their strength in the tabernacles of Ham: But made his own people to go forth like sheep, and guided them in the wilderness like a flock. And he led them on safely, so that they feared not: but the sea overwhelmed their enemies. And he brought them to the border of his sanctuary, even to this mountain, which his right hand had purchased. He cast out the heathen also before them, and divided them an inheritance by line, and made the tribes of Israel to dwell in their tents. Yet they tempted and provoked the most high God, and kept not his testimonies: But turned back, and dealth unfaithfully like their fathers: they were turned aside like a deceitful bow. For they provoked him to anger with their high places, and moved him to jealousy with their graven images. When God heard this, he was wroth, and greatly abhorred Israel: So that he forsook the tabernacle of Shiloh, the tent which he placed among men; And delivered his strength into captivity, and his glory into the enemy's hand. He gave his people over also unto the sword; and was wroth with his inheritance. The fire consumed their young men; and their maidens were not given to marriage. Their priests fell by the sword; and their widows made no lamentation. Then the Lord awaked as one out of sleep, and like a mighty man that shouteth by reason of wine. And he smote his enemies in the hinder parts: he put them to a perpetual reproach. Moreover he refused the tabernacle of Joseph, and chose not the tribe of Ephraim: But chose the tribe of

YESHUA IS OUR HIGH PRIEST

Judah, the mount Zion which he loved. And he built his sanctuary like high places, like the earth which he hath established for ever. He chose David also his servant, and took him from the sheepfolds: From following the ewes great with young he brought him to feed Jacob his people, and Israel his inheritance. So he fed them according to the integrity of his heart; and guided them by the skillfulness of his hands.

But how long before they took control of their own lives again?

When you exhaust your physical strength in time to come and can't defend yourself against bombardment from all sides, in your desperation you will cry out to God to send you a Savior. It will be Yeshua, your Messiah, who will make Himself real to you and cause your revival in Israel. The Holy Spirit led me to the following Scriptures. *O Israel, thou hast destroyed thyself; but in me is thine help. I'm the LORD, your Holy One, the creator of Israel, your King. This people have I formed for myself; they shall show forth my praise.*

(Hosea 13:9 and Isaiah 43:15 & 21). Confirmed in Psalm 91:1, 5–6, 11 & 15–16,

He that dwelleth in the secret place of the most High shall abide under the shadow of the Almighty. Thou shalt not be afraid for the terror by night; nor for the arrow that flieth by day; Nor for the pestilence that walketh in darkness; nor for the destruction that wasteth at noonday. For he shall give his angels charge over thee, to keep thee in all thy ways. He shall call upon me, and I will answer him: I will be with him in trouble; I will deliver him, and honour him. With long life will I satisfy him, and shew him my salvation. God confirmed it through Zechariah 4:6b, *Not by might, nor by power, but by my spirit, saith the LORD of hosts.*

Isn't He an awesome God?

CHAPTER 3

My Unexpected Trip to the Holy Land

Years ago, while I was conducting a successful real estate career, I bought several pieces of clothing at a shopping mall. A few years later, at the end of January 1985, God called me out of real estate to serve Him as a full-time evangelist. He had been preparing my heart for some time to leave my profession, so when the day came, I was ready. Although I ate, drank, and slept real estate, as we say, toward the end I was ready to give it up. When I looked back a year later, I was amazed at myself for not giving God an argument about it, or at least saying, "Lord, just one more year to save a little more money!" I believe He had it timed right or I would have missed my calling. If God is ready for a certain job to be done in His kingdom and you are not, He will pick the next person who makes himself or herself available to serve Him. We are told in Colossians 3:11, *Where there is neither Greek nor Jew, circumcision nor uncircumcision, Barbarian, Scythian, bond or free: but Christ is all, and in all.* Had I not obeyed the voice of the Holy Spirit, I would have become the loser.

Several weeks after quitting my job, I browsed through the same store I had shopped in a few years earlier and was surprised to see the same lady on duty. She greeted me by saying, "Hi, Mrs. Steward!" I was startled that she had remembered my name because I had not returned to the store for several years. Since she called me by name, I stopped and talked with her. Sometime later she told me that she had made it a point to remember my name because I knew what I wanted when I shopped and wasn't wasting her time, which really impressed her. During our conversation, I mentioned that I had just written a Christian book. She asked me to get her one from my car. Then she excitedly told me about an upcoming trip to Israel and Egypt that she was planning to take in the middle of March with several other ladies. She shared with me that one of them might have to back out because of an illness in the family. Since she knew that I was a Christian, she asked if I would be interested in taking this lady's place. Instead of saying no, I told her I would go home and pray about it. These were not my own words; the Holy Spirit had put them in my mouth. As I prayed, a peace came over me and, to my surprise, God even provided the money I needed for the trip—all of it, including my spending money.

Since my accountant had just passed away, his brother, also an accountant from Arizona, completed my taxes. I only had a short time in which to prepare for my trip. The other ladies all had about three months to get ready. Since I was taking someone else's place, I had little time to take care of my affairs, such as paying my property and income taxes, which were both due in April. The accountant told me on a Tuesday on the phone that I owed $3,400 in income tax, but when I met with him on Friday to pick up my papers after he processed the same figures through the computer he told me that I would actually be receiving a $671 refund. I said, "Praise the Lord." There is nothing impossible with God. I knew this was God's way of financing my unexpected trip. Remember, these were 1985 prices. Later that evening, the Lord revealed to me, "I take care of the sparrow. He eats every day. How much more precious do you think you are to me?" I almost jumped for joy. He truly is my heavenly Father and takes care of me.

Never in my life could I have visualized all the happenings we experienced. Seeing all the sites we read about in the Scriptures gave me a burning desire to know them even more. All in all I'm quoting over 2,500 Scriptures in this manuscript. We walked where Yeshua walked and even drank water from Jacob's well. There were only seven of us, of which one was our tour guide. She has been a tour guide in Mexico for over thirty years and had the opportunity to live with an Arabic Christian family just outside of Bethlehem for six months the year before, during which time she traveled extensively and gained enough knowledge to take us the following year. Because of her association with the local people, we saw some sites and places not known to most tourists. We were on the go every day. After we returned from our trip, I felt led by the Holy Spirit to write down what all we saw. I'll try to guide you through our once-in-a-lifetime experience by describing the many sites we visited and providing the Scriptures for biblical reference.

First we traveled by airplane from Seattle to New York where another lady joined us. Then we continued on to Paris. I got to see a couple of Jewish men put on their prayer shawls. To my surprise, they tied their phylacteries on their bodies.

The prayer shawl (*tallit*) is described in the book of Numbers 15:37–39,

And the LORD spake unto Moses, saying, Speak unto the children of Israel, and bid them that they make fringes in the borders of their garments throughout their generations, and that they put upon the fringe of the borders a ribband of blue. And it shall be unto you for a fringe, that ye may look upon it, and remember all the commandments of the LORD, and do them; and that ye seek not after your own heart and your own eyes, after which ye used to go awhoring.

Phylacteries are explained in Matthew 23:5, *But all their works they do for to be seen of men: they make broad their phylacteries, and enlarge the borders of their garments.* The following scriptures of the law are contained in: Exodus 13:2–17; Deuteronomy 6:4–9 & 13–23,

Sanctify unto me all the first-born, whatsoever openeth the womb among the children of Israel, both of man and of beast: it is mine. And Moses said unto the people, Remember, this day, in which ye came out of Egypt, out of the house of bondage; for by strength of hand the LORD brought you out from this place: there shall be no leavened bread be eaten. This day came ye out in the month Abib. And it shall be when the LORD shall bring thee into the land of the Canaanites, and the Hittites, and the Amorites, and the Hivites, and the Jebusites, which he sware unto thy fathers to give thee, a land flowing with milk and honey, that thou shalt keep this service in this month. Seven days thou shalt eat unleavened bread, and in the seventh day shall be a feast to the LORD. Unleavened bread shall be eaten seven days; and there shall no leavened bread be seen among thee, neither shall there be leaven seen with thee in all thy quarters. And thou shalt shew thy son in that day, saying, This is done because of that which the LORD did unto me when I came forth out of Egypt. And it shall be for a sign unto thee upon thine hand, and for a memorial between thine eyes, that the LORD's law may be in thy mouth: for with a strong hand hath the LORD brought thee out of Egypt. Thou shalt therefore keep this ordinance in his season from year to year. And it shall be when the LORD shall bring thee into the land of the Canaanites, as he sware unto thee and to thy fathers, and shall give it thee, that thou shalt set apart unto the LORD all that openeth the matrix, and every firstling that cometh of a beast which thou hast; the males shall be the LORD's. And every firstling of an ass thou shalt redeem with a lamb; and if thou wilt not redeem it, then thou shalt break his neck: and all the firstborn of man among thy children shalt thou redeem. And it shall be when thy son asketh thee in time to come, saying, What is this? That thou shalt say unto him, By strength of hand the LORD brought us out from Egypt, from the house of bondage: And it came to pass, when Pharaoh would hardly let us go, that the LORD slew all the firstborn in the land of Egypt, both the firstborn of man and the firstborn of beast: therefore I sacrifice to the LORD all that openeth the matrix, being males: but all the firstborn of my children I redeem. And it shall be for a token upon thine hand, and for frontlets between thine eyes: for by strength of hand the LORD brought us forth out of Egypt. And it came to pass, when Pharaoh had let the people go, that God led them not through the way of the land of the Philistines, although that was near; for God said, Lest peradventure the people repent when they see war, and they return to Egypt.

Hear, O Israel: The LORD our God, is one LORD: And thou shalt love the LORD thy God with all thine heart, and with all thy soul, and with all thy might. And these words which I command thee this day, shall be in thine heart: And thou shalt teach them diligently unto the children, and shalt talk of them when thou sittest in thine house, and when thou walkest by the way, and when thou liest down, and when thou risest up. And thou shalt bind them for a sign upon thine hand, and they shall be *as frontlets between thine eyes. And thou shalt write them upon the posts of thy house, and on thy gates. Thou shalt fear the LORD thy God, and serve him, and shalt swear by his name. Ye shall not go after other gods, of the gods of the people which are round about you: (for the LORD thy God is a jealous God among you) lest the anger of the LORD thy God be kindled against thee, and destroy thee from off the face of the earth. Ye shall not tempt the LORD your God, as ye tempted him in Massah. Ye shall diligently keep the commandments of the LORD your God, and his testimonies, and his statutes, which he hath commanded thee. And thou shalt do that which is right and good in the sight of the LORD: that it may be well with thee, and that thou mayest go in and possess the good land which the LORD sware unto thy fathers, to cast out all thine enemies from before thee, as the LORD hath spoken. And when thy son asketh thee in time to come, saying, What mean the testimonies, and the statutes, and the judgments, which the Lord our God hath commanded you? then thou shalt say unto thy son, We were Pharaoh's bondmen in Egypt and the LORD brought us out of Egypt with a mighty hand: and the LORD showed signs and wonders, great and sore, upon Egypt, upon Pharaoh, and upon all his household, before our eyes: and he brought us out from thence, that he might bring us in, to give us the land which he sware unto our fathers.*

It was probably not polite, but I hid and took a picture of these Jewish men. This scene was not going to escape me. I was stunned; I had never seen anyone dressed that way before. Later, I found out the meaning of these prayer boxes. Since many Jewish people still wait for their Messiah to come for the first time, they don't believe in the Brit Chadasha. Jesus Christ, the "Anointed One," was already here two thousand years ago to fulfill the Tanakh. Messiah means "Anointed One" in Hebrew.

In order to have those Scriptures close to their heart and between their eyes – in their brain – which contain passages of the law. The phylacteries contain the aforementioned Scriptures in two small black leather boxes attached to leather straps. One is wrapped around the left arm, which is close to the heart, and the other is wrapped around the forehead, close to the brain. They are worn by Jews with a strong belief in God. It is in obedience to their understanding of Exodus

13:16, *And it shall be for a token upon thine hand, and for frontlets between thine eyes: for by strength of hand the LORD brought us forth out of Egypt.*

By Yeshua's death on the cross and the shedding of His blood, the born-again believer knows that his or her sins are forgiven. The Holy Spirit now convicts us—what an assurance. *This is the covenant that I will make with them after those days, saith the LORD, I will put my laws into their hearts, and in their minds will I write them; and their sins and iniquities will I remember no more* (Hebrew 10:16–17). It takes place when we invite Him into our heart to become our Savior, whereas many Jewish people still wear theirs on the outside to this day. Yet Ezekiel wrote about it in chapter 36:26, *A new heart also will I give you, and a new spirit will I put within you: and I will take away the stony heart out of your flesh, and I will give you an heart of flesh.*

Israel, the land of the Bible, is a small country situated at the eastern end of the Mediterranean that could fit twenty-eight times into the state of Texas. It is surrounded by Lebanon, Syria, Jordan, and Egypt, all together twenty two seperate Islamic states spanning an area of more than five million square miles. Israel is only one state of three thousand square miles. World-wide there are one billion three hundred million Muslims, compared to a world-wide Jewish population between twelve and eighteen million. A world-wide re-gathering is taking place. In the 1890s, the population of Israel was forty thousand. After World War ll, the count was eight hundred thousand. They came from over hundred different countries. Israel's capital city of Jerusalem is mentioned over seven hundred times in the Scriptures, but not even once in the Quran.

When we arrived in Tel Aviv at Ben Gurion Airport, these Jewish men blended in with the local people. Our prearranged taxi driver chauffeured us to the home of the Arabic Christian family just outside of Bethlehem. It was to be our home base for over five weeks.

Since we lived so close, we could hardly wait to go up to the Church of the Nativity in the Bethlehem Square the next morning. It is one of the oldest churches in the world. Bethlehem was the birthplace of King David and, ten centuries later, it is the site where Yeshua was born in the manger. Yes, the Savior of the world was born in an animal stable, as described in Luke 2:1–7,

And it came to pass in those days, that there went out a decree from Caesar Augustus that all the world should be taxed. (And this taxing was first made when Cyrenius was governor of Syria.) And all went to be taxed, every one into his own city. And Joseph also went up from Galilee, out of the city of Nazareth, into Judea, unto the city of David, which is called Bethlehem; because he was of the house and lineage of David: to be taxed with Mary his espoused wife, being great with child. And so it was, while they were there, the days were accomplished that she should be delivered. And she brought forth her firstborn son, and wrapped him in swaddling clothes, and laid him in a manger, because there was no room for them in the Inn.

A silver star inlaid in the stone floor marks the spot where Yeshua was born. The church is walled in by three monasteries: Armenian, Greek, and Latin. Visitors must enter the basilica through a low, narrow entrance, which can be seen at the end of the long approach to the church. We obtained a special key from the monks to enter a side entrance. Steps lead down to the Tomb of the Innocent next to the Bell Tower. It displays the bones of many innocent children, separated by the bones of their mothers who refused to give them up. The wise men returned home via a different route. We read in Matthew 2:16, *Then Herod, when he saw that he was mocked of the wise men, was exceeding wroth, and sent forth, and slew all the children that were in Bethlehem, and in all the coasts thereof, from two years old and under, according to the time which he had diligently enquired of the wise men.*

The wise men—none of them Jews—came from the East and followed the star in the sky. They inquired from King Herod as to where they might find He who was born the King of the Jews so they could bring him gifts and worship Him. King Herod's jealousy of losing his position made him mass murder all those innocent babies. He could not distinguish the difference between a physical and a spiritual king. Although the wise men followed the star shown them by God, Satan had already set out to kill Yeshua in His infancy.

Around the corner from the Church of the Nativity is another church, the site where Mary took baby Yeshua in order to breastfeed him. She probably wanted some privacy away from all the visitors.

It is called the "Milk Grotto Street" and is the route taken by Joseph when he fled with Mary and the baby to Egypt. A life-size statue of a donkey with Mary and baby Yeshua settled on top, led by Joseph, can be seen in the courtyard of the Milk Grotto Church.

From there, it is only a short walk to Shepherd's Field, with its chapel and shepherd's cave to shelter the lambs from the weather. It was here that the angel appeared to tell the shepherds that a Savior, who was Christ the Lord, was born that day, as evidenced by a babe wrapped in swaddling clothes lying in a manger. Luke 2:8-20,

And there were in the same country shepherds abiding in the field, keeping watch over their flock by night. And, lo, the angel of the Lord came upon them, and the glory of the Lord shone round about them: and they were sore afraid. And the angel said unto them, Fear not: for, behold, I bring you good tidings of great joy, which shall be to all people. For unto you is born this day in the city of David a Savior, which is Christ the Lord. And this shall be a sign unto you;Ye shall find the babe wrapped in swaddling clothes, lying in a manger. And suddenly there was with the angel a multitude of the heavenly host praising God, and saying, Glory to God in the highest, and on earth peace, good will toward men. And it came to pass, as the angels were gone away from them into heaven, the shepherds said one to another, Let us now go even unto Bethlehem, and see this thing which is come to pass, which the Lord hath made known unto us. And they came with haste, and found Mary, and Joseph, and the babe lying in a manger. And when they had seen it, they made known abroad the saying which was told them concerning this Child. And all they that heard it wondered at those things which were told them by the shepherds. But Mary kept all these things, and pondered them in her heart. And the shepherds returned, glorifying and praising God for all the things that they had heard and seen, as it was told to them.

The Chapel at Shepherd's Field houses three most beautiful paintings, directly drawn inside on the stone walls in gold and blue. They depict the visit from the angel and the shepherd boys. I photographed the paintings and copied their explained meaning:

1. The shepherds heard the angels tell them, "Go to Bethlehem. Christ was born."

2. Their visit to Bethlehem and seeing the baby Yeshua.

3. After seeing the baby Yeshua, on their way back to the Shepherd's Field, the boy is dancing. The father plays the flute and the grandfather looks as if he has seen the glory!

God made sure that the arrival of the proper baby was confirmed. He sent the wise men on a long journey to follow the star in order to identify the real King of kings. He got plenty of exposure that King Herod could not deal with. I have heard it said that all the gifts brought to Yeshua by the wise men financed the trip and stay when they fled to Egypt. I don't know the validity of this. Here are the Scriptures to back it up: Matthew 2:1-16, & 19-23,

Now when Jesus was born in Bethlehem of Judea in the days of Herod the king, behold there came wise men from the east to Jerusalem, saying, Where is he that is born King of the Jews? For we have seen his star in the east, and are come to worship him. When Herod the king heard these things, he was troubled, and all Jerusalem with him. And when he had gathered all the chief priests and scribes of the people together, he demanded of them where Christ should be born. And they said unto him, in Bethlehem of Judea: for thus it is written by the prophet, And thou Bethlehem, in the land of Judah, are not the least among the princes of Judah: for out of thee shall come a Governor, that shall rule my people Israel. Then Herod, when he had privily called the wise men, inquired of them diligently what time the star appeared. And he sent them to Bethlehem, and said, Go and search diligently for the young child, and when ye have found him, bring me word again, that I may come and worship him also. When they had heard the king, they departed; and lo, the star, which they saw in the east, went before them, till it came and stood over where the young child was. When they saw the star, they rejoiced with exceeding great joy. And when they were come into the house, they saw the young child with Mary his mother, and fell down, and worshipped him: And when they had opened their treasures, they presented unto him gifts; gold, and frankincense, and myrrh. And being warned of God in a dream that they should not return to Herod, they departed into their own country another way. And when they were departed, behold the angel of the Lord appeared to Joseph in a dream, saying, Arise and take the young child and his mother, and flee into Egypt, and be thou there until I bring thee word: for Herod will seek the young child to destroy him. When he arose, he took the young child and his mother by night, and departed into Egypt: and was there until the death of Herod: that it might be fulfilled which was spoken of the Lord by the prophet, saying, Out of Egypt have I called my Son. But when Herod was dead, behold, an angel of the Lord appeareth in a dream to Joseph in Egypt saying, Arise, and take the young child and his mother, and go into the land of Israel: for they are dead which sought the young child's life. And he arose, and took the young child and his mother, and came into the land of Israel. But when he heard that Archelaus did reign in Judea in the room of his father Herod, he was afraid to go thither: notwithstanding, being warned of God in a dream, he turned aside into the parts of Galilee: And he came and dwelt in a city called Nazareth: that it might be fulfilled which was spoken by the prophets, He shall be a Nazarene.

Can anyone doubt the authenticity of the Scriptures? Even in the Tanakh, the prophets foretold of Him being born in Bethlehem, which means "house of bread." Yes, He is the Bread of Life. Seven centuries prior, the prophet Micah proclaimed one of the greatest prophecies about Yeshua when he announced Him to be the ruler in Israel! It might shock you what I'm going to tell you. In 1986 as I was ministering in Oregon, the Holy Spirit revealed to me Isaiah 19:18-25 and that I was to fulfill it. Verse 25 states: *"Whom the LORD of hosts shall bless, saying, Blessed be Egypt my people, and Assyria the work of my hands, and Israel mine inheritance."* Many years later on the 24th of July 2012 the Holy Spirit let me know the reason why Bethlehem is controlled by the Arabs. Because you don't believe in Yeshua, who was born in Bethlehem you have no claim to it and God gave it to the Muslims temporarily. According to Isaiah 19 some day you all be one. Although Yeshua's lineage can be traced back to King David, His roots go all the way back to the beginning, as described in Micah 5:2, (who lived between 704 BC and 696 BC) *But thou Bethlehem Ephrathah, though thou be among the thousands of Judah, yet out of thee shall he come forth unto me that is to be ruler in Israel; whose goings forth have been from of old, from everlasting.* To document the accuracy of the Scriptures, the prophet Hosea, who lived around 750 BC, prophesied His return from Egypt in Hosea 11:1b, *And called my son out of Egypt.* Many wars have been fought to deny this truth and much hatred and persecution of believers is experienced to this day. It is and always has been a war by Satan against Yeshua.

Close by is the field were Ruth the Moabitess met Boaz while she was gleaning barley in his field. *And Naomi had a kinsman of her husband's, a mighty man of wealth, of the family of Elimelech; and his name was Boaz. So Boaz took Ruth, and she was his wife: and when he went in unto her, the LORD gave her conception, and she bare a son. There is a son born to Naomi; and they called his name Obed: he is the father of Jesse, the father of David* (Ruth 2:1; 4:13 & 17b).

On the outskirts of Bethlehem, we visited Rachel's Tomb, where Jewish women came to pray, shed tears, and tell Rachel their problems until it fell under Arabic control. I heard that there is a high wall around it now and it is patrolled with machine guns. Maybe this is how the delicate glass tear bottle originated, which is a souvenir item. I read in Psalms 56:8, *Thou tellest my wanderings: put thou my tears into thy bottle: are they not in thy book?* Remember, anywhere something spiritual took place, a historical monument of some sort was erected. Rachel's tomb was no exception, built in remembrance of her death, which occurred while giving birth to Benjamin, as described in Genesis 35:16–20,

And they journeyed from Bethel; and there was but a little way to come to Ephrath: and Rachel travailed, and she had hard labor. And it came to pass, when she was in hard labor, that the midwife said unto her, Fear not; thou shalt have this son also. And it came to pass, as her soul was departing (for she died) that she called his name Ben-oni: but his father called him Benjamin. And Rachel died, and was buried on the way to Ephrath, which is Bethlehem. And Jacob set a pillar upon her grave: that is the pillar of Rachel's grave unto this day.

It is hard to imagine all these sites of old unless you can see them for yourself. It would surely change your life and enhance your knowledge of Israel, giving you a clear picture of the Old Testament, the Tanakh, and Yeshua's ministry as described in the New Testament— the Brit Chadasha. In fact, serious believers should have it on their priority list to visit Israel at least once in their lifetime. Starting with the first book of the Bible, Yes, we walked where Yeshua walked.

David's Well was at King David's Cinema, where we saw a presentation of the Jesus film. It must have been renamed later to David's Well. We read in 2 Samuel 23:14–27,

> And David was then in an hold, and the garrison of the Philistines was then in Bethlehem. And David longed, and said, Oh that one would give me drink of water of the well of Bethlehem, that was by the gate! And the three mighty men brake through the host of the Philistines, and drew water out of the well of Bethlehem, that was by the gate, and took it, and brought it to David: nevertheless he would not drink thereof, but poured it out unto the LORD. And he said, Be it far from me, O LORD, that I should do this: is not this the blood of the men that went in jeopardy of their lives? therefore he would not drink it. These things did these three mighty men.

It would not be fair if I didn't mention the many shops we encountered in Bethlehem. Our tour guide took us to the home of an olive wood carver, who displayed his workmanship. We visited several times and befriended the family. One of the sisters of their adult children made me a purse and matching belt out of olive wood beets. I bought my olive wood Nativity set from their brother which showed his outstanding workmanship. It is so expertly done that I display it year-round. Many of the handcrafted gift items are made from mother of pearl.

About five miles from Bethlehem is Herodium, one of King Herod's five desert fortresses, built as a sanctuary against enemy attack. It lies in the hollow of a manmade crater. After completion, the top of this massive mountain was cut off, leaving it without a roof. Archaeological excavations from the past allowed us to identify different rooms, including a Roman bathhouse and numerous other divided rooms. Documents prove that the fortress was used by Jewish forces during the first and second revolts against the Romans. It was a long walk up there. Because of the steep climb, even their horse stables were situated down below. It displayed an awesome view from the top.

Next we visited Jerusalem. We came with an awesome expectancy. On Mount Zion was King David's tomb and the upper room where Yeshua ate His last supper with the disciples. We saw the Dormition Abbey with the crypt where Mary fell into eternal sleep.

We passed the Citadel on the right near the Jaffa Gate as we came from Bethlehem, which is less than five miles away. Its high tower overlooks the ancient, walled-in city. This portion of Jerusalem is called the Old City, and was the fortified Jerusalem of the Bible. Today, the three-thousand-year-old city of Jerusalem, the capital of the Jewish faith, is also a holy city for Christianity and Islam.

Let me share with you some of the important history of the wall and recount what one person can accomplish for God. It is rather lengthy, but you will appreciate it as you read these important Scriptures. The king of Babylon, who had made war, carried thousands with him in to exile. All the gates were broken down and the people feared for their safety. God gave the prophet Nehemiah a burden for his people. I would like to illustrate with the help of the Scriptures how important our unshakable faith in God is, no matter what the circumstances might dictate or how bleak things look.

The words of Nehemiah the son of Hachaliah. And it came to pass in the month Chisleu, in the twentieth year, as I was in Shushan the palace, that Hanani, one of my brethren, came, he and certain men of Judah; and I asked them concerning the Jews that had escaped, which were left of the captivity, and concerning Jerusalem. And they said unto me, The remnant that are left of the captivity there in the province are in great affliction and reproach: the wall of Jerusalem also is broken down, and the gates thereof are burned with fire. And it came to pass, when I heard these words, that I set down and wept, and mourned certain days; and fasted, and prayed before the God of heaven, and said, I beseech thee, O LORD God of heaven, the great and terrible God, that keepeth covenant and mercy for them that love him and observe his commandments: let thine ear now be attentive, and thine eyes open, that thou mayest hear the prayer of thy servant, which I pray before thee now, day and night, for the children of Israel thy servants, and confess the sins of the children of Israel, which we have sinned against thee: both I and my father's house have sinned. We have dealt very corruptly against thee, and have not kept the commandments, nor the statutes, nor judgments, which thou commandest thy servant Moses. Remember, I beseech thee, the word that thou commandest thy servant Moses, saying, if ye transgress, I will scatter you abroad among the nations: but if ye turn unto me, and keep my commandments, and do them; though there were of you cast out unto the uttermost part of the heaven, yet will I gather them from thence, and will bring them unto the place that I have chosen to set my name there. Now these are thy servants and thy people, whom thou hast redeemed by thy great power, and by thy strong hand. O Lord, I beseech thee, let now thine ear be attentive to the prayer of thy servant, and to the prayer of thy servants, who desire to fear thy name: and prosper, I pray thee, thy servant this day, and grant him mercy in the sight of this man. For I was the king's cupbearer (Nehemiah 1:1–11).

Nehemiah found favor with the king.

And it came to pass in the month Nisan, in the twentieth year of Artaxerxes the king, that wine was before him: and I took up the wine, and gave it unto the king. Now I had not been beforetime sad in his presence. Wherefore the king said unto me, Why is thy countenance sad, seeing thou art not sick? this is nothing else but sorrow of heart. Then I was very sore afraid, and said to the king, Let the king live forever: why should not my countenance be sad, when the city, the place of my fathers sepulchers lieth waste, and the gates thereof are consumed with fire? Then the king said unto me, For what dost thou make request? So I prayed to the God of heaven. And I said unto the king, If it please the king, and if thy servant have found favor in thy sight, that thou wouldest send me unto Judah, unto the city of my fathers' sepulchres, that I may build it. And the king said unto me (the queen also sitting by him) For how long shall thy journey be? and when wilt thou return? So it pleased the king to send me; and I set him a time. Moreover I said unto the king, If it please the king, let letters be given me to the governors beyond the river, that they may convey me over till I come into Judah; and a letter unto Asaph the keeper of the king's forest, that he may give me timber to make beams for the gates of the palace which appertained to the house, for the wall of the city, and for the house that I shall enter into. And the king granted me, according to the good hand of my God upon me. Then I came to the governors beyond the river, and gave them the king's letters. Now the king had sent captains of the army and horsemen with me. When Sanballat the Horonite and Tobiah the servant, the Ammonite, heard of it, it grieved them exceedingly that there was come a man to seek the welfare of the children of Israel. So I came to Jerusalem and was there three days. And I arose in the night, I and some few men with me; neither told I any man what my God had put in my heart to do at Jerusalem: neither was there any beast with me, save the beast that I rode upon. And I went out by night by the gate of the valley, even before the dragon well, and to the dung port, and viewed the walls of Jerusalem, which were broken down, and the gates thereof were consumed with fire. Then I went on to the gate of the fountain and to the king's pool, but there was no place for the beast that was under me to pass. Then went I up in the night by the brook, and viewed the wall, and turned back, and entered by the gate of the valley, and so returned. And the rulers knew not whither I went, or what I did: neither had I as yet told it to the Jews, nor to the priests, nor to the nobles, nor to the rulers, nor to the rest that did not work. Then I said to them, Ye see the distress that we are in, how Jerusalem lieth waste, and the gates thereof are burned with fire: come, and let us build up the wall of Jerusalem, that we be no more a reproach. Then I told them of the hand of my God which was good upon me; as also of the king's words that he had spoken unto me. And they said, Let us rise up and build. So they strengthened their hands for this good work. But when Sanballat the Horonite, and Tobiah the servant, the Ammonite, and Geshem the Arabian, heard it, they laughed us to scorn, and despised us, and said, What is this thing that ye do? will ye rebel against the king? Then answered I them, and said unto them, The God of heaven, he will prosper us; therefore we his servants will arise and build: but ye have no portion, nor right, nor memorial, in Jerusalem (Nehemiah 2:1–20).

Then Nehemiah gives an account of who helped to repair the wall and the remarkable unity they displayed. We read of their tremendous challenge in Nehemiah 3:1, *Then Eliashib the high priest rose up with his brethren the priests, and they builded the sheep gate: they sanctified it, and set up the doors of it; even unto the tower of Meah they sanctified it, unto the tower of Hananeel.* When Sanballat heard that they were rebuilding the wall, he was furious and mocked the Jews. His friend Tobiah said, "Whatever they build, if even a fox goes up on it, he will break down their stone wall."

Nehemiah went to prayer, as we read in chapter 4:4–23,

Hear, O our God; for we are despised: and turn their reproach upon their own head, and give them for a pray in the land of captivity: and cover not their iniquity, and let not their sin be blotted out from before thee: for they have provoked thee to anger before the builders. So built we the wall; and all the wall was joined together unto the half thereof: for the people had a mind to work. But it came to pass, that when Sanballat, and Tobiah, and the Arabians, and the Ammonites, and the Ashdodit heard that the walls of Jerusalem were made up, and that the breaches began to be stopped, then they were very wroth and conspired all of them together to come and to fight against Jerusalem and to hinder it. Nevertheless we made our prayer to our God, and set a watch against them day and night, because of them. And Judah said, The strength of the bearers of burdens is decayed, and there is so much rubbish: so that we are not able to build the wall. And our adversaries said, They shall not know, neither see, till we come in the midst among them, and slay them, and cause the work to cease. And it came to pass, that when the Jews which dwelt by them came, they said unto us ten times, From all places whence ye shall return, unto us they will be upon you. Therefore set I in the lower places behind the wall, and on the higher places. I even set the people after their families with their swords, their spears, and their bows. And I looked, and rose up, and said unto the nobles, and to the rulers, and to the rest of the people, Be not ye afraid of them: remember the LORD, which is great and terrible, and fight for your brethren, your sons, and your daughters, your wives, and your houses. And it came to pass, when our enemies heard that it was known unto us, and God had brought their counsel to nought, that we returned all of us to the wall everyone unto his work. And it came to pass from that time forth, that the half of my servants wrought in the work, and the other half of them held both the spears, the shields, the bows, and the habergeons; and the rulers were behind all the house of Judah. They which builded on the wall, and they that bear burdens, with those that laded, everyone with one of his hands wrought in the work, and with the other hand held a weapon.

For the builders, every one had his sword girded by his side, and so builded. And he that sounded the trumpet was by me. Then I said unto the nobles, and to the rulers, and to the rest of the people, The work is great and large, and we are separated upon the wall, and far from another. In what place therefore ye hear the sound of the trumpet, resort ye thither unto us: our God shall fight for us. So we labored in the work: and half of them held the spears from the rising of the morning till the stars appeared. Likewise at the same time said I unto the people, Let every one with his servant lodge within Jerusalem, that in the night they may be a guard to us, and labor on the day. So neither I, nor my brethren, nor my servants, nor the men of the guard which followed me, none of us put off our clothes, saving that every one put them off for washing.

So the wall was finished in the twenty and fifth day of the month Elul, in fifty and two days. And it came to pass, that when all our enemies heard thereof, and all the heathen that were about us saw these things, they wrought of our God (Nehemiah 6:15–16).

As governor of the province of Judah, Nehemiah appointed his brother Hanani as governor of Jerusalem. In the next few verses, we learn how many people returned. Would you say that God was in this project all the way?

Now the city was large and great: but the people were few therein, and the houses were not builded. And my God put into mine heart to gather together the nobles, and the rulers, and the people, that they might be reckoned by genealogy. And I found a register of the genealogy of them which came up at the first, and found written therein, These are the children of the province, that went up out of the captivity, of those who had been carried away, whom Nebuchadnezzar the king of Babylon had carried away; and came again to Jerusalem and to Judah, every one unto his city. The whole congregation together was forty and two thousand three hundred and threescore, beside their man servants and their maidservants, of whom there were seven thousand three hundred thirty and seven: and they had two hundred forty and five singing men and singing women (Nehemiah 7:4–6, 66–67).

The ramparts, which are about seven feet wide, are reached via stairways. The walkway has been paved, guardrails have been installed, and observation points provided. The walkways are divided into different routes. From Damascus Gate to Lion's Gate is about fifteen hundred meters. From the Citadel to Zion Gate is about five hundred and fifty meters. From Zion Gate to Dung Gate is about seven hundred and fifty meters. Yes, we walked the ramparts almost around the whole Old City. As I continue, you will read what all goes on inside. The Jaffa Gate is close to the Citadel. Then we came across Zion Gate, Dung Gate, St. Stephen's Gate, New Gate, and Herod's Gate, which is also called the Gate of Flowers. The most famous of them all is the Golden Gate, which was permanently closed by the Turks in 1530. It faces the Mount of Olives and is in plain sight from the Church of all Nations. It is the location where Yeshua prayed and sweat blood. Damascus Gate is the main entrance in to the Old City. It marked the beginning of the highway to Damascus. Jews call the gate Shaar Shechem, since the highway passes through the town of Shechem, which was the capital of Samaria in biblical times.

Today this city is called Nablus, with a population of 126,132. It is also the place of Joseph's tomb. *And Joseph said to his brethren, I die: and God will surely visit you, and bring you out of this land unto the land which he sware to Abraham, to Isaac, and to Jacob. And Joseph took an oath of the children of Israel, saying, God will surely visit you, and ye shall carry up my bones from hence. So Joseph died, being an hundred and ten years old: and they embalmed him, and he was put in a coffin in Egypt* (Genesis 50:24–26). *And Moses took the bones of Joseph with him: for he had straitly sworn the children of Israel, saying, God will surely visit you; and ye shall carry up my bones away hence with you* (Exodus 13:19).

When we visited Joseph's tomb underground in 1985, several Jewish soldiers were standing guard above ground with machine guns. Now that Nablus is under Arabic rule, I wondered who was watching over Joseph's tomb now. Palestinians destroyed Joseph's tomb during the Arabic–Jewish uprising in October 2000. They must have restored it again, because I heard Minister Limor Livnat from Jerusalem in a speech here told us that her nephew went there to pray with some friends. I was very touched and asked for permission to mention it in my book. I received the following e mail: Ben Yosef Livnot, of blessed memory, was murdered by a Palistinian policeman at Joseph's Tomb in Shechem in May 2011. He left behind a wife and four children and was the nephew of MK Limor Livnat, Israel's Minister of Culture and Sport.

Jacob's Well is also in Nablus. We even had a cool drink from it. In earlier biblical times, Jacob's Well had been a traditional resting place for travelers. The Bible reads different to me now that I have visited so many sites.

And he must needs go through Samaria. Then cometh he to a city of Samaria, which is called Sychar, near to the parcel of ground that Jacob gave to his son Joseph. Now Jacob's well was there. Jesus therefore, being wearied with his journey, sat thus on the well: and it was about the sixth hour. There cometh a woman of Samaria to draw water: Jesus saith unto her, Give me to drink. (For his disciples were gone away unto the city to buy meat.) Then said the woman of Samaria unto him, how is it that thou, being a Jew, askest drink of me, which am a woman of Samaria? For the Jews have no dealings with the Samaritans. Jesus answered and said unto her, If thou knewest the gift of God, and who it is that said to thee, Give me to drink, thou wouldest have asked of him, and would have given thee living water. The woman saith unto him, Sir, thou hast nothing to draw with, and the well is deep: from whence then hast thou that living water? (John 4:4–11).

The extremely large church for this time period behind the well has been rebuilt many times, but it has always been destroyed again. In 1914, reconstruction was started once more but was never completed. I remember seeing a large cross cut in the back of the concrete wall, through which allows one to see daylight and the blue sky.

Deuteronomy chapter 27 speaks of two mountains outside Nablus. Mount Gerizim is to bless them and Mount Ebal is to curse them.

And Moses with the elders of Israel commanded the people, saying, Keep all the commandments which I command you this day. And it shall be on the day when ye shall pass over Jordan unto the land which the LORD thy God giveth thee, that thou shalt set thee up great stones, and plaster, and plaster them with plaster. And thou shalt write upon them all the words of this law, when thou art passed over, that thou mayest go in unto the land which the LORD thy God giveth thee, a land that floweth with milk and honey, as the

LORD God of thy fathers hath promised thee. Thou shalt therefore obey the voice of the LORD thy God, and do his commandments and his statutes, which I command thee this day. And Moses charged the people the same day, saying, These shall stand upon mount Gerizim to bless the people, when ye are come over Jordan, Simeon, and Levi, and Judah, and Issachar, and Joseph, and Benjamin (Deuteronomy 27:1–3, 10–12).

Verses 13–14 tell of Mount Ebal: *And these shall stand upon mount Ebal to curse, Reuben, Gad and Asher, and Zebulin, Dan and Naphtali. And the Levites shall speak, and say unto all the men of Israel with a loud voice...* Verses 15–16 describe the twelve curses.

Deuteronomy chapter 28 describes all the blessings.

We had an appointment with the Samaritan high priest Abraham Cohen, a descendant of Aaron, which visit I recorded on audio tape. He rode with us up to the summit of Mount Gerizim were he showed us their temple which contained an ancient Torah. He told us that he was 63 years old and never had his hair cut. When he took his covering off to show us, his hair was very, very long. He also mentioned, that when he was a boy their were only 180 Sameritans. They have only grown to 600 world-wide. Their believers leave Nablus on Friday to go up to the temple at Mount Gerizim. After sundown on Saturday, the Sabbath, they return home. They don't drive a car during that time and won't even touch a light switch. It is a time for total rest. He also showed us their sacrificial altar. On Friday they slaughter their animals and cook them underground, which keeps the food warm for the next day. He also told us, that they sacrifice lambs once a year for atonement of their sins.

The Mount of Olives is the site from which Yeshua ascended into heaven forty days after His resurrection, as described in Acts 1:1–5,

The former treatise have I made, O Theophilus, of all that Jesus began both to do and teach, until the day in which he was taken up, after that he through the Holy Ghost had given commandments unto the apostles whom he had chosen: To whom also he shewed himself alive after his passion by many infallible proofs, being seen of them forty days, and speaking of the things pertaining to the kingdom of God: And, being assembled together with them, commanded them that they should not depart from

Jerusalem, but wait for the promise of the Father, which, saith he, ye have heard of me. For John truly baptized with water; but ye shall be baptized with the Holy Ghost not many days hence.

The dome at the Chapel of the Ascension marks the place where it is traditionally accepted that Yeshua ascended to heaven. An imprint of the footstep of Yeshua is contained in this circular building, which was erected around the Rock of Ascension in 380 AD. Verses 6-13 a,

When they therefore were come together, they asked him, saying, Lord, wilt thou at this time restore again the kingdom to Israel? And he said unto them, It is not for you to know the times and the seasons, which the Father hath put in his own power. But ye shall receive power, after that the Holy Ghost is come upon you: and ye shall be witnesses unto me both in Jerusalem, and in all Judea, and in Samaria, and unto the uttermost part of the earth. And when he had spoken these things, while they beheld, he was taken up; and a cloud received him out of their sight. And while they looked steadfastly toward heaven as he went up, behold, two men stood by them in white apparel: which also said, Ye men of Galilee, why stand ye gazing up to heaven? This same Jesus, which is taken up from you into heaven, shall so come in like manner as ye have seen him go into heaven. Then returned they unto Jerusalem from the mount called Olivet, which is from Jerusalem a Sabbath day's journey. And when they were come in, they went up into an upper room.

As we walked down from the Mount of Olives on one of our visits we met a small, colorfully dressed Methodist group from Nigeria with their bishop. Their church is called Jerubim and Ceraphim. They sang "Halleluja, Halleluja, Halleluja Sa-Ba-Wa." Halleluja means glory to God.

The Mount of Olives got its name because of its many olive trees. From the fourth century, it has been honored as the site of Gethsemane. The life expectancy of an olive tree is five hundred years or more and new ones sometimes grow from the roots of fallen trunks. One olive tree can yield up to a thousand pounds of olive oil a year.

It was here in the Garden of Gethsemane that Yeshua was betrayed by Judas and arrested.

Gethsemane is described in Matthew 26:36–44,

Then cometh Jesus with them unto a place called Gethsemane, and said unto the disciples, Sit ye here, while I go and pray yonder. And he took with him Peter and the two sons of Zebedee, and began to be sorrowful and very heavy. Then saith he unto them, my soul is exceeding sorrowful even unto death: tarry ye here, and watch with me. And he went a little further, and fell on his face, and prayed, saying, O my Father, if it be possible, let this cup pass from me: nevertheless not as I will, but as thou wilt. And he cometh unto the disciples, and findeth them asleep, and saith unto Peter, What, could ye not watch with me one hour? Watch and pray, that ye enter not into temptation: and the spirit indeed is willing, but the flesh is weak. He went away the second time, and prayed, saying, O my Father, if this cup may not pass away from me, except I drink it. Thy will be done. And he came and found them asleep again: for their eyes were heavy. And he left them, and went away again, and prayed the third time, saying the same words.

High above the large, skull-like rock next to the Arabic bus station, three crosses are visible on Golgatha. In 1883, General Gordon of Khartoum recognized the similarity of the description in the Bible of the place of Yeshua's crucifixion to the skull-like rock. Eventually, the hill became known as Gordon's Calvary. *And he bearing his cross went forth into a place called the place of the scull, which is called in the Hebrew Golgatha: where they crucified him* (John 19: 17–18a).

The Church of All Nations was built around the large Rock of Agony, where Yeshua prayed and sweat blood. The rock is surrounded by a black, rod-iron fence of crown of thorns. On my last trip to Israel, I meditated for quite some time there. As I looked across, I realized that this thick Golden Gate would open one of these days and our Messiah will walk through it. This gate was actually built by the Byzantines. The original gate that Yeshua will walk through is about 10 feet under the present one. In His vision almost twenty-five hundred years ago, God showed it to Ezekiel, as we read in Ezekiel 44:1–3,

Then he brought me back the way of the gate of the outward sanctuary which looketh toward the east; but it was shut. Then said the LORD unto me; This gate shall be shut, it shall not be opened, and no man shall enter by it; because the LORD, the God of Israel, hath entered in by it, therefore it shall be shut. It is for the prince; the prince, he shall sit in it to eat bread before the LORD; he shall enter by the way of the porch of that gate, and shall go out by the way of the same.

Several Turks tried to open the gate many years ago, but all of them died instantly. Immediately outside the wall is a Muslim cemetery where it is believed that no one would walk through a cemetery. They are naive. Our Lord can do as He pleases.

It is awesome to read that Zechariah, who lived from 520 to 475 BC, prophesied that Yeshua will appear on the Mount of Olives. *And his feet shall stand in that day upon the mount of Olives, which is before Jerusalem on the east, and the mount of Olives shall cleave in the midst (split in two) thereof toward the east and towards the west, and there shall be a great valley; and half of the mountain shall remove toward the north, and half of it towards the south* (Zechariah 14:4). It is said that the instant the Messiah returns to the Mount of Olives, from which He ascended two thousand years ago, an earthquake will split the mountain in two and form a new canal that will make Jerusalem a major inland seaport. This geological shift will cause the Dead Sea to overflow southward. When questioned, He will show proof in Zechariah 13:6, *And one shall say unto him, What are these wounds in thine hands? Then he shall answer, Those with which I was wounded in the house of my friends.*

We read in Romans 10:1–5,

Brethren, my heart's desire and prayer to God for Israel is, that they might be saved. For I bear them record that they have a zeal of God, but not according to knowledge. For they being ignorant of God's righteousness, and going about to establish their own righteousness, have not submitted themselves unto the righteousness of God. For Christ is the end of the law for righteousness to every one that believeth. For Moses describeth the righteousness which is of the law, that the man which doeth those things shall live by them.

The Via Dolorosa, also called the Way of the Cross, winds along a narrow street in Jerusalem's Old City. Walking up the Via Dolorosa, we came to the Lirhostrotos, the site of the crowning with thorns and the mocking of Yeshua. Next was the Court of Flagelation, where Yeshua endured great pain. I will forever remember the place. Some spiritual experiences never leave your memory. *But he was wounded for our transgressions, he was bruised for our iniquities: the chastisement of our peace was upon him; and with his stripes we are healed* (Isaiah 53:5). In the same area was Pilate's Courtyard in the Antonia Fortress, as described in John 18:33, *Then Pilate entered into the judgment hall again, and called Jesus, and said unto him, Art thou the King of the Jews?* Though declared innocent by Pilate, He was bound to a pillar of scourging described in John 19:1–4, *Then Pilate therefore took Jesus, and scourged him. And the soldiers platted a crown of thorns, and put it on his head, and they put on him a purple robe, and said, Hail, King of the Jews! And they smote him with there hands. Pilate therefore went forth again, and said unto them, Behold, I bring him forth to you, that ye may know that I find no fault in him.*

Yeshua bore the cross from Pilate's Judgment Hall all the way to the place of the Skull, or Golgotha in Hebrew—the site of the crucifixion. *And they spit upon him, and took the reed, and smote him on the head. And after that they had mocked him, they took the robe off of him, and put his own raiment on him, and led him away to crucify him. And as they came out, they found a man of Cyrene, Simon by name: him they compelled to bear his cross* (Matthew 27:30–32).

Along the route he had to take are the Fourteen Stations of the Cross. Each marks an event of our Savior:

1. Yeshua is condemned to death.

2. Yeshua receives the cross.

3. Yeshua falls the first time.

4. Yeshua meets His mother.

5. Simon is made to bear the cross.

6. Veronica wipes the face of Yeshua.

7. Yeshua falls the second time.

8. Yeshua meets the woman of Jerusalem.

9. Yeshua falls the third time.

10. Yeshua is stripped of His garments.

11. Yeshua is nailed to the cross.

12. Yeshua dies on the cross.

13. Yeshua is taken down from the cross.

14. Yeshua is laid in the sepulchre.

The Garden Tomb, hewn out of the rock, was discovered in 1867 and has since been authentically validated as a Jewish tomb of the Herodian period.

And, behold, there was a man named Joseph, a counselor, and he was a good man, and a just: (The same had not consented to the counsel and deed of them;) he was of Arimathaea, a city of the Jews: who also himself waited for the kingdom of God. This man went unto Pilate, and begged the body of Jesus. And he took it down, and wrapped it in linen, and laid it in the sepulchre that was hewn in stone, wherein never man before was laid. And that day was the preparation, and the Sabbath drew on. And the women also, which came with him from Galilee, followed after, and beheld the sepulchre, and how his body was laid. And they returned and prepared spices and ointments; and rested the Sabbath day according to the commandment. Now upon the first day of the week, very early in the morning, they came unto the sepulchre, bringing the spices which they had prepared, and certain others with them. And they found the stone rolled away from the sepulchre. And they entered in, and found not the body of the Lord Jesus. And it came to pass, as they were much perplexed thereabout, behold, two men stood by them in shining garments: and as they were afraid, and bowed down their faces to the earth, they said unto them, Why seek ye the living among the dead? He is not here, but is risen: remember how he spake unto you when he was yet in Galilee, Saying, the Son of man must be delivered into the hands of sinful men, and be crucified, and the third day rise again, and they remembered his words, and returned from the sepulchre, and told all these things unto the eleven, and to all the rest. It was Mary Magdalene, and Joanne, and Mary the mother of Jesus, and other women that were with them, which told these things unto the apostles. And their words seemed to them as idle tales, and they believed them not. Then arose Peter, and ran unto the sepulchre; and stooping down, he beheld the linen clothes laid by themselves, and departed, wondering in himself at that which was come to pass (Luke 23:50–56; 24:1–12).

Only Yeshua lives beyond the grave. More then five hundred witnesses saw Him alive after He died on the cross and rose again three days later.

Like none other before Him, Yeshua bore the grief of all mankind under the weight of His cross. If we love Him, we also love His cross. That is what it took for Him to save us from going to hell. He told His disciples in Matthew 16:24, *If any man will come after me, let him deny himself, and take his cross, and follow me.* Be assured that He will not put more on us than we can handle. *And God said, Let us make man in our image, after our likeness. So God created man in his own image, in the image of God created he him; male and female created he them* (Genesis 1:26a & 27). *And have put on the new man, which is renewed in knowledge after the image of him that created him* (Colossians 3:10). *For there is one God, and one mediator between God and men, the man Christ Jesus* (1 Timothy 2:5). *And if Christ be not raised, your faith is vain; ye are yet in your sins* (1 Corinthians 15:17). Yeshua's resurrection is evidence of God's acceptance of that payment.

We visited Aceldama, the Field of the Blood. Peter describes Judas's death in Acts 1:16–20,

Men and brethren, this scripture must needs have been fulfilled, which the Holy Ghost by the mouth of David spake before concerning Judas, which was guide to them that took Jesus. For he was numbered with us, and had obtained part of his ministry. Now this man purchased a field with the reward of iniquity; and falling headlong, he burst asunder in the midst, and all his bowels gushed out. And it was known unto all the dwellers of Jerusalem; insomuch as that field is called in their proper tongue,

Aceldama, that is to say, The field of blood. For it is written in the book of Psalms, Let his habitation be desolate, and let no man dwell therein: and his bishopric let another take.

For betraying Yeshua, he was paid thirty pieces of silver. It is mind-boggling to me that it was prophesied in the Tanakh and recorded in Psalm 109:8, *Let his days be few; and let another take his office.* Desolate is right; I have been there two different times. It is a deserted, empty field. *Jesus answered them, Have not I chosen you twelve, and one of you is a devil? He spake of Judas Iscariot the son of Simon: for he it was that should betray him, being one of the twelve* (John 6:70 & 71). If you do not believe in Yeshua then please tell me for whom Judas was paid the thirty pieces of silver, after all it is printed in Psalm 109:8.

We were surprised to be able to visit the Church of St. Peter in Gallicantu, where it is said that Caiaphas lived. This was the scene of Yeshua's first trial and where Peter denied Yeshua when the cock crowed described in Matthew 26:31-35,

Then said Jesus unto them, All ye shall be offended because of me this night: for it is written, I will smite the shepherd, and the sheep of the flock shall be scattered abroad. But after I am risen again, I will go before you in Galilee. Peter answered and said unto him, though all men shall be offended because of thee, yet will I never be offended. Jesus said unto him, Verily I say unto thee, That this night, before the cock crow, thou shalt deny me trice. Peter said unto him, Though I should die with thee, yet will I not deny thee. Likewise also said all the disciples.

Christ Church is located near the Jaffa Gate in Jerusalem. Established in the nineteenth century, it was the first Protestant church in the Middle East. Built by the Church of England, Christ Church still holds regular services in several different languages.

In Peter Nostra Church, a corridor displays in fifty-seven languages, "Our Father," which his disciples asked our Lord to teach them.

And it came to pass, that, as he was praying in a certain place, when he ceased, one of his disciples said unto him, Lord, teach us to pray, as John also taught his disciples. And he said unto them, When ye pray, say, Our Father which art in heaven, Hallowed be thy name. Thy kingdom come. Thy will be done, as in heaven, so in earth. Give us day by day our daily bread. And forgive us our sins; for we also forgive every one that is indebted to us. And lead us not into temptation; but deliver us from evil (Luke 11:1–4).

Built in the fourth century, the Church of the Holy Sepulchre is a cluster of churches. Today, the church is home to six denominations: Roman Catholic, Greek Orthodox, Armenian Orthodox, Syrian Orthodox, Coptic Orthodox, and Ethiopian Orthodox. The church is of limited importance to Protestant Christians. A monk named Salomon was our tour guide through the Coptic Chapel. He explained to the people ahead of us that he was from Ethiopia. When our turn came, I mentioned the Ethiopian eunuch to him, and he responded, "Oh, you know the Bible?" From there we exchanged a few words and I asked him if he spoke in other tongues. "Why, I don't know," He answered no. I never plan what comes out of my mouth. I am led by the Holy Spirit.

He took me to his very small, primitive quarters in the back, where I prayed with him to receive the baptism in the Holy Spirit. He tried, but no response. I finally said, "Lord, hurry up, the others are waiting for me." Immediately, Salomon began to speak in other tongues. Since he was a foreigner with a language of his own, I asked him if he knew what he was saying. He said, "No, do you?" I met with him once more before we left for Egypt.

Upon my return from Cairo, I had another lengthy visit with Salomon. I laid my hands on him and prayed a stubborn headache away. We stayed in contact for a while. He last wrote to me from Germany, where he was continuing his education. He informed me that he studied during the week, but on the weekends he prays a lot in the spirit using other tongues. I was overjoyed about his enthusiasm for the Lord.

Catholics believe that the section of the holy Sepulchre under their control contains the tomb of Yeshua. They call it the angel room. Germans call it the Grave Church. In 1947, near Golgatha, a tomb was excavated. Protestants believe that this was Yeshua's grave. Why would they need Simon to help carry the cross to Golgatha if it was only around the corner?

And after that they had mocked him, they took the robe off from him, and put his own raiment on him, and led him away to crucify him. And as they came out, they found a man of Cyrene, Simon by name: him they compelled to bear his cross. And when they were come unto a place called Golgotha, that is to say, a place of a scull, they gave him vinegar to drink mingled with gall: and when he had tasted thereof, he would not drink. And they crucified him (Matthew 27:31–35a).

We saw the Church of Mary Magdalene. *Now there stood by the cross of Jesus his mother, and his mother's sister, Mary, the wife of Cleophas, and Mary Magdalene* (John 19:25).

Mary, Martha, and brother Lazarus were friends with Yeshua. I was amazed when we toured Mary and Martha's place in Bethany. Given the large property with vaulted ceilings, they were well off financially. We stepped inside the large, empty tomb close by where Lazarus once laid. The church next to it was a reminder of Yeshua raising Lazarus from the dead:

And when Mary was come where Jesus was, and saw him, she fell down at his feet, saying unto him, Lord, if thou hadst been here, my brother had not died. When Jesus therefore saw her weeping, and the Jews also weeping which came with her, he groaned in the spirit, and was troubled, and said, Where have ye laid him? They said unto him, Lord, come and see. Jesus wept. Then said the Jews, Behold how he loved him! And some of them said, Could not this man, which opened the eyes of the blind, have caused that even this man should not have died? Jesus therefore again groaning in himself cometh to the grave. It was a cave, and a stone lay upon it. Jesus said, Take ye away the stone. Martha, the sister of him that was dead, saith unto him, Lord, by this time he stinketh: for he had been dead four days. Jesus saith unto her, Said I not unto thee, that, if thou wouldest believe, thou shouldest see the glory of God? Then they took away the stone from the place where the dead was laid. And Jesus lifted up his eyes, and said, Father, I thank thee that thou hast heard me. And I knew that thou hearest me always: but because of the people which stand by I said it, that they may believe that thou hast sent me. And when he thus had spoken, he cried with a loud voice, Lazarus, come forth. And he that was dead came forth, bound hand and foot with grave clothes: and his face was bound about with a napkin. Jesus said unto them, Loose him, and let him go. Then many of the Jews which came to Mary, and had seen the things which Jesus did, believed in him (John 11:32–45).

After two days was the feast of the Passover, and of unleavened bread: and the chief priests and the scribes sought how they might take him by craft, (some trick) and put him to death. But they said, Not on the feast day, lest their be an uproar of the people. And being in Bethany in the house of Simon the leper, as he sat at meat, there came a woman having an alabaster box of ointment of spikenard very precious, and she brake the box, and poured it on his head (Mark 14:1–3).

Our taxi driver took us as far up the Mount of Olives as possible. We walked the rest of the way to the top from where we took part in the lengthy procession down hill on Palm Sunday in 1985. The following year, we watched ourselves on Christian television as the *700 Club* captured us with our beautifully decorated palms on camera.

At a Jewish cemetery at the bottom of the Mount of Olives, people placed rocks on the above-ground stone casket. I was also photographed on top of the Mount of Olives with Suzi the camel. It was hilarious to see my expression when she raised her long, hind legs to get up. My photo shows that I hung on for dear life, not knowing if she would throw me off.

On Resurrection day, we had coffee in the King David Hotel in Jerusalem. We met Richard Wurmbrand, who was a Christian prisoner for many years in Romania, and his wife. They invited us to hear him preach at the Garden Tomb. He had to take his shoes off when he preached, because his feet still hurt him a lot from the pain of the torture he had received in Romania over the years.

Dominus Flevit is the site of another structure on the slope of the Mount of Olives commemorating the tears Yeshua shed over His city before His entry into Jerusalem. *And when he was come near, he beheld the city, and wept over it, Saying, If thou hadst known, even thou, at least in this thy day, the things which belong unto thy peace! But now they are hid from thine eyes* (Luke 19:41–42).

It is believed that the Church of St. Anne and the Pool of Bethesda are the site of the home of Joachim and Anne, the parents of the Virgin Mary, described in John 5:2-9a,

> *Now there is at Jerusalem by the sheep market a pool, which is called in the Hebrew tongue Bethesda, having fife porches. In these lay a great multitude of impotent folk, of blind, halt, withered, waiting for the moving of the water. For an angel went down at a certain season into the pool, and troubled the water: whosoever then first after the troubling of the water stepped in was made whole of whatsoever disease he had. And a certain man was there, which had an infirmity thirty and eight years. When Jesus saw him lie, and knew that he had been now a long time in that case, he saith unto him, Wilt thou be made whole? The impotent man answered him, Sir, I have no man, when the water is troubled, to put me into the pool: but while I am coming, another steppeth down before me. Jesus saith unto him, Rise, take up thy bed, and walk. And immediately the man was made whole, and took up his bed, and walked.*

The Menorah is the symbol of light. This massive bronze seven-branched emblem of the state of Israel was presented to the nation by the British House of Parliament as a token of goodwill and friendship to the young state.

The Knesset building, the home of Israel's Parliament is to the left as we approached Jerusalem coming from Bethlehem.

In the Rockefeller Museum we saw many significant local archaeological excavations displayed.

When we toured the Dome of the Rock and the Al Aqsa Mosque, we were able to go inside, but we had to leave our purses and shoes outside in a pile. The octagonal Dome of the Rock is the third most important shrine in Islam. It was built in 691 on Mount Moriah and named after the large rock inside, which is actually the top of Mount Moriah. Tradition has it, Isaac was prepared for sacrifice by his father Abraham, and from where Mohammed supposed to have ascended to heaven on a horse. Was he ever that far from home?

These Scriptures prophecy the description of the Dome of the Rock. Ezekiel 42:15-20,

Now when he had made an end of measuring the inner house, he brought me forth toward the gate whose prospect is toward the east, and measured it round about. He measured the east side with the measuring reed, five hundred reeds, with the measuring reed round about. He measured the north side five hundred reeds, with the measuring reed round about. He measured the south side, five hundred reeds, with the measuring reed. He measured it by the four sides: it had a Wall round about, five hundred reeds long, and five hundred broad, to make a separation between the sanctuary and the profane place.

Which do you think is the profane place described in these Scriptures?

The Al Aqsa Mosque is the largest of the city's mosques and marks the farthest point of Mohammed's journey from Mecca. Here only the men meet.

The Dome of the Book is a modernistic building with a white Mexican sombrero looking roof – the Shrine of the Book. It displays the aged Isaiah scrolls behind the glass. While Zola Levitt, a Messianic Jewish Rabbi, was still alive, he read them once years ago on Christian television. Translated from Hebrew into English, the words are the same as in our King James version. These Dead Sea scrolls were found in different caves in the Judean Desert in 1948.

Yad Vashem is the national memorial to the six million Jews who were the victims of the Holocaust. Tourists with Jewish backgrounds from around the world can search on computers there for the names of relatives.

The Kidron Valley is located between the eastern wall of the Old City and the Mount of Olives. Refugees arrived in Jerusalem about the time of the fall of the northern kingdom (722 BC). Settlement spread to the western hill and a new wall was added for protection. Hezekiah was born in 736 BC and ruled for twenty-eight years from 715 to 687 BC. As a godly king, his first act was to reestablish the true worship of Jehovah, which had been neglected during the reign of his father. He had an underground aqueduct carved out of the solid rock to bring an ample water supply inside the city walls, enabling Jerusalem to survive the siege of Sennacherib in 701 BC.

From the beginning of the tunnel to the Pool of Siloam—meaning 'the Pool of One who will be sent' it will be He to pour water out on the dry dessert. It was symbolic of the Messiah's coming, who will pour the Holy Spirit out upon the people. Prior arrangements were made for a guide to walk us through Hezekiah's tunnel, which required us to roll our pant legs up as high as they could go. We considered ourselves privileged to have the experience of walking the full 1,777 feet through the very cold water of Hezekiah's tunnel from the Pool of the Virgins to the Pool of Siloam. What an unforgettable experience.

Absalom's Pillar was visible as we walked down the Kidron Valley. Absalom, King David's rebellious son, erected it for himself. *Now Absalom in his lifetime had taken and reared up for himself a pillar, which is in the king's dale: for he said, I have no son to keep my name in remembrance: and he called the pillar after his own name and it is called to this day, Absaloms place* (2 Samuel 18:18).

The miniature model of the second temple on the grounds of the Holyland Hotel enables the visitor to visualize life in the city at the time of the second temple, before the Jewish revolt against the Romans and the destruction of the city in 70 BC. This miniature temple complex is built of marble, granite, and limestone. The top of the fence that surrounds the place measured only up to my knees.

The Western Wall, or Wailing Wall, is the only remaining structure left from the majestic second temple built by King Herod. It is Jewry's most sacred site. Day and night, people of all nationalities come to pray at the wall and many leave their rolled up prayers in the crevasses of the wall's large stones, only for the eyes of God to be seen. Many bar mitzvahs are celebrated here. The area is divided in to two separate sections for males and females.

At Cana, the Wedding Church, Yeshua performed His first miracle as recorded in John 2:1-11,

And the third day there was a marriage in Cana of Galilee; and the mother of Jesus was there: and both Jesus was called, and his disciples, to the marriage. And when they wanted wine, the mother of Jesus saith unto him, They have no wine. Jesus saith unto her Woman, what have I to do

139

with thee? Mine hour is not yet come. His mother saith unto the servants, Whatsoever he saith unto you, do it. And there were set there six water pots of stone, after the manner of the purifying of the Jews, containing two or three firkins apiece. (18 or 27 gallons) Jesus saith unto them, Fill the water pots with water. And they filled them to the brim. And he saith unto them, Draw out now, and bear unto the governor of the feast. And they bear it. When the ruler of the feast had tasted the water that was made wine, and knew not whence it was: (but the servants which drew the water knew) the governor of the feast called the bridegroom, and saith unto him, Every man at the beginning doth seth forth good wine; and when men have well drunk, then that which is worse: but thou hast kept the good wine until now. This beginning of miracles did Jesus in Cana of Galilee, and manifested forth his glory; and his disciples believed on him.

An earthenware pitcher stands on a stone slab as a reminder of the six jars mentioned in the Scriptures.

Herod built Caesarea, a lavish, Roman-style palace, in honor of Caesar Augustus. It was the center of Roman government for nearly five hundred years. A moat protects the property from intruders. Philip lived here. *And the next day we that were of Paul's company departed and came to Caesarea: and we entered into the house of Philip the evangelist, which was one of the seven; and abode with him. And the same man had four daughters, virgins, which did prophesy* (Acts 21:8–9). The apostle Paul defended the gospel before King Agrippa, who answered him in Acts 26:28, *Then Agrippa said unto Paul, almost thou persuadest me to be a Christian.* During our visit, we observed an American college theater group practice at the old Roman theater, with its enormous seating hewn out of the rocks with the blue Mediterranean Sea in view.

The Dead Sea, the lowest spot on Earth is approximately 1,350 feet or 413 meters below sea level. It gave us a lot to laugh about. Some of us tried to swim in the salty water with its curative qualities and minerals. All I was able to do is float with one of my legs sticking straight up. I could not get it in the water. The high salt content of the water and the extreme evaporation that takes place causes salt deposits, which can be seen along the entire length of the lake. The mineral content of the Dead Sea is one of Israel's richest natural treasures. Thousands of tons of potash and bromine are produced annually and marketed abroad. The combination of the climate and mineral salts in the water makes the Dead Sea famous for its healing powers.

Yeshua warns the people in Luke 17:26–32,

And as it was in the days of Noe, so shall it be also in the days of the Son of man. They did eat, they drank, they married wives, they were given in marriage, until the day that Noe entered into the ark, and the flood came, and destroyed them all. Likewise also as it was in the days of Lot; they did eat, they drank, they bought, they sold, they planted, they builded; But the same day that Lot went out of Sodom it rained fire and brimstone from heaven, and destroyed them all. Even thus shall it be in the day when the Son of man is revealed. In that day, he which shall be upon the housetop, and his stuff in the house, let him not come down to take it away: and he that is in the field, let him likewise not return back. Remember Lot's wife. Whosoever shall seek to save his life, shall lose it; and whosoever shall lose his life shall preserve it.

Lot's wife turned around and looked back. Was she not willing to leave home? It is said that she turned into a pillar of salt. There is a huge pillar five or more feet high deposited at the edge of the Dead Sea for tourists to see. I asked a Jewish educator who told me that tradition claims it to be Lot's wife.

Qumran is where the Dead Sea scrolls were discovered between 1947 and 1956 in eleven caves throughout the area.

Masada was the ancient Herodian fortress. It has no biblical reference. Here, 960 zealots held out for three years against the Romans encamped below until the walls were breached. In an act of defiance against the anticipated slavery and slaughter, the group committed mass suicide, denying the Romans their "prize." Ascend by cable car to view the remains of the Roman wall, the water system, Roman baths, storerooms, swimming pool and synagogue.

Ein Karem – Here is John the Baptist's birthplace and Church

On the wall of the courtyard of the Church of the Visitation, the Magnificat is displayed in numerous different languages. We can read what Mary said in Luke 1:46–55,

My soul doth magnify the Lord, and my spirit hath rejoiced in God my Saviour. For he hath regarded the low estate of his handmaiden: for, behold, from henceforth all generations shall call me blessed. For he that is mighty hath done to me great things; and holy is his name. And his mercy is on them that fear him from generation to generation. He hath shewed strength with his arm; he hath scattered the proud in the imagination of their hearts. He hath put down the mighty from their seats; and exalted them of low degree. He hath filled the hungry with good things; and the rich he hath sent empty away. He hath holpen his servant Israel, in remembrance of his mercy; as he spake to our fathers, to Abraham, and to his seed for ever.

The church shows the birthplace of John the Baptist, with the grotto leading to the house. A large stone in the church marks the spot where he was born. It is a beautiful church. His father, Zacharias, could not speak until his son was born.

The Basilica of the Annunciation is probably Nazareth's best-known monument and the largest Christian Curch in Israel. Next to it was Yeshua's boyhood home when he returned from Egypt where He learned and helped Joseph in the carpenter shop. Matthew 2:19-21 & 23,

But when Herod was dead, behold, an angel of the Lord appeareth in a dream to Joseph in Egypt, Saying, Arise, and take the young child and his mother, and go into the land of Israel: for they are dead which sought the young child's life. And he arose, and took the young child and his mother, and came into the land of Israel. And he came and dwelt in a city called Nazareth: that it might be fulfilled which was spoken by the prophets, He shall be called a Nazarene.

Yeshua begins His ministry in Luke 4:16–22,

And he came to Nazareth, where he had been brought up: and, as his custom was, he went into the synagogue on the Sabbath day, and stood up for to read. And there was delivered unto him the book of the prophet Esaias. And when he had opened the book, he found the place where it was written, the Spirit of the Lord is upon me, because he hath anointed me to preach the gospel to the poor; he hath sent me to heal the brokenhearted, to preach deliverance to the captives, and recovering of sight to the blind, to set at liberty them that are bruised, to preach the acceptable year of the Lord. And he closed the book, and he gave it again to the minister, and sat down. And the eyes of all them that were in the synagogue were fastened on him. And he began to say unto them, this day is this scripture fulfilled in your ears. And all bare him witness, and wondered at the gracious words which proceeded out of his mouth. And they said, is not this Joseph's son?

Many people from around the world marvel at the beautiful representation donated of Mary to be seen on the second floor. I was not at all impressed with the one from the USA.

In Nazareth we hired a taxi driver. The ride up to Mount Tabor which rises 1,650 feet above the Jezreel Valley in the Galilee region was very steep. There are beautiful murals on the walls and ceiling in the Church of the Transfiguration, including the appearance of Yeshua with Moses and Elijah. It is something to be seen. Next to the beautiful old synagogue are the ruins of the one from Byzantine times. There is also a magnificent view of the valley and surrounding mountains from the terrace outside the church. Let's read the scenario described in Luke 9:27–36,

But I tell you of a truth, there be some standing here, which shall not taste of death, till they see the kingdom of God. And it came to pass about an eight days after these sayings, he took Peter and John and James, and went up into a mountain to pray. And as he prayed, the fashion of his countenance was altered, and his raiment was white and glistering. And behold, there talked with him two men, which were Moses and Elias: Who appeared in glory, and spake of his decease which he should accomplish at Jerusalem. But Peter and they that were with him were heavy with sleep: and when they were awake, they saw his glory, and the two men that stood with him. And it came to pass, as they departed from him, Peter said unto Jesus, Master, it is good for us to be here: and let us make three tabernacles; one for Thee, and one for Moses, and one for Elias: not knowing what he said. While he thus spake, there came a cloud. And there came a voice out of the cloud, saying, This is my beloved Son: hear him. And when the voice was past, Jesus was found alone. And they kept it close, and told no man in those days any of those things which they had seen.

The oak tree at Mamre outside of Beersheba is old, withered, and leaning, but it was still standing at the time of our visit when I took this picture. We went to see the leftover place, which consisted of a pile of scattered rocks outside of Beersheba where Abraham lived, or so we were told. He had three visitors, who were on their way to Sodom and Gomorrah to destroy it. He fed them before he let them go. He displayed hospitality recorded in Genesis 18:1-4,

And the LORD appeared unto him in the plains of Mamre: and he sat in the tent door in the heat of the day; and he lift up his eyes and looked, and, lo, three men stood by him and when he saw them, he ran to meet them from the tent door, and bowed himself toward the ground, and said, My Lord, if now I have found favor in thy sight, pass not away, I pray thee, from thy servant: Let a little water, I pray you, be fetched, and wash your feet, and rest yourself under the tree.

It was here that Sarah, Abraham's wife, was told she would have a child in a year. Genesis 21:27, 30-31, & 33,

And Abraham took sheep and oxen, and gave them unto A-bim-e-lech; and both of them made a covenant. And he said, For these seven ewe lambs shalt thou take of my hand, that they may be a witness unto me, that I have digged this well. Wherefore he called that place Beer-sheba; because there they sware both of them. And Abraham planted a grove in Beer-sheba, and called there on the name of the LORD, the everlasting God.

I have a group picture of us standing in front of Abraham's Well in Beersheba, which is the Capital of the Negev. Another time, we went there for the market and livestock auction.

The city of Hebron is one of the most ancient cities in the world, built seven years before Zoan and even older then Damascus, located twenty-four miles south of Jerusalem. Here are the tombs of the patriarchs Abraham, Isaac, and Jacob and their wives. Abraham was called "the friend of God." The Hebrew name for Hebron is Al Khulil. Abraham's family tombs attract all who profess to believe in God—Muslims, Jews, and Christians. He bought the property from

Ephron the Hittite over two thousand years ago. Genesis 23:19; 25:9 &10,

> *And after this, Abraham buried Sarah his wife in the cave of the field of Machpelah before Mamre: the same is Hebron in the land of Canaan. And his sons Isaac and Ishmael buried him in the cave of Machpelah, in the field of Ephron the son of Zohar the Hittite, which is before Mamre, the field which Abraham purchased of the sons of Heth: there was Abraham buried, and Sarah his wife.*

After the death of Saul, it was David's royal residence for seven and a half years before he relocated to Jerusalem. In Hebron, he was crowned king over all Israel.

> *And it came to pass after this, that David inquired of the LORD, saying, Shall I go up into any of the cities of Judah? And the LORD said unto him, Go up. And David said, Whither shall I go up? And he said, Unto Hebron. And the men of Judah came, and there they anointed David king over the house of Judah* (2 Samuel 2:1, 4a).

We watched glass blowers fashion beautiful articles in their shops, and I acquired several pieces to bring home. The gift shops in town had a nice selection of goods, including pottery, which I display in my home to this day.

Abner's tomb was across the street from the tombs of the patriarchs. He was Saul's cousin and commander-in-chief of his army.

> *So Joab and Abishai his brother slew Abner, because he had slain their brother Asahal at Gibeon in the battle. And David said to Jaob, and to all the people that were with him, Rend your clothes, and gird you with sackcloth, and mourn before Abner. And king David himself followed the bier. (coffin) And they buried Abner in Hebron: and the king lifted up his voice, and wept at the grave of Abner, and all the people wept* (2 Samuel 3:30–32).

It was here that we saw the beginning of an Arabic funeral procession. The women were wailing as the body was carried past us on a thin mattress. It is their custom to bury the body right away.

In order to see inside the church in Nain, we had to pick up the key from a neighbor.

He went into the city called Nain; and many of his disciples went with him, and much people. Now when he came nigh to the gate of the city, behold, there was a dead man carried out, the only son of his mother, and she was a widow: and much people of the town was with her. And when the Lord saw her, he had compassion on her, and said unto her, Weep not. And he came and touched the bier (coffin) and they that bare him stood still. And he said, Young man. I say unto thee, Arise. And he that was dead sat up, and began to speak. And he delivered him to his mother (Luke 7:11b–15).

An enormous hedge of Bougainvillea blossoms surrounded the entrance gate at Capernaum. The ruins of a large, fourth-century synagogue can be seen to this day. Under it is supposed to be the synagogue where Yeshua taught during His time. He teaches of the bread of heaven in Capernaum in John 6:53–59,

Then Jesus said unto them, Verily, verily, I say unto you, Except ye eat the flesh of the Son of man, and drink his blood, ye have no life in you. Whoso eateth my flesh, and drinketh my blood, hath eternal life; and I will raise him up at the last day. For my flesh is meat indeed, and my blood is drink indeed. He that eateth my flesh, and drinketh my blood, dwelleth in me, and I in him. As the living Father hath sent me, and I live by the Father: so he that eateth me, even he shall live by me. This is that bread which came down from heaven: not as your fathers did eat manna, and are dead: he that eateth of this bread shall live for ever. These things said he in the synagogue, as he taught in Capernaum.

Yeshua casts out a demon in Luke 4:31–37,

And came down to Capernaum, a city of Galilee, and taught them on the Sabbath days. And they were astonished at his doctrine: for his word was with power. And in the synagogue there was a man, which had a spirit of an unclean devil and cried out with a laud voice, Saying, Let us alone; what have we to do with thee, thou Jesus of Nazareth? Art thou come to destroy us? I know thee who thou art, the Holy One of God. And Jesus rebuked him, saying, Hold thy peace, and come out of him, and hurt him not. And they were all amazed, and spake among themselves, saying, What a word is this! For with authority and power he commanded the unclean spirits, and they came out. And fame of him went out into every place of the country round about.

Yeshua heals Peter's mother-in-law in Luke 4:38–39,

And he arose out of the synagogue and entered into Simon's house. And Simon's wife's mother was taken with a great fever, and they besought him for her. And he stood over her, and rebuked the fever; and it left her: and immediately she arose and ministered unto them.

Yeshua heals the paralytic in Luke 5:18–20,

And behold, men brought in a bed a man which was taken with a palsy: and they sought means to bring him in, and to lay him before him. And when they could not find by what way they might bring him in because of the multitude, they went upon the housetop, and let him down through the tiling with his couch into the midst before Jesus. And when he saw their faith, he said unto him, Man, thy sins are forgiven thee.

We stayed in a nice hotel right on the Sea of Galilee in Tiberias, where we had an appointment with a pastor at the baptismal site at Yardenit on the Jordan River. The Jordan River has its origination up north as it runs from the slopes of Mount Hermon and the Sea of Galilee to the Dead Sea.

The Sea of Galilee, also called the Sea of Gennesaret, measures eight miles wide and thirteen miles long, according to my studies. *After these things Jesus went over the sea of Galilee, which is the sea of Tiberias. And a great multitude followed him, because they saw his miracles which he did on them that were diseased. And Jesus went up into a mountain, and there he sat with his disciples* (John 6:1–3).

We visited the Church of the Loves and the Fishes in Tabgha after we crossed the Lake by boat. It is the traditional site of the Miracle of the Multiplication of the Loves and the Fishes and viewed the beautiful mosaic floor displaying the loves and the fishes inlayed from a church dating back to the 4th century.

And when it was evening, his disciples came to him, saying, This is a desert place, and the time has now past, send the multitudes away, that they may go into the villages, and buy themselves victuals. (food) But Jesus said unto them, they need not depart give ye them to eat. And they say unto him, We have here but five loaves, and two fishes. He said, Bring them hither to me. And he commanded the multitude to sit down on the grass, and took the five loaves, and the two fishes, and looking up to heaven, he blessed, and brake, and gave the loaves to his disciples, and the disciples to the multitude. And they did all eat, and were filled: and they took up of the fragments that remained twelve baskets full. And they that had eaten were about five thousand men, beside women and children (Matthew 14:15–21).

The Church of the Beatitudes on the Mount of the Beatitudes is a beautiful church with a view of the Sea of Galilee. The way the church is structured, two different services can be conducted at the same time. Matthew describes in chapters 5 through 7 the standard of righteousness that Yeshua taught. We read in chapter 5:20: *For I say unto you, That except your righteousness shall exceed the righteousness of the scribes and Pharisees, ye shall in no case enter into the kingdom of heaven.* These are strong words from Yeshua.

In His sermon on the mount, Yeshua describes the Beatitudes in Matthew 5:3–12,

Blessed are the poor in spirit, for theirs is the kingdom of heaven. Blessed are they that mourn: for they shall be comforted. Blessed are the meek: for they shall inherit the earth. Blessed are they which do hunger and thirst after righteousness, for they shall be filled. Blessed are the merciful: for they shall obtain mercy. Blessed are the pure in heart: for they shall see God. Blessed are the peacemakers: for they shall be called the children of God. Blessed are they which are persecuted for righteousness' sake: for theirs is the kingdom of heaven. Blessed are ye, when men shall revile you, and persecute you, and say all manner of evil against you falsely, for my sake. Rejoice, and be exceeding glad: for great is your reward in heaven; for so persecuted they the prophets which were before you.

On a rack in the Church of Peter's Landing on the Sea of Galilee hang several different robes for the clergy to wear as they bring their congregations and preach sermons.

Now when he had left speaking, he said unto Simon, Launch out into the deep, and let down your nets for a draught. And Simon answering said unto him, Master, we have toiled all the night, and have taken nothing: nevertheless at thy word I will let down the net. And when they had this done, they enclosed a great multitude of fishes and their net brake (Luke 5:4–6).

It was here that Peter walked on the water, as described in Luke 14:24–33, Yeshua also calmed the storm in Luke 8:22–25.

The Round Tower dates back seven thousand years. Jericho is the oldest walled city in the world and lies 820 feet below sea level. The first excavation began in 1908 and was finished in 1956. Remains of the ancient city of Jericho which had a population of around 2,500 at the time of Joshua's conquest were found to a depth of fifteen meters and show evidence of three civilizations. Modern Jericho, a West Bank city lies in a fertile plain in the Judean Dessert where date palms, bananas, oranges, figs, and many other fruits and vegetables flourish. They grow enough to supply Europe. A symbol in the form of a Menorah, the emblem of Israel, is all that is left on the mosaic floor of an ancient synagogue from the sixth century in Jericho.

Elijah's Spring is very close to the excavation site. My friend Ellen and I, who was influential to have me go on this trip played in it.

And the word of the Lord came unto him, saying, Get thee hence, and turn thee eastward, and hide thyself by the brook Cherith, that is before Jordan. And it shall be, that thou shalt drink of the brook: and I have commanded the ravens to feed thee there. So he went and did according unto the word of the Lord: for he went and dwelt by the brook Cherith, that is before Jordan. And the ravens brought him bread and flesh in the morning, and bread and flesh in the evening: and he drank of the brook (1 Kings 17:2–6).

And Jesus entered and passed through Jericho. And behold there was a man named Zacchaeus, which was the chief among the publicans, and he was rich. And he sought to see Jesus who he was: and could not for the press, because he was little of stature. And he run before, and climbed up into a sycamore tree to see him: for he was to pass that way. And when Jesus came to the place, he looked up, and saw him, and said unto him, Zacchaeus, make hast, and come down, and received him joyfully (Luke 19:1–6).

149

In the middle of town, we saw the biggest Bougainvillea tree, with hundreds or even thousands of beautiful purple flowers.

The Mount of Temptation overlooks ancient Jericho. Halfway up the towering cliffs is the Greek Orthodox monastery of the Quarantal. This is the traditional site of the temptation of Jesus during forty days of fasting in the wilderness. A cluster of small buildings and a chapel comprise the monastery. Hermit cells are carved into the mountains. The community of monks, which once numbered six thousand, now consists of only seven souls.

And Jesus being full of the Holy Ghost returned from Jordan, and was led by the Spirit into the wilderness, being forty days tempted of the devil. And in those days he did eat nothing: and when they were ended, he afterward hungered. And the devil said unto him, If thou be the Son of God, command this stone that it be made bread. And Jesus answered him, saying, it is written, That man shall not live by bread alone, but by every word of God. And the devil taking him on into a high mountain, shewed unto him all the kingdoms of the world in a moment of time. And the devil said unto him, All this power will I give thee, and the glory of them: for that is delivered unto me; and to whomever I will give it. If thou therefore wilt worship me, all shall be thine. And Jesus answered and said unto him, Get thee behind me, Satan: for it is written, Thou shalt worship the Lord thy God, and him only shalt thou serve. And he brought him to Jerusalem, and set him on a pinnacle of the temple, and said unto him, If thou be the Son of God, cast thyself down from hence: For it is written, He shall give his angels charge over thee, to keep thee (Luke 4:1–10).

Caesarea Philippi, also called Banjas, is up north, close to the Golan Heights where the River Jordan originates. Mount Hermon reaches an altitude of 6,398 feet or 1,950 meter. Sacrificial altars are carved in the mountain where certain people prayed to their pagan gods. Near the Banjas Cave are the remains of a Greek temple to Pan, the Greek god of nature and woods. We had a small Bible study.

It was here that Yeshua had the following conversation with His disciples.

When Jesus came into the coast of Caesarea Philippi, He asked His disciples, saying, Who do men say that I the Son of man am? And they said, Some say that thou art John the Baptist: some Elias, and others, Jeremias, or one of the prophets. He said unto them, But whom say ye that I am? And Simon

Peter answered and said, Thou art the Christ, the Son of the living God. And Jesus answered and said unto him, Blessed art thou, Simon Barjona: for flesh and blood hath not revealed it unto thee, but my Father which is in heaven. And I say also unto thee, That thou art Peter, and upon this rock I will build my church; and the gates of hell shall not prevail against it. And I will give unto thee the keys of the kingdom of heaven: and whatsoever thou shalt bind on earth shall be bound in heaven: and whatsoever thou shalt loose on earth shall be loosed in heaven (Matthew 16:13–19).

Looking across up to the mountaintop, we could see buildings belonging to the Druze community, who are an independent religious group. The Druze speak Arabic and are believed to have split from Islam in the eleventh century. They are friendly and hospitable people.

I can still picture us walking up to the ruins of Nimrod's Castle. Behind it to the north of the castle sits Mount Hermon. Genesis 10:8 & 9 tells us, And Cush begot Nimrod: he began to be a mighty one in the Earth. He was a mighty hunter before the LORD for it is said, Even as Nimrod the mighty hunter before the LORD. The footnotes in my bible tells us, that he led the first organized rebellion against God. He hunted people, not animals. It refers to opposition to the Lord.

The Golan Heights are at the most northern part of Israel, where the Syrians can threaten the Jewish people. News from Israel came to me on July 14th, that Syria is taking their chemical warfare out of storage. The following information was seen here on television several years ago: A former Iraqi general ... alleged that in June 2002 Saddam Hussein transported weapons of mass destruction out of his country to Syria aboard several refitted commercial jets, under the pretense of conducting a humanitarian mission for flood victims after a irrigation dam collapsed in Zeyzoun, Syria. He shipped the weapons under cover of an aid project to the flooded region. When the United Nations weapons inspection team searched for them in Iraq they could not find any. Insted, two commercial jets, a 747 and 727, were converted to cargo jets. In order to carry raw materials and equipment related to WMD projects, the general said. The passenger seats, galleys, toilets and storage compartments were removed. New flooring was installed. Hundreds of tons of chemicals were reportedly included in the cargo shipment. Two Iraq Airways captains who were reportedly flying the sorties came immediately and told the general. A sortie is one mission or attack by a single plane. All in all fifty-six sorties were done between Baghdad and Damascus.

The Jezreel Valley is the largest valley in Israel, stretching between the mountains of Galilee in the north and the mountains of Samaria in the south. It is one of the most fertile regions in Israel.

The Battle of Armageddon-in the Hebrew tongue, will be fought in the Valley of Megiddo, as described in Zachariah 14:2–3 and Revelation 14:19–20,

> *For I will gather all nations against Jerusalem to battle; and the city shall be taken, and the houses rifled, and the women ravished; and half of the city shall go forth into captivity, and the residue of the people shall not be cut off from the city. Then shall the LORD go forth, and fight against those nations, as when he fought in the day of battle. And the angel thrust in his sickle into the earth, and gathered the vine of the earth, and cast it into the great winepress of the wrath of God. And the winepress was trodden without the city, and blood came out of the winepress, even unto the horse bridles, by the space of a thousand and six hundred furlongs.*

It tells us that the horses will stand in blood all the way up to their bridles for a distance of two hundred miles.

What an unforgettable education this trip was! I better stop now from describing any more places.

Who do you think will be the winner? Yeshua said in Revelation 22:13, *I am Alpha and Omega, the beginning and the end, the first and the last.* If the truth be told, this battle is for the control of Jerusalem.

CHAPTER 4

Biblical Prophecy

A good portion of the Bible deals with Israel, the Holy Land. Israelites are God's chosen people and are geographically at the center of the world. I have heard it said that Jerusalem is the navel of the earth. More than a dozen different prophets made hundreds of prophetic statements in the Bible. They describe the birth, life, crucifixion, and resurrection of Yeshua. No other leader has ever been willing to lay his life down for his followers. The mystery of calvary and the cross is hard for our human intellect to understand, but God ordained it even before the creation of the world. So let's believe Him in faith. As the prophets foretold the birth of Yeshua in the Scriptures, they also told exactly how, and by whom, Yeshua, the promised Messiah, would be born.

As we have already read, every prophecy regarding Yeshua was fulfilled to the last detail. He was nailed to the cross out of love for us, including the preservation of His bones as stated in John 19:31–37,

The Jews therefore, because it was the preparation, that the bodies should not remain upon the cross on the sabbath day, (for that sabbath day was a high day) besought Pilate that their legs might be broken, and that they might be taken away. Then came the soldiers, and brake the legs of the first, and of the other, which was crucified with him. But when they came to Jesus, and saw that he was dead already, they brake not his legs: But one of the soldiers with a spear pierced his side, and forthwith came there out blood and water. And he that saw it bare record, and his record is true: and he knoweth that he saith true, that ye might believe. For these things were done, that the scripture should be fulfilled. A bone of him shall not be broken. And again another scripture saith, They shall look on him whom they pierced.

We're experiencing more and more earthquakes, famines touch nearly every country, and terrorism and warfare steadily increase, causing many people to be killed, even by fear, throughout the world.

Men's hearts failing them for fear, and for looking after those things, which are coming on the earth: for the powers of heaven shall be shaken (Luke 21:26). Yeshua also told His disciples about these last days before His return in Matthew 24:1–51,

And Jesus went out, and departed from the temple: and his disciples came to him to show him the buildings of the temple. And Jesus said unto them, See ye not all these things? Verily I say unto you, there shall not be left there one stone upon another that shall not be thrown down. And as he sat upon the Mount of Olives, the disciples came unto him privately, saying, Tell us, when shall these things be? And what will be the sign of thy coming, and of the end of the world? And Jesus answered and said unto them, Take heed that no man deceive you. For many shall come in my name, saying, I am Christ: and shall deceive many. And ye shall hear of wars and rumors of wars; see that ye be not troubled: for all these things must come to pass, but the end is not yet. For nation shall rise against nation, and kingdom against kingdom: and there shall be famines, and pestilences, and earthquakes, in divers places. All these are the beginning of sorrows. Then shall they deliver you up to be afflicted, and shall kill you: and ye shall be hated of all nations for my name's sake. And then shall many be offended, and shall betray one another, and shall hate one another. And many false prophets shall rise, and shall deceive many. And because iniquity shall abound, the love of many shall wax cold. But he that shall endure unto the end, the same shall be saved. And this gospel of the kingdom shall be preached in all the world for a witness unto all nations; and then shall the end come. When ye therefore shall see the abomination of desolation, spoken of by Daniel the prophet, stand in the holy place, (whoso readeth, let him understand) Then let them which be in Judaea flee into the mountains: Let him which is on the housetop not come down to take any thing out of his house: Neither let him which is in the field return back to take his clothes. And woe unto them that are with child, and to them that give suck in those days! But pray ye that your flight be not in the winter, neither on the sabbath day: For then shall be great tribulation, such as was not since the beginning of the world to this time, no, nor ever shall be. And except those days should be shortened, there should no flesh be saved: but for the elect's sake those days shall be shortened. Then if any man shall say unto you, Lo, here is Christ, or there, believe it not. For there shall arise false Christs, and false prophets, and shall shew great signs and wonders; insomuch that, if it were possible, they shall deceive the very elect. Behold, I have told you before. Wherefore if they shall say unto you, Behold, he is in the desert; go not forth: behold, he is in the secret chambers; believe it not. For as the lightning cometh out of the east, and shineth even unto the west; so shall also the coming of the Son of man be. For wheresoever the carcase is, there will the eagles be gathered together. Immediately after the tribulation of those days shall the sun be darkened, and the moon shall not give her light, and the stars shall fall from heaven, and the powers of the heavens shall be shaken: And then shall appear the sign of the Son of man in heaven: and then shall all the tribes of the earth mourn, and they shall see the Son of man coming in the clouds of heaven with power and great glory. And he shall send his angels with a great sound of a trumpet, and they shall gather together his elect from the four winds, from one end of heaven to the other.

Now learn a parable of the fig tree; When his branch is yet tender; and putteth forth leaves, ye know that summer is nigh: So likewise ye, when ye shall see all these things, know that it is near, even at the doors. Verily I say unto you, This generation shall not pass, till all these things be fulfilled. Heaven and earth shall pass away, but my words shall not pass away. But of that day and hour knoweth no man, no, not the angels of heaven, but my Father only. But as the days of Noah were, so shall also the coming of the Son of man be. For as in the days that were before the flood they were eating and drinking, marrying and giving in marriage, until the flood came, and took them all away; so shall also the coming of the Son of man *be. Then shall two be in the field; the one shall be taken, and the other left. Two women shall be grinding at the mill; the one shall be taken, and the other left. Watch therefore: for ye know not what hour your Lord doth come. But know this that if the good man of the house had known in what watch the thief would come, he would have watched, and would not have suffered his house to be broken up. Therefore be ye also ready: for in such an hour as ye think not the Son of man cometh. Who then is a faithful and wise servant, whom his lord hath made ruler over his household, to give them meat in due season? Blessed is that servant, whom his lord when he cometh shall find so doing. Verily I say unto you, That he shall make him ruler over all his goods. But if that evil servant shall say in his heart, my lord delayeth his coming; and shall begin to smite his fellow-servants, and to eat and drink with the drunken; the lord of that servant shall come in a day when he looketh not for him, and in an hour that he is not aware of. And shall cut him asunder, and appoint him his portion with the hypocrites: there shall be weeping and gnashing of teeth.*

I strongly believe that we are the generation who will see all these things come to pass. Yes, we don't know the day or the hour, but as a student of Bible prophecy, we know the season. More people are accepting Yeshua as their Messiah, but this is only a drop in the bucket. As our revival spreads, people are convicted by the Holy Spirit of their need for a Savior to keep them out of hell. John, one of Yeshua's disciples, tells us in 1 John 4:1, *And we have seen and do testify that the Father sent the Son to be the Savior of the world.*

He says in Revelation 1:11, *I am Alpha and Omega, the first and the last...* In this Scripture, He tells us that He was God in the beginning and will be God over everything and Everyone until the end. It was not His wish to scatter Israel to the four corners of the world, but because of the Israelites' disobedience, they rejected Yeshua as Messiah. Hosea 4:6–7 tells us, *My people are destroyed for lack of knowledge: because thou hast rejected knowledge, I will also reject thee, that thou shalt be no priest to me: seeing thou hast forgotten the law of thy God, I will also forget thy children. As they were increased, so they sinned against me: therefore will I change their glory into shame.*

For this reason, God offered salvation to the Gentiles, as quoted in Luke 21:24, *And they shall fall by the edge of the sword, and shall be led away captive into all nations: and Jerusalem shall be trodden down of the Gentiles, until the times of the Gentiles be fulfilled.* I believe we are very close to the rapture. Yeshua will appear in the clouds to take us up in to heaven before the antichrist appears on the scene. If you obey, you will be blessed; if not, you will pay the consequences. God has not changed the Scriptures He gave in the Torah thousands of years ago.

Since the prophecies given in the Bible include the past, present, and future, let's look at some of them Ezekiel 38:1-23.

And the word of the LORD came unto me, saying, Son of man, set thy face against Gog, the land of Magog, the chief prince of Meshech and Tubal, and prophecy against him. And say, Thus saith the Lord God; Behold, I am against thee, O Gog, the chief prince of Meshech and Tubal: and I will turn thee back, and put hooks into thy jaws, and I will bring thee forth, and all thine army, horses and horsemen, all of them clothed with bucklers and shields, all of them handling swords: Persia, Ethiopia, and Libya with them; all of them with shield and helmet: Gomer, and all his bands; and many people with thee. Be thou prepared, and prepare for thyself thou, and all thy company that are assembled unto thee, and be thou a guard unto them. After many days thou shalt be visited: in the latter years thou shalt come into the land that is brought back from the sword, and is gathered out of many people, against the mountains of Israel, which have been always waste: but it is brought forth out of the nations, and they shall dwell safely all of them. Thou shalt ascent and come like a storm, thou shalt be like a cloud to cover the land, thou and all thy bands, and many people with thee. Thus saith the Lord God; It shall also come to pass, that at the same time shall things come into thy mind, and thou shalt think an evil thought: And thou shalt say, I will go up to the land of unwalled villages; I will go to them that are at rest, and dwell safely, all of them dwelling without walls, and having neither bars nor gates, to take a prey; to turn thine hand upon the desolate places that are not inhabited, and upon the people that are gathered out of the nations, which have gotten cattle and goods, that dwell in the midst of the land. Sheba, and Dedan, and the merchants of Tarshish, with all the young lions thereof, shall say unto thee, 'Art thou come to take a spoil? Hast thou gathered thy company to take a prey? To carry away silver and gold, to take away cattle and goods, to take a great spoil?' Therefore, son of man, prophesy and say unto Gog, Thus saith the Lord God; In that day when my people of Israel dwelleth safely, shalt thou not know it? And thou shalt come from thy place out of the north parts, thou, and many people with thee, all of them riding upon horses, a great company, and a mighty army: And thou shalt come up against my people of Israel, as a cloud to cover the land; it shall be in the latter days, and I will bring thee against my land, that the heathen may know me, when I shall be sanctified in thee, O Gog, before their eyes. Thus saith the Lord God; 'Art thou he of whom I have spoken in old time by my servants the prophets of Israel, which prophesied in those days many years that I would bring thee against them?' And it shall come to pass at the same time when Gog shall come against the land of Israel, saith the Lord God, that my fury shall come up in my face. For in my jealousy and in the fire of my wrath have I spoken, Surely in that day there shall be a great shaking in the land of Israel; So that the fishes of the sea, and the fowls of the heaven, and the beasts of the field, and all creeping things that creep upon the earth, and all the men that are upon the face of the earth, shall shake at my presence, and the mountains shall be thrown down, and the steep places shall fall, and every wall shall fall to the ground. And I will call for a sword against him throughout all my mountains, saith the Lord God: every man's sword shall be against his brother. And I will plead against him with pestilence and with blood; and I will rain upon him, and upon his bands, and upon the many people that are with him, an overflowing rain, and great hailstones, fire and brimstone. Thus will I magnify myself, and sanctify myself; and I will be known in the eyes of many nations, and they shall know that I am the LORD.

He continues in Ezekiel 39:1–29,

Therefore, thou son of man, prophesy against Gog, and say, Thus saith the Lord God; Behold I am against thee, O Gog, the chief prince of Meshech and Tubal: And I will turn thee back, and leave but the sixth part of thee, and I will cause thee to come up from the north parts, and will bring thee upon the mountains of Israel: And I will smite thy bow out of thy left hand, and will cause thine arrows to fall out of thy right hand. Thou shalt fall upon the mountains of Israel, thou, and all thy bands, and the people that is with thee: I will give thee unto ravenous birds of every sort, and to the beasts of the field to be devoured. Thou shalt fall upon the open field: for I have spoken it, saith the Lord GOD. And I will send a fire on Magog, and among them that dwell carelessly in the isles: and they shall know that I am the LORD. So will I make my holy name known in the midst of my people Israel; and I will not let them pollute my holy name any more: and the heathen shall know that I am the LORD, the Holy One in Israel. Behold, it is come, and it is done, saith the Lord GOD; this is the day whereof I have spoken. And they that dwell in the cities of Israel shall go forth, and shall set on fire and burn the weapons, both the shields and the bucklers, the bows and the arrows, and the handstaves, and the spears, and they shall burn them with fire seven years: so that they shall take no wood out of the field, neither cut down any out of the forests; for they shall burn the weapons with fire: and they shall spoil those that spoiled them, and rob those that robbed them, saith the Lord GOD. And it shall come to pass in that day that I will give unto Gog a place there of the graves in Israel, the valley of the passengers on the east of the sea: and it shall stop the noses of the passengers: and there shall they bury Gog and all his multitude: and they shall call it The Valley of Hamongog. And seven months shall the house of Israel be burying of them, that they may cleanse the land. Yea, all the people of the land shall bury them; and it shall be to them a renown the day that I shall be glorified, saith the Lord GOD. And they shall sever out men of continual employment, passing through the land to bury with the passengers those that remain upon the face of the earth, to cleanse it: after the end of seven months shall they search. And the passengers that pass through the land, when any seeth a man's bone, then shall he set up a sign by it, till the buriers have buried it in the Valley of Hamongog. And also the name of the city shall be Hamonah. Thus shall they cleanse the land. And thou son of man, thus saith the Lord GOD; Speak unto every feathered fowl, and to every beast of the field, Assemble yourselves, and come gather yourselves on every side to my sacrifice that I do sacrifice for you, even a great sacrifice upon the mountains of Israel, that ye may eat flesh, and drink blood. Ye shall eat the flesh of the mighty, and drink the blood of the princes of the earth, of rams, of lambs, and of goats, of bullocks all of them fatlings of Bashan. And ye shall eat fat till ye be full, and drink blood till ye be drunken, of my sacrifice which I have sacrificed for you. Thus ye shall be filled at my table with horses and chariots, with mighty men, and with all men of war, saith the Lord GOD. And I will set my glory among the heathen, and all the heathen shall see my judgment that I have executed, and my hand that I have laid upon them. So the house of Israel shall know that I am the Lord their GOD from that day and forward. And the heathen shall know that the house of Israel went into captivity for their iniquity: because they trespassed against me, therefore hid I my face from them, and gave them into the hand of their enemies: so fell they all by the sword. According to their uncleanness and according to their transgressions have I done unto them, and hid my face from them. Therefore thus saith the Lord GOD: Now will I bring again the captivity of Jacob, and have mercy upon the whole house of Israel, and will be jealous for my holy name; After that they have borne their shame, and all their trespasses whereby they have trespassed against me, when they dwelt safely in their land, and none made them afraid. When I have brought them again from the people, and gathered them out of their enemies' lands and am sanctified in them in the sight of many nations; Then shall they know that I am the LORD their God, which caused them to be led into captivity among the heathen: but I have gathered them unto their own land, and have left none of them any more there. Neither will I hide my face any more from them: for I have poured out my spirit upon the house of Israel, saith the Lord GOD.

We can see several references made to "And they shall know that I am their God." The mighty nation of Russia and her allies will attack the tiny country Israel. Common sense tells us that the Russians, with their large warfare capabilities, will win. But then God will step in and take over the situation. This is why Israel has been winning battles against her modern-day attackers time and time again. Israel will not lose, according to God's plan. If only the Arab countries would read and study the Bible. The future has long been foretold. It was prophesied several thousand years ago. They would save themselves a lot of money. The amount they've spent on weapons would feed many of their poor people, not to mention the many lives that would have been saved. God's Word, as given to man, will be fulfilled. God told the prophet in Ezekiel 38:4 that He will "put hooks into their jaws." Ezekiel 39:11 even indicates where they will be buried and verse 12 tells how long it will take to bury them. In verse 29, God tells His people that He will not hide His face from them anymore, but will pour out His spirit upon them. When His spirit is poured, it will be as if He is taking the scales away from their eyes. They will be finally able to see that Yeshua is, and has always been, their Messiah.

The prophet Daniel had a similar vision that revealed God's plan for the future. It is estimated that he wrote it around the year 535 BC. Here are some excerpts.

In the third year of Cyrus king of Persia a thing was revealed unto Daniel, whose name was called Belteshazzar; and the thing was true, but the time appointed was long: and he understood the thing, and had understanding of the vision. And in the four and twentieth day of the first month, as I was by the side of the great river, which is Hiddekel; Then I lifted up mine eyes, and looked, and behold a certain man clothed in linen, whose loins were girded with fine gold of Uphaz: His body also was like the beryl, and his face as the appearance of lightning, and his eyes as lamps of fire, and his arms and his feet like in color to polished brass, and the voice of his words like the voice of a multitude. And I Daniel alone saw the vision: for the men that were with me saw not the vision; but a great quaking fell upon them, so that they fled to hide themselves. Then said he, Knowest thou wherefore I come unto thee? and now will I return to fight with the prince of Persia: and when I am gone forth, lo, the prince of Grecia shall come. And at the time of the end shall the king of the south push at him: and the king of the north shall come against him like a whirlwind, with chariots, and with horsemen, and with many ships; and he shall enter into the countries, and shall overflow and pass over. He shall enter also into the glorious land, and many countries shall be overthrown: but these shall escape out of his hand, even Edom, and Moab, and the chief of the children of Ammon. He shall stretch forth his hand also upon the countries: and the land of Egypt shall not escape. But he shall have no power over the treasures of gold and silver, and over all the precious things of Egypt: and the Libyans and the Ethiopians shall be at his steps. But tidings out of the east and out of the north shall trouble him: therefore he shall go forth with great fury to destroy, and utterly to make away many. And he shall plant the tabernacles of his palace between the seas in the glorious holy mountain; yet he shall come to his end, and none shall help him. And at that time shall Michael stand up, the great prince which standeth for the children of thy people: and there shall be a time of trouble, such as never was since there was a nation even to that same time: and at that time thy people shall be delivered, every one that shall be found written in the book. And many of them that sleep in the dust of the earth shall awake, some to everlasting life, and some to shame and everlasting contempt. And they that be wise shall shine as the brightness of the firmament and they that turn many to righteousness as the stars forever and ever. But thou, O Daniel, shut up the words, and seal the book, even to the time of the end: many shall run to and fro, and knowledge shall be increased. Then I Daniel looked, and, behold, there stood other two, the one on this side of the bank of the river, and the other on that side of the bank of the river. And one said to the man clothed in linen, which was upon the waters of the river, How long shall it be to the end of these wonders? And I heard the man clothed in linen, which was upon the waters of the river, when he held up his right hand and his left hand unto heaven, and sware by him that liveth for ever that it shall be for a time, times, and an half; and when he shall have accomplished to scatter the power of the holy people, all these things shall be finished. And I heard, but I understood not: then said I, O my Lord, what shall be the end of these things? And he said, go thy way, Daniel: for the words are closed up and sealed till the time of the end. Many shall be purified, and made white, and tried, but the wicked shall do wickedly: and none of the wicked shall understand; but the wise shall understand. And from the time that the daily sacrifice shall be taken away, and the abomination that maketh desolate set up, there shall be a thousand two hundred and ninety days. Blessed is he that waiteth, and cometh to the thousand three hundred and five and thirty days. But go thou thy way till the end be: for thou shalt rest, and stand in thy lot at the end of the days (Daniel 10:1, 4–7, 20; 11:40–45; 12:1–13).

These prophecies should make every one of us realize that it is not the things we do or say in our own strength, but rather it is in the power of God, who controls the whole universe. Prophecy has been fulfilled until now, to the point that the Russian army and its allies are able to attack Israel at any time. They will be destroyed, as I mentioned earlier in this chapter, as described in Ezekiel 39:2–3, 11–12. We also read in the Scriptures that Yeshua will return once again to receive all who are looking for Him in the clouds.

Just as some of these foregoing events have come true, even to the minutest detail, we can know that those that still remain to be fulfilled will also come true in the exact same manner and in God's precise timing. Yeshua promised to return for the saints. We call this event the Rapture because it refers to the time when believers in Yeshua (both dead and alive) will, in the twinkling of an eye, rise up to meet Him in the air. The apostle Paul explains this in 1 Thessalonians 4:13–18,

> *But I would not have you to be ignorant, brethren, concerning them which are asleep, that ye sorrow not, even as others which have no hope. For if we believe that Yeshua died and rose again, even so them also which sleep in Jesus will God bring with him. For this we say unto you by the word of the Lord, that we which are alive and remain unto the coming of the Lord shall not prevent them which are asleep. For the Lord Himself shall descend from heaven with a shout, with the voice of the archangel, and with the trump of God: and the dead in Christ shall rise first: Then we which are alive and remain shall be caught up together with them in the clouds, to meet the Lord in the air: and so shall we ever be with the Lord. Wherefore comfort one another with these words.*

Yeshua will come quickly and unexpectedly without any prior warning, as He states in Luke 17:34–36, *I tell you, in that night there shall be two men in one bed; the one shall be taken, and the other shall be left. Two women shall be grinding together; the one shall be taken, and the other left. Two men shall be in the field; the one shall be taken, and the other left.*
Yeshua confirms His return in Luke 21:27–28, 32, 36,

> *And then shall they see the Son of man coming in a cloud with power and great glory. And when these things begin to come to pass, then look up, and lift up your heads; for your redemption draweth nigh. Verily I say unto you, This generation shall not pass away, till all be fulfilled. Watch ye therefore, and pray always, that ye may be accounted worthy to escape all these things that shall come to pass, and to stand before the Son of man.*

The apostle Paul wrote in 2 Timothy 3:1-5,

> *This know also, that in the last days perilous times shall come. For men shall be lovers of their own selves, covetous, boasters, proud, blasphemers, disobedient to parents, unthankful, unholy, without natural affection,*

trucebreakers, false accusers, incontinent, fierce despisers of those that are good, traitors, heady, high-minded, lovers of pleasures more than lovers of God; Having a form of godliness, but denying the power thereof: from such turn away.

As it was in Noah's days, which was five hundred years before Abraham, man had drifted so far from God that He destroyed most of humankind with a great flood. Why did God save Noah and his family? Because they were the only righteous ones He could find among the whole population. The rest drowned. What good came from all their riches? Their lifestyles caused their destruction. Why not donate some of your time and money to the kingdom of God now to spread the good news. There are many people who, through no fault of their own, are deprived and have never heard the gospel of Yeshua. Somehow, God opens these doors now through supernatural channels. Wouldn't you like to have a part in what could be our last great harvest? God will reward you for it. Are you certain you're among those who are redeemed by the blood of Yeshua and are looking for His return? Without the shedding of His blood, there would be no remission of sins. Yeshua is the Son of God who died for our sins. He was raised from the dead for our justification. He ascended on high and is sitting at the right hand of the Father, interceding for us.

Before the antichrist arrives, Yeshua will return and rapture the true believers in the air. This will begin an eternal chain of events from which there will be no deviation. God has determined the outcome. Man himself cannot change this plan, although I believe there are men at work in different countries who are undermining the principles of truth. They take a news story totally out of context and often twist it to such a degree that it points in a direction far from the truth, thereby blaming innocent people in order to cover themselves or gain for their own profitable interests. Some day soon, they will have to stand before Yeshua and He will judge them according to all the evil they have done. It all starts with a love of money and power, as is described in 1 Timothy 6:10, *For the love of money is the root of all evil: which while some coveted after, they have erred from the faith, and pierced themselves through with many sorrows.* Greed has been the cause of many wars and is to blame for the loss of many innocent lives. By acting in this manner, we see that the time of the antichrist is near, as the Scriptures foretold.

Human teachings are overtaking our school system and quickly becoming a way of life. Man is trying to be his own god and decide his own fate. Everything seems all right and is accepted everywhere. As this teaching takes the power of authority away from the teachers, it also is visible in the disrespect children give to their parents. God's spirit is in conflict with the world we live in. Slowly but surely, we are being conditioned to accept a new global monetary system while important powers are working toward a one-world government. Everything will be tightly controlled in these days to come. Everyone will have to have a number or "mark of the beast," as foretold in Revelation 13:16–18, *And he causeth all, both small and great, rich and poor, free and bond, to receive a mark in their right hand, or in their foreheads: And that no man might buy or sell, save he that had the mark, or the name of the beast, or the number of his name. Here is wisdom. Let him that hath understanding count the number of the beast: for it is the number of a man; and his number is Six hundred threescore and six.*

You may ask who the antichrist is. The Bible gives some key characteristics that will show us his true identity. *And every spirit that confesseth not that Jesus Christ is come in the flesh is not of God: and this is that spirit of antichrist, whereof ye have heard that it should come; and even now already is it in the world* (1 John 4:3). Also Revelation 13:3–4, *And I saw one of his heads as it were wounded to death; and his deadly wound was healed: and all the world wondered after the beast. And they worshipped the dragon which gave power unto the beast: and they worshipped the beast, saying, Who is like unto the beast? who is able to make* war with him?

The antichrist will be a world dictator and break his peace treaty with Israel in order to persecute those who are left during this time. He does not know when he will take over; the antichrist (Satan) will possess him later. It will be in the same manner as with Judas, who betrayed Yeshua when Satan entered him. He will be able to bring peace in the Middle East. The false prophet, a religious leader will direct all worship to the antichrist.

The next seven-year period, called the tribulation, is a time of great turmoil for this world. The antichrist will become world leader, setting himself as God upon the newly constructed temple in Jerusalem. People around the world will be willing to worship him because of the great sense of false peace he will be able to bring during the first half of this seven-year period. Then, after his false identity is exposed, he will make war with the nations and none will be able to defeat him. He will insist that everyone wear his mark or number to purchase food. Eventually, he will wage war against the Son of God. By then, we, the born-again believers, will have already been raptured by Yeshua because we refused the mark of the beast. Our security is in Him.

The antichrist has no respect for the religion or beliefs of his fathers or nation. Daniel 11:37 says, *He will have no regard for the God of his fathers, nor the desire of women, nor regard any god: for he shall magnify himself above all.* We read in 2 Thessalonians 2:4, *Who opposeth and exalteth himself above all that is called God, or that is worshipped; so that he as God sitteth in the temple of God, showing himself that he is God.* Because of his pride, he will have no trouble changing territorial boundaries to benefit himself, as described in Daniel 11:39, *Thus shall he do in the most strong holds with a strange god, whom he shall acknowledge and increase with glory: and he shall cause them to rule over many, and shall divide the land for gain.* This is possible because 2 Thessalonians 2:11–12 reveals, *And for this cause God shall send them strong delusion, that they should believe a lie: That they all might be damned who believed not the truth, but had pleasure in unrighteousness.*

He will be a skilled negotiator, as described in Daniel 8:23–25,

And in the latter time of their kingdom, when the transgressors are come to the full, a king of fierce countenance, and understanding dark sentences, shall stand up. And his power shall be mighty, but not by his own power: and he shall destroy wonderfully, and shall prosper, and practice, and shall destroy the mighty and the holy people. And through his policy also he shall cause craft to prosper in his hand; and he shall magnify himself in his heart, and by peace shall destroy many: he shall also stand up against the Prince of princes; (Yeshua) but he shall be broken without hand.

God has his fate recorded. Satan or the antichrist will be defeated and cast into the lake of fire (hell). It will take place as shown in Revelation 19:20–21,

And the beast was taken, and with him the false prophet that wrought miracles before him, with which he deceived them that had received the mark of the beast, and them that worshipped his image. These both were cast alive into a lake of fire burning with brimstone. And the remnant were slain with the sword of him that sat upon the horse, (Yeshua and his army) which sword proceeded out of his mouth: and all the fowls were filled with their flesh.

Daniel saw the antichrist in a vision long ago. He told in Daniel 9:27, *And he shall confirm the covenant with many for one week: and in the midst of the week he shall cause the sacrifice and the oblation to cease, and for the overspreading of abominations he shall make it desolate, even until the consummation, and that determined shall be poured upon the desolate.*

Yeshua will have His way in the bloody battle to prove that Israel is His land and the land of the people. At the end of the seven years, Yeshua will return and trample Israel's enemies, putting an end to Satan's short reign of authority as antichrist and preparing a place of safety for the Israelites. This return is referred to in the Bible as the second coming of Yeshua.

Who is this that cometh from Edom, with dyed garments from Bozrah? This that is glorious in his apparel, traveling in the greatness of his strength? I that speak in righteousness, mighty to save. Wherefore thou are red in thine apparel, and thy garments like him that treadeth in the winevat? I have trodden the winepress alone; and of the people there was none with me: for I will tread them in mine anger, and trample them in my fury; and their blood shall be sprinkled upon my garments, and I will stain all my raiment. For the day of vengeance is in mine heart, and the year of my redeemed is come (Isaiah 63:1–4).

We, His saints, will rule the world with Him for a thousand years after we return from heaven, where we have celebrated for seven years the marriage supper of the lamb.

It strongly effected my mind again as I stood looking at the Eastern (Golden) Gate in Jerusalem on my second trip. The gate is made of huge stones in a seven-foot-thick wall. Ezekiel 44:2–3 tells us,

Then said the LORD unto me; This gate shall be shut, it shall not be opened, and no man shall enter in by it; because the LORD, the God of

Israel, hath entered in by it, therefore it shall be shut. It is for the Prince; the Prince, he shall sit in it to eat bread before the LORD; he shall enter by the way of the porch of that gate, and shall go out by the way of the same.

The Golden Gate will open when Yeshua returns for the second time and sets His feet upon the Mount of Olives, which is in a direct line to the gate. Zechariah 14:3–4 says, *Then shall the LORD go forth, and fight against those nations, as when he fought in the day of battle. And his feet shall stand in that day upon the mount of Olives, which is before Jerusalem on the east, and the mount of Olives shall cleave in the midst thereof toward the east and toward the west, and there shall be a very great valley; and half of the mountain shall remove toward the north, and half of it toward the south.*

The Euphrates River will dry up so that the two-hundred-million-strong army from the East can approach as the Messiah returns from heaven with His saints to destroy the enemy at a place called Armageddon. Chinese Muslims, who are part of the ten non-Han Chinese ethnic groups, are part of this large army from the East. They occupy one half of the land in China. They are the Uygur, Kazak, Dongxiang, Kirghiz, Salar, Tadjik, Uzbek, Bonan, Tatar, and Hui and have a population that numbers between twenty and forty million. The Hui are by far the largest group and the Uygur are second. They are exempt from the one child per family policy and can reproduce at will. Many call Tibet home. Islam came to China via Abu Waggas, one of Mohammed's contemporaries. He preached Islam in southern China and had the Beacon Tower Mosque built in memory of Mohammed in 627 AD. More and more Arabic and Persian Muslim merchants and mercenaries arrived in China, where they married local women and settled down to raise the first Chinese-Muslim families with the goal of spreading Islam. No matter how far away they live, all of them want to annihilate the Jews. I have been told the very same here by some Arabic and Iranian Muslims.

Yeshua alone can bring peace to Jerusalem and to the entire Middle East region as He gathers these vast armies from Megiddo, the southern rim of the Jezreel Valley, all the way south to Kidron Valley, which lies just east of Jerusalem. The world's final battle, the battle of Armageddon, will then take place and become the battle-ground for the greatest blood bath the world has ever seen.

I will also gather all nations, and will bring them down to the valley of Jehoshaphat, (which means judgment of the Eterrnal. In our days it is called the Kidron Valley) and will plead with them there for my people and for my heritage Israel, whom they have scattered among the nations, and parted my land. Proclaim ye this among the Gentiles; prepare war, wake up the mighty men, let all the men of war draw near; let them come up: Beat your plowshares into swords, and your pruning hooks into spears: let the weak say, I am strong. Assemble yourselves, and come, all ye heathen, and gather yourselves together round about: thither cause thy mighty ones to come down, O LORD. Let the heathen be wakened, and come up the valley of Jehoshaphat: for there will I sit to judge all the heathen round about. Put ye the sickle, for the harvest is ripe: come, get you down; for the press is full, the fats overflow; for their wickedness is great. Multitudes, multitudes in the valley of decision: for the day of the LORD is near in the valley of decisions. The sun and the moon shall be dark-ened, and the stars shall withdraw their shining. The LORD also shall roar out of Zion, and utter his voice from Jerusalem; and the heavens and the earth shall shake: but the LORD will be the hope of his people, and the strength of the children of Israel (Joel 3:2 & 9–16).

In that day shall the LORD defend the inhabitants of Jerusalem; and he that is feeble among them at that day shall be as David; and the house of David shall be as God, as the angel of the LORD before them. And it shall come to pass in that day that I will seek to destroy all the nations that come against Jerusalem. And I will pour upon the house of David, and upon the inhabitants of Jerusalem, the spirit of grace and of supplication: and they shall look upon me whom they have pierced and they shall mourn for him, as one mourneth for his only son, and shall be in bitterness for him, as one that is in bitterness for his firstborn (Zechariah 12:8–10).

Their intent is to destroy Jerusalem and take over world leader-ship, but they have no idea that Yeshua is returning from heaven with His saints to set the record straight, as told in Revelation 14:14 & 19–20,

And I looked, and behold a white cloud, and upon the cloud one sat like unto the Son of man, having on his head a golden crown, and in his

hand a sharp sickle. And the angel thrust in his sickle into the earth, and gathered the vine of the earth, and cast it into the great winepress of the wrath of God. And the winepress was trodden without the city, and blood came out of the winepress, even unto the horse bridles, by the space of a thousand and six hundred furlongs.

Another translation said that blood flowed in a stream two hundred miles long and as high as a horse's bridle.

Revelation 9:14b–19 says,

Loose the four angels which are bound in the great river Euphrates. And the four angels were loosed, which were prepared for an hour, and a day and a month, and a year, for to slay the third part of men. And the number of the army of the horsemen were two hundred thousand thousand: and I heard the number of them. And thus I saw the horses in the vision, and them that sat on them, having breastplates of fire, and of jacinth, and brimstone; and the heads of the horses were as the heads of lions; and out of their mouths issued fire and smoke and brimstone. By these three was the third part of men killed, by the fire, and by the smoke, and by the brimstone, which issued out of their mouth. For their power is in their mouth, and in their tails: for their tails were like unto serpents and had heads, and with them they do hurt.

At the time, John had a vision but no knowledge of atomic warfare, so he had to describe future events in terms that he knew. That is why he describes war machines as horses. Once this great battle between the armies of the antichrist and the East (Red China) has begun, they will realize that a great army from heaven led by Yeshua is attacking them.

And I saw heaven opened, and behold a white horse; and he that sat upon him was called Faithful and True, and in righteousness he doth judge and make war. His eyes were as a flame of fire, and on his head were many crowns; and he had a name written, that no man knew, but he himself. And he was clothed with a vesture dipped in blood; and his name is called The Word of God. And the armies which were in heaven followed him upon white horses, clothed in fine linen, white and clean. And out of his mouth

*goeth a sharp sword, that with it he should smite the nations: and he
shall rule them with a rod of iron: and he treadeth the winepress of the
fierceness and wrath of Almighty God. And he hath on His vesture and
on his thigh a name written, KING OF KINGS, and LORD OF LORDS*
(Revelation 19:11–16).

The armies that followed Yeshua from heaven on white horses
are comprised of the saints who were raptured earlier and are now
returning with Him to rule the world from Jerusalem.

*And he gathered them together into a place called in the Hebrew tongue
Armageddon. And the seventh angel poured out his vial into the air; and
there came a great voice out of the temple of heaven, from the throne, saying,
It is done. And there were voices, and thunders, and lightnings; and there
was a great earthquake, such as was not since men were upon the earth, so
mighty an earthquake, and so great. And the great city was divided into
three parts, and the cities of the nations fell: and great Babylon came in
remembrance before God, to give unto her the cup of the wine of the fierceness of his wrath. And every island fled away, and the mountains were not
found. And there fell upon men a great hail out of heaven, every stone about
the weight of a talent: and men blasphemed God because of the plague of the
hail; for the plague thereof was exceeding great* (Revelation 16:16–21).
Another translation says that the hailstones weighed one hundred
pounds each.

What will happen after this great battle has been fought? We turn,
once again, to the vision John received from God for the outcome in
Revelation 20:1–3,

*And I saw an angel come down from heaven having the key of the bottom-
less pit and a great chain in his hand. And he laid hold on the dragon,
that old serpent, which is the Devil, and Satan, and bound him a thousand
years, and cast him into the bottomless pit, and shut him up and set a seal
upon him that he should deceive the nations no more till the thousand
years should be fulfilled.* This thousand-year imprisonment of Satan
and Yeshua's rule on Earth are referred to as the millennium.

The millennium will not yet be heaven but will be a government
in which God is recognized as supreme civil ruler and His laws are

taken as the laws of the land. The Lord will choose Jerusalem to be the center of all spiritual blessing. During these thousand years of peace, health, happiness, and prosperity that will prevail, many children will be born with an abundance of everything. Believers who have been previously raptured (met Yeshua in the clouds) are the ones who will be given positions of responsibility when we return to rule the world with Yeshua from Jerusalem.

God, in His justice and mercy, will allow Satan one more chance to be loosened from His bonds and will test those who were not satisfied. Revelation 20:7–10 says,

And when the thousand years are expired, Satan shall be loosed out of his prison, and shall go out to deceive the nations which are in the four quarters of the earth, Gog and Magog, to gather them together to battle: the number of whom is as the sand of the sea. And they went up on the breadth of the earth, and compassed the camp of the saints about, and the beloveth city: and fire came down from God out of heaven, and devoured them. And the Devil that deceived them was cast into the lake of fire and brimstone, where the beast and the false prophet are, and shall be tormented day and night forever and ever.

After this final and everlasting defeat of Satan will come a time of judgment when every person who has ever lived will have his or her life and work judged. 1 Corinthians 3:13–14 tells us,

Every man's work shall be made manifest: for the day shall declare it, because it shall be revealed by fire; and the fire shall try every man's work of what sort it is. If any man's work abide which he hath built thereupon, he shall receive a reward

John describes his vision of this final judgment in Revelation 20:11–15,

And I saw a great white throne, and him that sat on it, from whose face the earth and the heaven fled away; and there was found no place for them. And I saw the dead, small and great, stand before God; and the books were opened: and another book was opened, which is the book of life; and the

dead were judged out of those things which were written in the books, according to their works. And the sea gave up the dead which were in it; and death and hell delivered up the dead which were in them: and they were judged every man according to their works, and death and hell were cast into the lake of fire.

It seems as if each one of these leaders tried to take control of Israel at one time or another. Forget it. It was prophesied thousands of years ago exactly the way it will be fulfilled.

Yeshua promised us in Revelation 22:12–20,

And behold, I come quickly; and my reward is with me, to give every man according as his work shall be. I am Alpha and Omega, the beginning and the end, the first and the last. Blessed are they that do his commandments, that they may have right to the tree of life, and may enter in through the gates into the city. For without are dogs, and sorcerers, and whoremongers, and murderers, and idolaters, and whomsoever loveth and maketh a lie. I Jesus have sent mine angel to testify unto you these things in the churches. I am the root and the offspring of David, and the bright and morning star. And the Spirit and the bride say, Come. And let him that heareth say, Come. And let him that thirst come. And whosoever will, let him take the water of life freely. For I testify unto every man that heareth the words of the prophecy of this book. If any man shall add unto these things, God shall add unto him the plagues that are written in this book. And if any man shall take away from the words of the book of this prophecy, God shall take away his part out of the book of life, and out of the holy city, and from the things which are written in this book. He which testefieth these things saith, Surely I come quickly. Amen. Even so, come, Lord Jesus.

Some of these last Scriptures are also given in the Tanakh. For your confirmation, they are in Daniel 12:1–2 and 7–12; 2 Samuel 7:2–16; Isaiah 9:7; Jeremiah 23:5; Numbers 24:16–19; Deuteronomy 4:2; and 12:32; Proverbs 30:6; and Exodus 32:33. At the end, He tells us in Joel 3:17, *So that ye know that I am the LORD your God dwelling in Zion, my holy mountain: then shall Jerusalem be holy, and there shall no strangers pass through her any more.*

Remember, A friend of Israel is a friend of God.

Since the Scriptures are the living Word of God, what He said to the Israelites so long ago still applies today. *Every Word of God is pure: He is a shield unto them that put their trust in him* (Proverbs 30:5).

CHAPTER 5

The Names of God

Names throughout the Bible have meanings and often show the attributes or character of that person, revealing their personality. An example of this is when God changed Abram to Abraham. Abram means "high father" and Abraham means "father of a multitude." Sarai was his wife's name to begin with, which translates to domineering and bossy, but God changed it to Sarah, which translates to "female royalty, princess, or queen." Jacob, meaning "supplanter" had his name changed to Israel, which means "He will rule as God." This was typical of God's posterity, as described in Genesis 17:4–5, 15–16; 35:10. Many people give their children biblical names in hopes that the child will become what the name represents or just because they liked that character in the Bible.

When we study the meanings of the names used for "God" and try to put them into one word, it is an almost impossible task. How can finite man hope to discern the glories of an infinite and eternal God? One may attempt it by understanding the meaning of the names by which God revealed Himself to His people. Some of those names are general names, mostly falling under three different words: Yahweh, Adonai, and Elohim. A bit of research in the Torah and the Brit Chadasha reveals some of their meanings. The English word *god* is given in the Bible dictionary 4,408 times with at least fourteen different meanings. The word *Yeshua* is given almost a thousand times. Other forms, such as Jehovah, are almost impossible to search for.

Let us start with Genesis 1:1, *In the beginning God...* The English word *God* is a translation of the Hebrew word *Elohim*, which is a compound of *El* (Hebrew for "mighty strength," as used in Genesis 14:18), and *elah,* implying faithfulness. The Aramaic *El Elohim* is the first of three primary names for deity. *Deity* means having a divine nature. All the names for God give a glimpse of his attributes. Elohim is seen in its plural form in Genesis 1:26, *And God said, Let us make man in our image...* and Genesis 3:2, *And the LORD God said, Behold, the man is become as one of us, to know good and evil...* So the English word *God* in Genesis 1:1 is plural and shows that the trinity was active in the creation of Father, Son, and Holy Spirit. This name is used twenty-five hundred times in the Torah. It can also be seen in Isaiah 9:6, *For unto us a child is born, unto us a son is given; and the government shall be upon his shoulder: and his name shall be called Wonderful, Counselor, The mighty God, The everlasting Father, The Prince of Peace...* It is speaking of Yeshua, born of a virgin, yet His name shall be the mighty God, the everlasting Father. Yes, Yeshua, as we generally call the Jewish Messiah, was active in the creation of the world.

In the beginning was the Word, and the Word was with God, and the Word was God. The same was in the beginning with God. All things were made by him; and without him was not anything made that was made. In him was life; and the life was the light of men. And the light shineth in darkness; and the darkness comprehended it not. That was the true Light, which lighteth every man that cometh into the world. He was in the world, and the world was made by him, and the world knew him not. He came unto his own, and his own received him not. But as many as received him, to them gave he power to become the sons of God, even to them that believe on his name: Which were born, not of blood, nor of the will of the flesh, nor of the will of man, but of God. And the Word was made flesh, and dwelt among us, (and we beheld his glory, the glory as of the only begotten of the Father,) full of grace and truth. And to make all men see what is the fellowship of the mystery, which from the beginning of the world hath been hid in God, who created all things by Jesus Christ. God, who at sundry times and in divers manners spake in time past unto the fathers by the prophets, hath in these last days spoken unto us by his Son, whom he hath appointed heir of all things, by whom also he made the worlds (John 1:1–5, 9–14; Ephesians 3:9; Hebrews 1:1–2).

The God of Genesis 1:1 is the Trinity: God the Father, God the Son, and God the Holy Spirit created the cosmos as an orderly, harmonious system. *In the beginning God created the heaven and the earth.* It was the Holy Spirit moving in Genesis 1:2, *And the earth was without form, and void; and darkness was upon the face of the deep. And the spirit of God moved upon the face of the waters.*

Jacob, on his journey away from home, laid his head on a pillar of stone and dreamed of a ladder reaching to heaven. The next morning, he called the place Beth-el, "House of God, in Genesis 28:11–19. Twenty years later, as he journeyed back to his homeland, he was instructed by God to go back to Beth-el in Genesis 35:1 & 7. Jacob built an altar there and this time called it El Beth-el. It wasn't the place that impressed him, but the *God* of the place. El Beth-el means God of the house.

Then there is Eloha. It is singular for Elohim.

In Genesis 21:33, Abraham called upon El Olam, which is translated in English as everlasting God. Olam is a Hebrew word meaning secret or hidden things. *Before the mountains were brought forth, or ever thou hadst formed the earth and the world, even from everlasting to everlasting, thou art God* (Psalms 90:2). It is the Hebrew word *Aion*, meaning age or dispensation. The ideas of things kept secret and of duration are combined in the word. Both ideas exist in the doctrine of the dispensations. They are among the mysteries of God, In Ephesians 1:9–10; 3:2–6, the everlasting God El Olam is that name of the deity by virtue of which He is God. His wisdom has divided all time and eternity into the mystery of successive ages. It is not merely that He is everlasting, but that He is God over everlasting things.

El Elyon is the Hebrew word for Most High God—in Genesis 14:18–19, the possessor of heaven and earth. It means *highest.* The first revelation of this name indicates its distinctive meanings. Abraham met Melchizedek, king of Salem (Jerusalem), who was priest of the Most High God and blessed Abraham in the name of

El Elyon, possessor of heaven and earth. This impressed Abraham remarkably, and he gave tithes of all the spoils of the battle he had just won.

El Shaddai is the Hebrew word for Almighty God, as in Genesis 17:1. The significance of the word is both interesting and touching. *El* signifies strong one and *Shaddai* is formed from the Hebrew *ahad*, which is the breast. God is Shaddai because He is the nourisher, the strength-giver. As a mother nourishes her baby by breastfeeding, so is El Shaddai the satisfier of His people. He pours Himself into believers' lives. Almighty God as used here could be expressed as all sufficient. He not only enriches, but also makes fruitful. This is brought out in the context of Genesis 17:1–5, where Abraham was to be father of many nations. It was God's enablement, even at the age of ninety-nine, when Abraham had not yet had the child promised by God.

Going to Genesis 2:4, we find the Lord God made heaven and earth. Lord God here is the English translation of the Hebrew Jehovah, meaning self-existing one who reveals himself. The external I AM of Exodus 3:14. Jehovah is the same as Yahweh and points to a continuous and increasing self-revelation. He is the self-existent one who reveals Himself. The name suggests a certain attribute of deity such as strength rather than His essential being. The name indicates a special relation of deity in His Jehovah character to man. Jehovah is the distinctive redemption name. When sin entered and redemption became necessary, it was Jehovah-Elohim who sought the sinning ones (Genesis 3:9–13) and clothed them with skins. Genesis 3:21 is a beautiful picture of righteousness provided through sacrifice. It was the first shedding of blood to provide a cover for man's sins. Lord God is Jehovah Elohim (Hebrew 9:22 and Matthew 26:28). Jehovah is the distinctive name of El Ohim, as in the covenant with Israel (Exodus 19:3 & 20:1–2). In His redemptive relation to man, Jehovah has seven compound names that reveal Him as meeting every need of man from his lost state to the end. Jehovah is the Jews' national name for the English God.

Jehovah-Jireh, in Genesis 22:1–14, means the Lord will provide.

Abraham had taken his beloved son of promise, Isaac, up to Mount Moriah to offer him as a sacrifice, at God's instruction. This was an act of deep faith, since God had told him *in Isaac shall thy seed be called.* But if he sacrificed him as a young lad, how could this prophecy be fulfilled? Could Abraham believe that even though he had slain the lad, God would bring him back to life? He may not have reasoned out how things would work out, but when Isaac said, *"Behold, the fire and the wood: but where is the lamb for a burnt offering?"* Abraham showed his implicit faith by answering, *"My son, God will provide Himself a lamb."* Jehovah-Jireh: God will provide. And He did! Not only here, but on the cross of calvary when He offered His own Son (John 3:16). This is the only time this name is used in Scripture. It is the symbolic name of Mount Moriah (1 Chronicles 21:18 & 2 Chronicles 3:1). David had bought the threshing floor for the purpose of erecting an altar. Yeshua was crucified, so the Son of God became the lamb of God, slain from the foundation of the earth (Revelation 13:8). After that, Abraham was reminded on Mount Moriah that Jehovah is the one who provides help in the severest tests of faith.

Believers in our day, no matter how deep the trials that come, should always remember that God knows and that Jehovah-Jireh will provide for our deepest needs.

Jehovah-Rophe, in Exodus 15:26, means the Lord that healeth thee.

That this refers to physical healing is shown by the context of the passage. It can also be seen when Moses was instructed to put a brass snake on a pole and those who had been bitten had only to look at the snake to be healed and saved from death (Numbers 21:6–9). Yet brass is the symbol of sin and the brass snake is a type of Yeshua on the cross, dying for our sins. The deeper healing of the soul malady is also implied.

Jehovah-Nissi, in Exodus 17:8–15, means, the Lord our banner.

The name is interpreted by the context. The enemy was Amalek, a type of flesh, and the conflict that day stands for the conflict of Galatians 5:17—the war of the spirit against the flesh. Victory was wholly due to divine help. This word is used only once in Scripture, but clearly shows that *his banner over us is love* (Isaiah 59:19). In the midst of life's battles, by whose power are battles won? Only by the power of Jehovah-Nissi, for He is the Lord of our banner. *When the enemy shall come in like a flood, the spirit of the Lord shall lift up a standard against him* (Isaiah 59:19b).

Jehovah-Rohi, in Psalm 23, means the Lord is my shepherd.

Jehovah makes peace by the blood of the cross in Psalm 22. In Psalm 23, He is shepherding His own in the world (John 10:7). The shepherd work of Jehovah-Raah has three aspects: As the good shepherd, He gives His life for His sheep (John 10:11) and is therefore the door by which *if any man enter in he shall be saved* (John 10:9). This answers Psalm 22:2. He is the great shepherd brought again from the dead in Hebrew 13:20 to care for and make perfect the sheep. He is the chief shepherd who is *coming in glory to give crowns of rewards to the faithful undershepherds* (1 Peter 5:4). This answers Psalm 24.

Jehovah-Shammah, in Ezekiel 48:35, means the Lord is present, or the Lord is there.

This name signifies Jehovah's abiding presence. We have Yeshua's own promises: *I will never leave thee, nor forsake thee* from Hebrews 13:5, and *Lo, I am with you always, even unto the end of the world* from Matthew 28:20. The Lord is present among His own today. Believers know this precious truth. He takes up residence in our hearts when we receive Yeshua as our Savior (Ephesians 1:13–14). He never departs as long as we abide in Him (John 15:4). And Jehovah promised never to leave His people Israel (1 Samuel 12:22; & 1 Kings 6:13). When Yeshua returns again, the whole world, including Israel, will be under the rule of the Messiah. He will then be in the midst of His people, never again to depart from them. How wonderful it will be that day when Israel will at last claim Him as Messiah and possess their Beulah land (Isaiah 62:4). At that time, God will be Jehovah-Shammah. The Lord is there. This is the symbolic name of Jerusalem.

Jehovah-Tsidkenou, in Jeremiah 23:6, means the Lord our righteousness.

In his days Judah shall be saved, and Israel shall dwell safely: and this is his name whereby he shall be called, THE LORD OUR RIGHTEOUSNESS. This name of Jehovah occurs in a prophecy concerning the future restoration and conversion of Israel. They will then hail Him by the name Jehovah-Tsidkenou. This is the epithet of Yeshua as their Messiah.

Jehovah-Shalom, in Judges 6:24, means the Lord our peace.

Gideon built an altar and called it Jehovah-Shalom. It means the Lord our peace or the Lord sent peace. Jehovah hates and judges sin (Judges 6:1–5) but loves and saves sinners—only through sacrifice (Romans 5:1; Ephesians 2:14; Colossians 1:20). He shall be called the Prince of Peace (Isaiah 9:6). The word *shalom* is the common greeting word used by Israelis and generally means peace, but it can have a variety of other meanings depending on the context. In Gideon's experience, it also meant "a comfort to my soul" because the Lord was going to deliver His people so they could live in comfort and rest. But this variation in meaning is only slight. If my soul is comforted by the Lord, I certainly could say, The Lord is peace. He can be a nation's *shalom* as well, when people realize that righteousness exalts a nation, but there is no *shalom* when a nation's sins bring disgrace upon her.

Yahweh (also spelled Yah or Jah), in Psalm 68:4, means It is the sacred name used as most forceful, strong and ardent.

It is much used in worship. Hallelujah is a word used in all languages and is a form of praise that combines the words hallelu, meaning praise ye, and jah, meaning Lord. It is used in Revelations 19:1–6. *Praise ye Jah, PRAISE YE THE LORD!*

Adonai (Adonajah) Jehovah is God, in Genesis 15:2 & 18:3, means *He is sovereign, master, owner.* This name is the distinctive name of the deity as in the covenants he made with Israel—Exodus 19:3 & 20:1–2; Jeremiah 31:31–39. It is often translated as the Lord God and appears frequently in the psalms and prophets, such as in Psalm 68:4. The word Adonai, compounded with *Jah,* is the meaning of the title the Lord Jesus Christ? Emphasis is on God as master or owner of every believer, since He bought us for a price—his own precious blood. Paul borrows this Torah concept of Lord as master from Deuteronomy 10:17 and applies it to Yeshua in 1 Timothy 6:15. He expounds on it when he refers to Yeshua the only king of kings or sovereign. In doing so, he not only exalts Him to the highest level, but also emphasizes that Yeshua has the absolute right to be master. He has not forgotten meeting Yeshua on the Damascus Road. Thomas, in John 20:28, uses the word *kurios* when he says, My Lord and my God, which is the Greek word with the same meaning as the Hebrew *Adonai*. Peter also uses the concept of master in 2 Peter 2:1 and stresses the right of Yeshua to unquestionable obedience. Malachi uses this name in his indictment *A son honors his father and a servant his master* (Malachi 1:6). The relation here is national, not personal (Jeremiah 3:18–19). The Jews, apparently, were calling Jehovah father, but yielding Him no filial obedience. Like Israel, we need to learn to respect and honor Adonai, the Lord.

Jehovah-Mikkadesh, in Leviticus 20:7–8, means I am the Lord who sanctifies you.

He tells us to consecrate ourselves and be holy. To keep His statutes and perform them. He is our sanctifier.

Lord of Sabaoth, in Isaiah 1:9; 1 Samuel 1:3; Romans 9:29 & James 5:4, means Lord of hosts.

It has a special reference to warfare or service. In use, the two ideas are united. Jehovah is Lord of (warrior) hosts. It is the name of Jehovah in manifestation of power. *The LORD of Hosts, He is the King of Glory* (Psalms 24:10). This name was revealed in the time of Israel's need (2 Kings 6:8–17). It is used in Jeremiah eighty times. Haggai uses it fourteen times in two chapters. Zechariah calls upon the Lord of hosts fifty times in fourteen chapters and in Malachi the name occurs about twenty-five times. Psalms 46:7 & 11 say, *The LORD of Hosts is with us...* The hosts are heavenly. Primarily the angels are meant, but the name gathers into itself the idea of all divine, or heavenly power, available for the need of God's people (Genesis 32:1–2; Isaiah 6:1–5; 1 Kings 22:19 & Luke 2:13–15). When we see the word Sabaoth, we immediately think it is a different spelling for Sabbath, the day of rest. This is not the same word, nor does it have the same meaning. Sabaoth carries the meaning of military armies organized for war. It is the military epithet of God (Jehovah). Lord (Jehovah) of hosts (Sabaoth) is the name used to demonstrate God's care for Israel and to emphasize the fact that a host (large numbers, a multitude, an army) of created beings, and indeed all creation, is at God's command to be used on behalf of His people of Israel. It also carries over into the Brit Chadasha (James 5:4). While John does not mention the phrase, we can see a demonstration of Yeshua as Lord of hosts (Sabaoth) riding forth with the armies of heaven at His command to wage war against antichrist and the nations who would oppose Him in the great battle of Armageddon (Revelations 19:11–16). In fact, from the description given in verse 14, it seems that we, the redeemed believers, will be that army *clothed in fine linen, white and clean* (Zechariah 14:5 & Revelations 19:8). Believers today should learn that no matter what happens, the ever-abiding presence of the Lord of Sabaoth is with us and His gracious purpose on our behalf is always accomplished. He *is* Jehovah-Sabaoth, our Lord of hosts.

Angel of the Lord is a name that has rich significance. It can be shown in many places in the Tanakh that the Angel of the Lord is identified as Jehovah Himself. In the appearance to Gideon, Judges 6:11–16, we see Him in His leadership of Israel on the way to the land of Canaan, where He is described as having power to forgive sins (Exodus 23:20–21). Since no mere angel can forgive sins, this is evidently none other than the Angel of the Lord—Yeshua incarnate. In the account of Genesis 8:1–33, three men came to Abraham. They talked and ate with him (verse 8). At this time, Sarah was promised to bear a son (verse 10) and one of the three (identified in verses 17 and 22 as the Lord) informed Abraham of the coming destruction of Sodom and Gomorrah. Abraham became the intercessor for the few righteous in the city. Although the name Angel of the Lord is not used in this Scripture, it does confirm that Yeshua showed Himself to Abraham, as the Scripture concerning the Angel of the Lord indicates. In the Brit Chadasha, there is no further reference to the Angel of the Lord, except in Matthew 1:18–25, where the Angel of the Lord appeared to Joseph and announced the coming birth of the Messiah. Once the Messiah appears in the flesh, in the incarnation, there was no further need to speak of the Torah designation. This unique person now reveals himself as Yeshua, the Messiah. In the Torah, the Angel of the Lord was the pre-incarnate Messiah, known to us as Lord Yeshua.

The Lord (Adonai-Jehovah) Yeshua, the earthly name of the Messiah (Matthew 1:21 and Luke 1:28–33), was conceived by Mary through the power of the Holy Spirit. He is the son of God (Luke 1:32). Therefore, He is the second member of the trinity and was in the word God in Genesis 1:1 & John 1:1–4. He is the lamb of God slain from the foundations of the world (Revelation 13:8). He is the Messiah promised to Israel, yet He was rejected when He appeared. He is the Savior, the redeemer of all mankind, including the saints of the church age as well as His chosen people of Israel. He is the one who is coming again (Matthew 28:18–20; Acts 1:10–11). The church age is hastening to its close and soon we will hear that trumpet call (1 Corinthians 15:51–52; 1 Thessalonians 4:13–18).

Theos, in Mark 15:29 & Matthew 3:9, means exceeding, supreme divinity.

This was Yeshua's cry on the cross: My God, my God, Why have you forsaken me? *Kurios* is the word used in Acts 19:20 to mean supreme in authority. *Tsur* is the word used in Deuteronomy 32:15 for God which also made Him the rock of His salvation. *Tsur* is the rock that laid the foundation of the earth, with its meaning of rock, refuge, strong one. Do we not refer to Yeshua as the rock of ages? He is also spoken of as the holy one of Israel (Isaiah 1:4).

There are probably many other names for God (Elohim) throughout the Scriptures, but these are enough to show that the attributes of God revealed through His names are numerous. In our fellowship with Jehovah, let us reflect the *divine power* of Elohim, the *all sufficiency* of El Shaddai, our confidence in El Elyon, *the most high,* and our personal encounter with Jehovah-Savior, who is the Alpha and Omega, *the beginning and the end,* the judge of all the earth, and glorify Him!

CHAPTER 6

The Names of Yeshua

In the Tanakh, God spoke directly to his chosen leaders, but through the redemption of the blood of Yeshua that occurred on the cross, we read in Hebrews 4:16, *Let us therefore come boldly unto the throne of grace, that we may obtain mercy, and find grace to help in time of need.* No longer do we need to wait for God to speak to only a chosen few in order to know what His will is for our lives. Since the creation of Adam, God has longed for intimate fellowship with man, which sin destroyed by its conception through the temptation of Satan. Even though man fell out of fellowship with God, He longed for a way to restore Himself to that perfect place. Sacrifices were instituted and performed in order to receive forgiveness for their sins.

However, from the beginning of time, even before the creation of humankind, God knew that man's sinful nature and the sacrifices of animals would not be enough to restore the broken communication that sin had caused. Hebrew 9:19–20 & 22–28 tell us about it this way:

For when Moses had spoken every precept to all the people according to the law, he took the blood of calves and of goats, with water, and scarlet wool, and hyssop, and sprinkled both the book and all the people, Saying, This is the blood of the testament which God has enjoined unto you. And almost all things are by the law purged with blood; and without shedding of blood is no remission. So Christ was once offered to bear the sins of many; and unto them that look for him shall he appear the second time without sin unto salvation.

Therefore Yeshua knew that He would be the only acceptable perfect sacrifice that could be given to restore man to fellowship with God. *He was willing to die so that none should perish but that all should come to repentance* (2 Peter 3:9). He is all we need to be able to participate in our eternal inheritance, allowing His blood to cleanse us from all our unrighteousness by accepting Yeshua as our personal Savior and making Him Lord of our lives.

Since Yeshua is our all-sufficiency, we learn to know Him and to know of Him through the many meanings of His name, which are:

God the Son: *And lo a voice from heaven, saying, This is my beloved Son, in whom I am well pleased* (Matthew 3:17).

Equal to the Father: *I and my Father are one* (John 10:30).

The Leader: *Who is the image of the invisible God, the firstborn of every creature* (Colossians 1:15).

The Firstborn*: For unto which of the angels said he at any time, Thou art my son, this day have I begotten thee? And again, I will be to him a father, and he shall be to me a son? And again, when he bringeth in the firstbegotten into the world, he saith, and let all the angels of God worship him* (Hebrews 1:5–6).

The Image of God: *Who being the brightness of his glory, and the express image of his person, and upholding all things by the word of his power, our sins, sat down on the right hand of the Majesty on high* (Hebrews 1:3).

Lord of Lord, King of Kings: *These shall make war with the Lamb, and the Lamb shall overcome them: for he is Lord of lords, and King of kings: and they that are with him are called, and chosen, and faithful* (Revelation 17:14).

The Creator: *All things were made by him; and without him was not anything made that was made* (Colossians 1:16–17). *For by him were all things created, that are in heaven, and that are in earth, visible and invisible, whether they be thrones, or dominions, or principalities, or powers: all things were created by him, and for him. And he is before all things, and by him all things consist* (John 1:3).

The Savior: *For unto you is born this day in the city of David a Savior, which is Christ the Lord* (Luke 2:11). *And it shall be for a sign and for a witness unto the LORD of hosts in the land of Egypt: for they shall cry unto the LORD because of the oppressors, and he shall send them a savior, and a great one, and he shall deliver them* (Isaiah 19:20). *And the Lord gave Israel a Savior, so that they went out from under the hand of the Syrians* (2 Kings 13:5a).

The Holy One: *For I am the Lord thy God, the Holy One of Israel, thy Savior: I gave Egypt for thy ransom, Ethiopia and Seba for thee* (Isaiah 43:3).

The Mediator: *For there is one God, and one mediator between God and men, the man Christ Jesus* (1 Timothy 2:5).

The Prophet: *Repent ye therefore, and be converted, that your sins may be plotted out, when the times of refreshing shall come from the presence of the Lord; and he shall send Jesus Christ, which before was preached unto you: Whom the heaven must receive until the times of restitution of all things, which God hath spoken by the mouth of all his holy prophets since the world began. For Moses truly said unto the fathers, A prophet shall the Lord your God raise up unto you of your brethren, like unto me; him shall ye hear in all things whatsoever he shall say unto you. And it shall come to pass, that every soul, which will not hear that prophet, shall be destroyed from among the people* (Acts 3:19–23).

The Priest: *This High Priest of ours understands our weaknesses, since he had the same temptations we do, though he never once gave away to them and sinned* (Hebrew 4:15).

The Judge: *For the Son of man shall come in the glory of his Father with His angels; and then he shall reward every man according to his works* (Matthew 16:27).

When the Son of man shall come in his glory: and before him shall be gathered all nations: and he shall separate them one from another, as a shepherd divideth his sheep from the goats: and he shall set the sheep on his right hand, but the goats on the left. Then shall the King say unto them on his right hand, Come, ye blessed of my Father, inherit the kingdom prepared for you from the foundation of the world: For I was an hungered, and ye gave me meat: I was thirsty, and ye gave me drink: I was a stranger, and ye took me in: Naked, and ye clothed me: I was sick, and ye visited me: I was in prison, and ye came unto me. Then shall the righteous answer him, saying, Lord, when saw we thee an hungered, and fed thee? or thirsty and gave thee drink? When saw we thee a stranger, and took thee in? or naked, and clothed thee? Or when saw we thee sick, or in prison, and came unto thee? And the King shall answer and say unto them, Verily I say unto you, Inasmuch as ye have done it unto one of the least of these my brethren, ye have done it unto me. Then shall he say also unto them on the left hand, Depart from me, ye cursed, into everlasting fire, prepared for the devil and his angels: For I was an hungered, and ye gave me no meat: I was thirsty, and ye gave me no drink: I was a stranger, and ye took me not in: naked, and ye clothed me not: sick, and in prison, and ye visited me not. Then shall they also answer him, saying, Lord, when saw we thee an hungered, or athirst, or a stranger, or naked, or sick, or in prison, and did not minister unto thee? Then shall he answer them, saying, Verily I say unto you, Inasmuch as ye did it not to one of the least of these, ye did it not to me. And these shall go away into everlasting punishment: but the righteous into life eternal. (Matthew 25:31–46)

For the Father judgeth no man, but hath committed all judgment unto the Son: That all men should honour the Son, even as they honour the Father. He that honoureth not the Son honoureth not the Father which hath sent him. Verily, verily, I say unto you, He that heareth my word, and believeth on him that sent me, hath everlasting life, and shall not come into condemnation; but is passed from death unto life. Verily, verily, I say unto you, The hour is coming, and now is, when the dead shall hear the voice of the Son of God: and they that hear shall live. For as the Father hath life in himself; so hath he given to the Son to have life in himself; and hath given him authority to execute judgment also, because he is the Son of man. Marvel not at this: for the hour is coming, in the which all that are in the graves shall hear his voice, and shall come forth; they that have done good, unto the resurrection of life; and they that have done evil, unto the resurrection of damnation. I can of mine own self do nothing: as I hear, I judge: and my judgment is just; because I seek not mine own will, but the will of the Father which hath sent me. (John 5:22–30)

He is the Shepherd: *He shall feed his flock like a shepherd: he shall gather the lambs with his arm, and carry them in his bosom, and shall gently lead those that are with young* (Isaiah 40:11). *I am the good shepherd: the good shepherd giveth his life for the sheep* (John 10:11).

The Head of the Church: *And God has put all things under his feet and gave him to be the head over all things to the church, which is his body, the fullness of him that filleth all in all* (Ephesians 1:22–23).

He is the Way: *Jesus saith unto him, I am the way, the truth and the life: no man cometh unto the Father, but by me* (John 14:6). *Having therefore, brethren, boldness to enter into the holiest by the blood of Jesus, by a new and living way, which he had consecrated for us, through the veil, that is to say, his flesh* (Hebrews 10:19–20).

He is the Truth: *And we know that the Son of God is come, and hath given us an understanding, that we may know him that is true, and we are in him that is true, even in his Son Jesus Christ. This is the true God, and eternal life* (1 John 5:20).

He is the Life: *When Christ, who is our life, shall appear, then shall ye also appear with him in glory* (Colossians 3:4).

And this is the record, that God hath given to us eternal life, and this life is in his Son (1 John 5:11).

In John 1:49, *Nathaniel declared, Rabbi, you are the Son of God; you are the King of Israel.*

In fact, Yeshua is mentioned in every book of the Bible, from Genesis to Revelation. Here are a few examples:

He is the breath of Life: *And the LORD God formed man of the dust of the ground, and breathed into his nostrils the breath of life; and man became a living soul* (Genesis 2:7).

He is the Passover Lamb: *It is the LORD'S Passover. On that same night I will pass through Egypt and strike down every firstborn—both men and animals—and I will bring judgement on all the gods of Egypt. I am the LORD. The blood will be a sign for you on the houses where you are; and when I see the blood, I will pass over you. No destructive plague will touch you when I strike Egypt* (Exodus 12:11b–13).

He is our Fire by night: *And on the day that the tabernacle was reared up the cloud covered the tabernacle, namely, the tent of the testimony: and at even there was upon the tabernacle as it were the appearance of fire, until the morning. So it was always: the cloud covered it by day, and the appearance of fire by night* (Numbers 9:15-16).

He is our kinsman Redeemer: *If thou wilt redeem it, redeem it: but if thou wilt not redeem it, then tell me, that I may know: for there is none to redeem it beside thee; and I am after thee. And he said, I will redeem it* (Ruth 4:4b).

He is the Prince of peace: *For unto us a child is born, unto us a son is given: and the government shall be upon his shoulder; and his name shall be called Wonderful, Counselor, The mighty God, The everlasting Father, The Prince of Peace* (Isaiah 9:6).

Following are samples that describe Yeshua in each book of the Bible. In the Tanakh He is concealed, in the Brit Chadasha He is revealed.

GENESIS
The Creator Genesis 1:1; Colossians 1:16
The Beginning 1:1; Revelations 1:8
The Seed of the Woman 3:15; Matthew 1:23
The Ark of Salvation 6:18; 7:23; Luke 2:30
Isaac, Only Begotten Son 22:1–19; John 3:16
Joseph, Beloved Son 37:4; Matthew 3:17

EXODUS
The Deliverer Exodus 3; 6:1–18; Acts 5:31
The Mediator 3:13–15; 32:30–35; Hebrews 8:6; 33:12–14
The Lawgiver 20:24; Hebrews 8:10
High Priest 28; 39; Hebrews 2:17
Passover Lamb 12:1; Corinthians 5:7
Tabernacle of God With Men 40:34–35; John 1:14

LEVITICUS
Sacrifice and Oblation Leviticus 9; Hebrews 10:12
Holy High Priest 8–10; Hebrews 7:26
The Atonement 16; Hebrews 9:14
Way of Approach To God 16; Hebrews 7:25

NUMBERS
The Tabernacle Numbers 3, 4, 9; John 1:14
Sanctuary in Wilderness 3, 4, 7; Ezekiel 11:16
The Nazarite 6:2–3; Hebrews 7:26
The Son of Man/Serpent of Brass 21:8–9; John 3:14

The Smitten Rock 20:8–13; 1 Corinthians 10:4
The Star out of Jacob 24:17; Matthew 2:2

DEUTERONOMY
The True Prophet Deuteronomy 18:15–19; Act 3:22
The Rock 32:4, 18, 31; 1 Corinthians 10:4

JOSHUA
Joshua (Jehoshua) Joshua 1–24; Hebrews 4:8
Captain of our Salvation 5:13–15; Hebrews 2:10
The Man with the Sword 5:13–15; Ephesians 6:12–18
Inheritance Giver 13–19; Hebrews 1:4; Ephesians 1:3, 14

JUDGES
Judge/Deliverer/Savior Judges 2:13–23; Matthew 1:21–23

RUTH
The Mighty Man Ruth 2:1
Lord of the Harvest 2:14–17
Kinsman-Redeemer 4:1–12

1 SAMUEL
Anointed Prophet/Priest 1 Samuel 16:1, 13
King/Intercessor

2 SAMUEL
Sceptre/Throne/Kingdom Holder 2 Samuel 7:13, 16; Luke 1:31–35

1 KINGS
The Son of David 1 Kings 1:13; 2:4, 12, 45; Mat 1:1
King of Peace and Glory 3:10–14, 28; 4:20–21, 25, 29, 30
The Wisdom of God 3:4; 1 Corinthians 1:30
Temple Builder 5:7; Ephesians 2:20–22
Greater than Solomon 10; Matthew 12:42
The Prophet of God/Word 13:1–3; John 1:14
King of kings/Lord of lords 22:19; Revelation 19:16

2 KINGS
The Righteous King 2 Kings 3:12
The Man of God 1:12
The Word of the Lord Personified 3:12; John 1:14

1 CHRONICLES
The Greater King David 1 Chronicles 11:1–3; Matthew 1:1

2 CHRONICLES
Prophet/Priest/King 2 Chronicles 20:14–21; Hebrews 9:11; 2:17; Revelations 19:16
Temple Cleanser 1:11, 12; 7:6; 9:22; Matthew 21:12–13
Reformer 29:1–19

EZRA
Governor/Priest Ezra 6:7; 4:25; 9:10; Hebrews 5:1–5; Matthew 2:6
Scribe and Restorer 6:2–7; Isaiah 58:12

NEHEMIAH
Governor of Judah Nehemiah 8:9; Matthew 2:6
Man of Prayer and Work 2:4–8; 3 John 17; Matthew 16:18

ESTHER
The Great King and His Bride Esther 1:1–8; 2:17; Revelations 19:7
Yeshua in the Old Testament Poetical Books:

JOB
Patient Suffering Priest Job 40:8, 10; 1:20–22; Hebrews 5:1–5

PSALMS
The Beloved Shepherd/King Psalm 23; John 3:15; Hebrews 13:20
The Sweet Singer 139–145; Hebrews 2:12

PROVERBS
The Wisdom of God Proverbs 1, 2; 1 Corinthians 1:24, 30; Colossians 2:3

ECCLESIASTES
The Preacher in Jerusalem Ecclesiastes 1:1
The Son of David 1:1
The Wisdom of God 1 Corinthians 1:24
The King "from above" Galatians 4:26

SONG OF SOLOMON
King of Peace
Beloved Bridegroom Lover Song 1–8; Ephesians 5:32
Yeshua in the Old Testament Prophetical Books:

ISAIAH
The Holy One of Israel Isaiah 30:11, 12, 15, 29; Mark 1:24
Our Salvation 12; Matthew 1:21
Our Righteousness 51:4–8; 1 Corinthians 1:30
Our Comfort 51:3; 66:13; John 14:16, 18
The True Judges 2:4; John 5:22

JEREMIAH
The Appointed Prophet Jeremiah 1:5
The Righteous Branch, the King 23:5
The Lord our Righteousness 23:4–6

LAMENTATIONS
The Weeping Prophet Lamentations 1:16
The Man of Sorrows 1:12, 18; Luke 19:41–44; Matthew 23:27, 38

EZEKIEL
The Son of Man Ezekiel 2:1, 3, 6, 8; 3:1, 3, 4, 10, 17, 25; John 1:51
The Shekinah Glory 43:1–4

DANIEL
The Son of Man Daniel 7:13
The Crushing Stone 2:34–45; Matthew 21:42–44
The Kingdom of God personified 7:27
King of Kings/Lord of lords 7:27; Revelations 19:16

HOSEA
The Prophet of Law and Love Hosea 1:2; Acts 3:22–23; Matthew 5:17–18; John 3:16

JOEL
Jehovah-God, Promiser and Joel 2:28–32; Luke 24:49; Acts 2:33; John 1:31–33
Baptizer With the Holy Spirit

AMOS
Burden-bearer
Judge and Punisher of Nations Amos 1; 2 Thessalonians 1:7–9
Building of David's Tabernacle 9:11–15; Matthew 16:18–19; Acts 15:15–18

OBADIAH
Servant and Worshipper Hebrews 2:12
Executor of Divine Wrath Obadiah 17, 21, 15; 2 Thessalonians 1:6–10

JONAH
The Greater than Jonah 1:17; Matthew 12:39–41

MICAH
Heavenly Micah "like God" Micah 7:17; Hebrews 1:2–4
Rejected King of the Jews 5:1; John 19:15
Establisher of His House 4:1–2; Hebrews 3:6

NAHUM
Prophet of Comfort Nahum 1:7, 15; 2:2; 1:2–6; John 14:16; 2 Thessalonians 1:8
and Vengeance

HABAKKUK
The Judge of Babylon Habakkuk 1:5–11; Revelation 17, 18
The Rewarder 2:1–4; Hebrews 10:38; 11:6

ZEPHANIAH
The Jealous God Zephaniah 1:18; 2 Corinthians 11:2
Executor of Gods Wrath 1 Romans 2:5–6

HAGGAI
Prophet/Priest/Prince
Builder of the Lord's House Matthew 16:18; Hebrews 3:5

ZECHARIAH
One Whom Jehovah Remembers
The Branch Zechariah 3:8; Matthew 2:23
Jehovah's Servant 3:8; Philippians 2:7
The Smitten Shepherd 13:7; Mark 14:27
King-Priest and Temple Builder 6:9–12; Hebrews 5:5–6
King Over All the Earth 14:9; Revelations 19:16

MALACHI
The Messenger of the Covenant Matthew 26:26–28
Refiner/Purifier/Cleanser of the Temple Malachi 3:1–3; Matthew 3:11; John 2:13–17

CHAPTER 7

Angels and Demons—Who Are They?

Angels are spiritual beings, created by God, and therefore are not to be worshipped or prayed to. The word *angel* means messenger, which in Hebrew is *malak*. Yet there are some people who worship angels, and even pray to them, substituting the honor and reverence that is due to Almighty God. We are told in Colossians 2:18, *Let no man beguile you of your reward in a voluntary humility and worshipping of angels, intruding into those things which he hath not seen, vainly puffed up by his fleshly mind.*

Angels have fascinated people throughout the centuries. From Genesis to Revelation, the Scriptures tell us about their activities in service to God and men. We read in Hebrews 1:14, *Are they not all ministering spirits, sent forth to minister for them who shall be heirs of salvation?* Angels are innumerable (Jeremiah 33:22). They are strong and powerful (Isaiah 37:36). Their appearance is awesome (Judges 13:20–22). They protect us (Psalm 34:7). They have limited knowledge (Mark 13:32). They lead sinners to the Gospel (Acts 10:3 & 22).

The Scriptures describe five types of angels

1. Seraphims who understand the revelation of God in His nature (Daniel 10).

2. Cherubims who understand the work of the Holy Spirit and lead the worship of heaven (Revelation 4:8).

197

3. Living creatures, who protect the throne of God (Ezekiel 1).

4. Archangels, who reveal or manifest God's authority, dominion, and rule.

5. Common angels, who appear to the saints and minister for the heirs of salvation

In the Middle East, hospitality to strangers is very common to this day which I experienced myself. The most widely known example of entertaining angels unaware is the time when Abraham invited three strangers into his tent and fed them a calf he had butchered. One of the three was the Lord Himself. He prophesied to Abraham and Sarah, who was long past childbearing age, that she would give birth to a son next year. In the Torah, God appeared to people with angels who sometimes looked like ordinary people, where in the Brit Chadasha, after Yeshua's ascension to heaven, it is the function of the Holy Spirit. I am sure Abraham never forgot this meeting. Their conversation was such that the people knew it had to be God's presence. By being hospitable and taking care of strangers, he received much information and bargained with God not to destroy all of Sodom, where his nephew Lot lived. You will find the destruction of Sodom and Gomorrah described in Genesis chapter 19.

On our trip to Israel in 1985, we visited Mamre, the site of the oak tree outside Hebron, where Abraham lived. Although leaning, the tree was still alive when we saw it. I believe we can all learn if we take the content and experience of these heavenly visitors to heart in Genesis 18:1–8,

And the LORD appeared unto him in the plains of Mamre: and he sat in the tent door in the heat of the day; and he lift up his eyes and looked, and, lo, three men stood by him: and when he saw them, he ran to meet them from the tent door, and bowed himself toward the ground, and said, My LORD, if now I have found favor in thy sight, pass not away, I pray thee, from thy servant: Let a little water, I pray you, be fetched, and wash your feet, and rest yourselves under the tree: And I will fetch a morsel of bread, and comfort ye your hearts; after that ye shall pass on: for therefore are ye come to your servant. And they said, So do, as thou hast said. And

Abraham hastened into the tent unto Sarah, and said, Make ready quickly three measures of fine meal, knead it, and make cakes upon the hearth. And Abraham ran unto the herd, and fetched a calf tender and good, and gave it unto a young man; and he hasted to dress it. And he took butter, and milk, and the calf, which he had dressed, and set it before them; and he stood by them under the tree, and they did eat.

People wore sandals back then, so anytime a visitor arrived, he or she would be offered water to wash the dust off their feet. It is a Bedouin custom still practiced in some areas for the host to stand while the visitors eat. It shows respect toward the visitor. We read in Hebrews 13:2, *Be not forgetful to entertain strangers: for thereby some have entertained angels unaware.*

When I was in Ghana, West Africa, the woman of the house never once sat at the table while her husband, sons, and I ate. In another house on a different trip, the wife and daughter had always eaten before I sat down for a meal. If the husband was home, I ate with him.

In the next excerpt, they asked for Sarah by name. How would strangers know her name if they had not yet seen her? They also knew she was barren. From that, Abraham could tell he was not dealing with men of human wisdom.

And they said unto him, Where is Sarah thy wife? And he said, Behold, in the tent. And he said, I will certainly return unto thee according to the time of life; and, lo, Sarah thy wife shall have a son. And Sarah heard it in the tent door, which was behind him. Now Abraham and Sarah were old and well stricken in age; and it ceased to be with Sarah after the manner of women. Therefore Sarah laughed within herself, saying, After I am waxed old shall I have pleasure, my lord (husband) being old also? And the LORD said unto Abraham, Wherefore did Sarah laugh, saying, Shall I of a surety bear a child, which am old? Is anything to hard for the LORD? At the time appointed I will return unto thee, according to the time of life, and Sarah shall have a son. Then Sarah denied, saying, I laughed not; for she was afraid. And he said, Nay, but thou didst laugh. And the men rose up from thence, and looked toward Sodom: and Abraham went with them to bring them on the way. And the LORD said, Shall I hide from Abraham that thing which I do; Seeing that Abraham shall surely become a great and mighty nation, and all the nations of the earth shall be blessed in him? For I know him, that he will command his children and his household after him, and they shall keep the way of the LORD, to do justice and judgment; that the LORD may bring upon Abraham that which he hath spoken of him. And the LORD said, Because the cry of Sodom and Gomorrah is great, and because their sin is very grievous; I will go down now, and see whether they have done altogether according to the cry of it, which is come unto me; and if not, I will know. And the men turned their faces from thence, and went toward Sodom: but Abraham stood yet before the LORD. And Abraham drew near, and said, Wilt thou also destroy the righteous with the wicked? Peradventure there be fifty righteous within the city: wilt thou also destroy and not spare the place for fifty righteous that are therein? That be far from thee to do after this manner, to slay the righteous with the wicked: and that the righteous should be as the wicked that be far from thee: Shall not the Judge of all the earth do right? And the LORD said, If I find in Sodom fifty righteous within the city, then I will spare all the place for their sakes. And Abraham answered and said, Behold now, I have taken upon me to speak unto the LORD, which am but dust and ashes: Peradventure there shall lack five of the fifty righteous: wilt thou destroy all the city for lack of five? And he said, If I find there forty and five, I will not destroy it. And he spake unto him yet again, and said, Peradventure there shall be forty found there. And he said I will not do it for forty's sake. And he said unto him, Oh let not the LORD be angry, and I will speak: Peradventure there shall thirty be found there. And he said, I will not do it, if I find thirty there. And he said, Behold now I have taken upon me to speak unto the LORD: Peradventure there shall be twenty found there. And he said I will not destroy it for twenty's sake. And he said Oh let not the LORD be angry, and I will speak yet but this once: Peradventure ten shall be found there. And he said, I will not destroy it for ten's sake. And the LORD went his way, as soon as he had left communing with Abraham: and Abraham returned unto his place (Genesis 18:9–33).

The following Scripture in the Brit Chadasha is confirmation of the above writings and should want to caution and alarm us, as described in Matthew 13:41, *The Son of man shall send forth his angels, and they shall gather out of his kingdom all things that offend, and them which do iniquity.* In other words, Yeshua will send His angels so that people can be struck dead if they offend anything in His kingdom. This is a powerful scripture. Ananias and Sapphira, who were not honest about how much profit they made on the sale of their property, are proof of it. They were struck dead for lying. Be very careful what you say about God's anointed!

I believe in the pre-tribulation rapture of the church, which I hope will take place soon so that we will join Yeshua in heaven when He comes for us in the air. The unbelievers and the wicked will stay on earth. The righteous saints—those waiting for Yeshua to return—will be caught up by Him in the twinkling of an eye. Those who remain will be in for seven years of destruction.

Angels come to our assistance simply by us speaking the Word of God. Let's keep them occupied by praying and quoting Scriptures to God so that He will dispatch them on our behalf. How many are there? The Bible tells us in Psalm 68:17, *The chariots of God are twenty thousand, even thousands of angels: the Lord is among them, as in Sinai, in the holy place.* Many books have been written about angels, but let us find out what the Bible has to say about this subject. They are not at all the tiny, childlike cherubs we see in paintings and in pictures, nor are they cute porcelain and ceramic figurines. Instead, they are very powerful, with different functions as God's messengers, since we are the heirs of salvation. We read in 2 Kings 19:35 that one angel by himself destroyed 185,000 Assyrian soldiers in one night in their own camp. King David wrote that angels fight for us in Psalm 35:5–6, *Let them be like chaff before the wind: and let the angel of the LORD chase them. Let their way be dark and slippery: and let the angel of the LORD persecute them.* Some of them are guardian angels assigned to Christians to rescue us when we are unaware. I would like to share several personal experiences.

Years ago, I was about to be confronted by a couple of very large men in a remote area. One was walking slowly toward me while the other came from behind the bushes to meet me head-on as I approached. Way off in the distance, I saw some young people and, in a calm voice, as if I was part of their group, I yelled to them and waved my arms, saying, Hey, you guys, don't run off, wait for me. By doing so, I pretended that I was with some other people that had gone ahead of me. God put these words in my mouth. I was too scared to think for myself, knowing what might happen to me. It was a divine intervention from the Holy Spirit. The men backed up so that I could pass them where before they came towards me. Many years later, the Holy Spirit revealed to me that those people I had waved to had been angels; there was not one human in sight. Did God let a certain number of angels show up on the scene in the form of young people for my protection? It had just rained and no one was in this large park, which I had to cross to get to my car. We read in Psalm 91:11, *For he shall give his angels charge over thee, to keep thee in thy ways.* Isn't that comforting? Angels move at the command of God, as we read in Psalm 103:20, *Bless the LORD, ye his angels, that excel in strength, that do his commandments, hearkening unto the voice of his Word.* This brings another appropriate Scripture to my mind. *For the eyes of the LORD run to and fro throughout the whole earth, to shew himself strong in the behalf of them whose heart is perfect toward him* (2 Chronicles 16:9a).

Let me give you an illustration of what I firmly believe was an attack by Satan that turned out to be the command of God to an angel. I was about to have a possible fatal fall. You see, when you are on the frontline in God's army, Satan is furious and tries to wipe you out. But all he can do is try, because the Scripture says in 1 John 4:4, *Ye are of God, little children, and have overcome them: because greater is he that is in you, than he that is in the world.* Yes, he attacks us, but he will not succeed in eliminating us. What the devil meant for evil, God turns to good. Angels are assigned to Christians and rescue us when we are in danger.

On May 13, 1997, I locked the front door of a vacant residence. I was by myself, and as I stepped back on what was supposed to be the platform, I lost my balance and fell backward, with no railing to hold on to. The ground several feet below was my destination, which I would hit with my back or head. But God had other plans. In the process of falling backward, all at once and without my effort or being conscious of it, my body turned to the left so that I could run at full speed down the steps and halfway across the lawn before I came to a stop. A strong force must have turned my body because I twisted my back and knees. Had an angel turned my body to keep me from being hurt or even killed?

My doctor referred me to an orthopedic surgeon who X-rayed my knees. I required an MRI, which confirmed torn cartilage in the back of my right knee, requiring arthroscopic surgery. While we were waiting for approval from the insurance company, the doctor sent me to physical aqua therapy. This delay allowed me to attend a healing crusade, where I was totally healed. Was God in this or not?

I traveled about twenty-five miles to the crusade in Seattle on August 22. All the way there, I talked to the Lord and prayed that He would heal me. I was desperate and told Him so. I pleaded with Him to fix my knee. The following week, I was to tell the doctor when to schedule my surgery. While I was at pool therapy, I told the attendant that I was going to the crusade and expected to be healed. I already knew she didn't believe in God. She laughed in disbelief when I said it. I remembered a song I had learned in a church in Ghana, West Africa, where I ministered several years earlier, and started to sing it several times in all sincerity. Here are the words: "Hallelujah, He is a prayer answering God, Hallelujah; He is a prayer answering God. I prayed in Jesus Name and then the answer came, Hallelujah, He's a prayer answering God."

When the minister preached, he called out different sicknesses and diseases. He asked us to step into the aisles in faith. I was fourteen rows up in the large arena and obeyed. With my pain still present, I made my way down to the main floor. The anointing was very strong and my faith was so great that I received my healing by the time I was down on the main floor. I had to take the first steps in pure faith and was able to give God all the glory. I tell you, I was on a spiritual high all day and was now able to sing, "Hallelujah. You're my prayer answering God." Now I needed to protect my healing from Satan, as Yeshua Himself said in John 10:10a, *The thief cometh not, but for to steal, and to kill, and to destroy.*

I kept my 8:30 a.m. pool therapy appointment on the follow-ing Monday, since I needed to tell the doctor, but I did not go in the water. I shared my healing with the unbelieving physical therapist. I told her that I would most likely cancel the rest of my appointments since I was healed. She told me that the chart read that I was to come twice a week for a month. I explained to her that now since I was healed, I no longer needed any kind of therapy. Since she was not a believer, it was too much for her to comprehend. Afterward, I went to see the doctor without an appointment and shared my story with him. To have clinical proof would require another MRI, which was too costly, but he could see me swinging my leg, which was proof enough for him. He said he would close my case and was happy for me. So was I.

Angels will escort a dying saint into the presence of God, yet an unsaved person will experience torment. First I will prove it to you from the Scriptures in the Bible and then I will give you two personal experiences of dying men whom I knew. One told me he heard the angels singing in his presence when I visited him in the hospital. The other... Well, you will read it.

There was a certain rich man, which was clothed in purple and fine linen, and fared sumptuously every day: And there was a certain beggar named Lazarus, which was laid at his gate, full of sores, and desiring to be fed with the crumbs which fell from the rich man's table: moreover the dogs came and licked his sores. And it came to pass, that the beggar died, and was carried by the angels into Abraham's bosom: the rich man also died, and was buried; and in hell he lift up his eyes, being in torments, and seeth Abraham afar off, and Lazarus in his bosom. And he cried and said, Father Abraham, have mercy on me and send Lazarus that he may dip the tip of his finger in water, and cool my tongue; for I am tormented in this flame. But Abraham said, Son, remember that thou in thy lifetime receivedst thy good things and likewise Lazarus evil things: but now he is comforted, and thou art tormented. And beside all this, between us and you there is a great gulf fixed; so that they, which would pass from hence to you, cannot; neither can they pass to us that would come from thence. Then he said, I pray thee therefore, father, that thou wouldest send him to my father's house: For I have five brethren; that he may testify unto them, lest they also come into this place of torment. Abraham saith unto him, they have Moses and the prophets; let them hear them. And he said Nay, father Abraham: but if one went unto them from the dead, they will repent. And he said unto him, If they hear not Moses and the prophets, neither will they be persuaded, though one rose from the dead (Luke 16:19–31).

Now you see how important it is to accept Yeshua as your Savior while you're here on earth, alive. Afterward, it is too late. How true it is. People go to hell by their own choices, even though God planned it only to be a place for the devil.

One morning as I awoke, the Lord showed me in the spirit how two men I had known died—one in peace, the other in torment. Using these examples seemed to be the only way I could witness to my accountant the next day. I made the acquaintance of a certain builder and his wife during my real estate career. Not only did I become their real estate agent, I was also their friend. A few years later, he became seriously ill and ended up in the hospital. He was improving and it looked as though he would be released from the hospital. I went to see him, hoping to ask if he would see heaven if he didn't survive. At that time, over thirty years ago, I was a fairly new Christian and not yet grounded in the Word of God. On top of that, I was a foreigner with a limited vocabulary about spiritual things since I had not learned about them in my native country. Although I had this question in mind, I couldn't think of the right words to ask him. Yet I continued to be concerned about his salvation.

As we visited, he asked me to tell the people who were singing outside his room to stop. I couldn't hear anything, but I listened to see if his hearing was that much better than mine. When I told him there was no one outside singing, he said, "Can't you hear them?" Once I even opened the door to prove no one was out there. He even named the song they were singing. At that time in my Christian walk, my knowledge of the works of God was limited and I did not understand the meaning of all that was happening. The song was referring to angels, but the significance of the situation still did not register in my mind, nor did I think to write down the words of the song. But he continued to hear them singing. It was only a day or two before he passed away. Years later, the Lord revealed to me that my builder-friend heard the voices of angels. Angels were hovering around his bed, preparing him to be with Yeshua in heaven. This is why I could not hear or see them—my time had not yet come. It all took place in the spiritual realm, not visible to the eye. God assured me that he went in peace.

On another occasion, over thirty years ago, I could not sleep and wrestled all night in bed. I had such an unusual feeling in my chest that I sat up and asked the Lord if my mother was dying. Why would I ask such a question? Why did I even associate this feeling with death? This awful sensation didn't go away all night. At about noon the next day, I stopped at another real estate agent's house, which I had passed by daily for years but had never visited. Once there, I found out that one of our coworkers, a relative of his, had passed away during the night. Then it occurred to me that he had recently sold a house I had just listed. The owners of the house had asked the purchasers how they had found out that their home was for sale. They were curious as to why it had sold in a few days. The purchasers said they had called my office the evening I placed the first ad in the newspaper. According to our office policy, I should have received the prospective buyer's phone number. Instead of referring them to me, this particular agent sat in the office that evening and stole my client. He not only showed my buyer the house the next day, but he sold it to them. They were supposed to be my clients since I had paid for the ad. Since this coworker claimed to be a Christian, I never suspected he would steal from me. However, through the curiosity of my sellers, it came to light. I never told him that I knew. As he struggled in his last hours, with his life flashing before him, I assumed his sins did also and he sought forgiveness for what he had done. This explained the mysterious feeling that would not leave me all night. My spirit had alerted me. We might think we can cheat a little here and there, but one day we will need to give an account for our life before God, our creator. The Bible tells us that rivers of living water will flow from out from our bellies when we are born again, until then it lies dormant and we need the Holy Spirit to activate it. It is like the suction of a vacuum, which is not satisfied until we fill it with Yeshua. New clothes and cars, or even a new home will only fix the emptiness for a while. Nothing can satisfy in its place. Yeshua is the only way.

I shared these death experiences with my coworkers after we lost another agent to a bee sting on a hunting trip. As an evangelist, I have a burden for souls and use every opportunity to share the gospel. Some of our agents who know Yeshua thanked me. I hope it convicted some of the others.

Which outcome will you face in your last hours? You have heard people testify on television or in books that they died for a short period of time while on the operating table or after an accident. Some testify that they went to heaven or hell, only to return and relate their unusual experiences. The ones who went to heaven saw all kinds of pleasant things, while those who received a glimpse of hell were confronted with the lake of fire. The Bible teaches us that hell is a reality under the earth. There are different places called hell. Their locations are Paradise, Shoal or Hell, Tartars, the Pit, and Gahanna—the lake of fire. God allowed me to explain what He showed me while in the spirit that particular morning. My friends had already died several years earlier; why was God taking me back? Why did I need to know in the first place? At that time, I could not understand why He would show me their dying hours. I didn't know I was to be used for a witness the following day.

I had the same accountant for a number of years. Whenever he changed to a different company, I would follow him. Eventually, he started his own business. One day, he came to my house in the afternoon to pick up my paperwork for my income tax. I had my papers well organized, and since he came early with ample time before his next appointment, we had quite a long visit. He was also German-born, so we had some nice visits when we got together. He always talked about his lively four- and five-year-old boys. He was a good daddy.

During this visit, he told me how much he and his brother were looking forward to seeing their grandmother in Germany after the tax season was over. She was in a nursing home and he wanted to visit her once more before she passed away. I told him that I had left real estate at the end of the previous January because God had called me to serve him. He could not believe I was giving up my successful career of fourteen years. I told him I had walked away because I was completely sold out to the Lord and my time was now His time. (That was in 1985, but since then, the Lord had me return to real estate in 1991). Since he was not receptive before, I could never share what a difference Yeshua had made in my life. This very day, though, I told him I had written a Christian book and shared with him in detail what God had shown me only the day before about the two men who had passed on. I am convinced that God had planned everything in advance and had timed it just right, knowing that my accountant had lots of time that day to listen.

Neither one of us had any idea that when he left my house, he would come face-to-face with tragedy and lose his life. An hour and a half after he left, my friends called to see how much longer it would be before the accountant would arrive for his appointment with them. He never got that far. Less than two miles from my house, he was hit broadside by a seventeen-year-old young man who had ignored the stop sign. A few hours later, he died in the hospital.

I believe that God allowed me to share with him the story of the two men in order for him to have the opportunity to invite Yeshua into his heart in the last few hours of his life. My friend's curiosity led them to check on the accountant at the fire department. He was told that they had to cut the door open and remove his seatbelt in order to get him out. He was a very tall, large man. The fireman said his injuries were not that bad because he walked around after they got him out of the car. My friend's, who's tax return he was to prepare next couldn't believe he had died.

Can you see how important it is to be ready to meet your maker? After the funeral, his brother told me that they came to this country at ages ten and eleven and never took the time to practice their faith. It is possible that my accountant may never have known how to ask the Lord into his heart if I had not been able to speak with him just a short time before his death. It sure seems as though God placed me in the right place at the right time. After the funeral service, I was able to share with all the people present at his widow's home the experience I had had with him just prior to his death. You see, there never was a need for God in their lives before. They were success-ful. Is that what you are saying? You don't have time for God either? Do you think it can wait until later, just before you die? How do you know if you will have a chance then? You might run out of time! At age thirty-three, my accountant certainly had not thought on that day that he would never see his family again. Give it some thought so that you will be ready, because no one knows the hour.

He suffered several broken ribs and internal injuries. One of the doctors informed his wife that he had had trouble breathing upon arriving at the hospital. Five doctors tried in vain to save his life. Can you imagine how shocked his wife was when she received a telephone call, upon returning home from shopping, that her husband had died? Neither she nor her husband would have believed that that morning they would share their last breakfast together. She told me that their oldest boy tried to take a piece of pizza home to daddy, while the little one asked who their new daddy was going to be. What a cruel question! But what else would you expect to hear from a four-year-old who was conveying his feelings?

My accountant liked classical music. He was playing the Funeral March on tape at the time of his accident. Later, his wife was puzzled when she found the tape. I thank God that He allowed him the privilege of choosing where he was going to spend eternity by keeping him alive for a few hours after the accident. His college professor conducted the service at the funeral home. He talked about everything but God to the many people present. At a time like this, people are receptive to inviting Yeshua as their Savior, which in my opinion should be offered at each funeral service. People that never otherwise attend church come to funerals and should be reminded to reflect on where they will spend eternity—in heaven or hell. I did not shed a tear at the funeral. I had an inner peace knowing that I would see him again in heaven. It means that the angels that surrounded my builder friend also encamped around my accountant, no matter how short the time was that he accepted Yeshua into his heart. Read where Yeshua Himself said in Luke 15:10 *Likewise, I say unto you, there is joy in the presence of the angels of God over one sinner that repenteth.*

Angels played a great role in Yeshua's life, as we see in the following verses:

An angel announced the birth of John, the forerunner of Yeshua (Luke 1:11–17).

The angel told Zacharias, his father, to name him John (Luke 1:13).

The announcement of Yeshua's birth to Mary came from an angel (Luke 1:26–37).

An angel foretold Joseph of the birth of Yeshua (Matthew 1:20–21).

The angel told him to call His name Jesus—Yeshua (Matthew 1:21).

Angels announced Yeshua's birth to shepherds nearby (Luke 2:8–15).

An angel directed the child's flight into and the return from Egypt (Matthew 2:13, 20).

Angels ministered to Yeshua on the pinnacle at His temptation (Matthew 4:5, 11).

An angel strengthened Yeshua in the Garden of Gethsemane (Luke 22:43).

An angel descended from heaven, rolling back the stone at His tomb (Matthew 28:2).

And telling the women not to fear: He is not here, for He is risen (Matthew 28:5–7).

Two angels at the sepulchre presented Yeshua to Mary Magdalene (John 20:11–14).

Yeshua could have called on twelve legions of angels to deliver Him (Matthew 26:53).

All the angels come with Yeshua when He sits on the throne of His glory (Matthew 26:31).

Yeshua said that the angels rejoice when one sinner repents (Luke 15:10).

If we confess Yeshua before men, He will confess us before the angels (Luke 12:8).

Yeshua will send His angels to remove the wicked out of His kingdom (Matthew 13:41).

Yeshua will send His angels to gather His elect (Matthew 24:31).

In the book of Acts, angels had many roles:

An angel opened the prison by night to let the apostles escape (Acts 5:19–23).

An angel directed Philip to go south, he met the Ethiopian eunuch (Acts 8:26–39).

An angel appeared to Cornelius and told him to send for Peter (Acts 10:1–23).

An angel shined a light on Peter in prison and led him to freedom (Acts 12:7–9).

Those gathered to pray at Mary's house said it was Peter's angel (Acts12:12–17).

An angel smote Herod for not giving God the glory for his release (Acts 12:18–23).

An angel stood by Paul during the storm, saving those sailing with him (Acts 27:23).

In the Torah, angels took care of many situations:

An angel found Hagar in the wilderness and told her to return (Genesis 16:7–9).

He told Hagar that her offspring would be too numerous to count (Genesis 16:10).

An angel said she was pregnant and to call her son Ishmael (Genesis 16:11).

Three heavenly visitors announced the birth of Isaac (Genesis 18:1–1).

Angels speak of the destruction of Sodom and Gomorrah (Genesis 18:16–33).

Two angels visit Lot, rescue him, and destroy Sodom (Genesis 19:1–29).

An angel called from heaven unto Abraham not to slay his son (Genesis 22:9–13).

An angel told Moses in the burning bush to deliver the Israelites (Genesis 24:7).

An angel went before them and guided the Israelites on their journey (Exodus 3:2–12).

God told Moses to lead the people: Mine angel shall go before thee (Exodus 23:20–23).

And I will send an angel before thee; and drive out your opposition (Exodus 32:34).

An angel rebuked Balaam, telling him only to speak what he was told (Exodus 33:2).

An angel said to Gideon: The LORD is with thee, man of valor (Numb. 22:31–35).

There are many more Scriptures in which angels had an important role. As I continue, you will see that angels have a large part in the visions and writing of the book of Revelation. We read in Revelation 1:1–2 that Yeshua passed His revelation through his angel unto His servant John, who recorded His testimony in the Book of the Revelation.

The seven stars are the angels of the seven churches (Revelation 1:20).

Yeshua sent His angel to testify of these things in the churches (Revelation 22:16).

A strong angel proclaimed, "Who is worthy to open the book?" (Revelation 5:2).

Ten thousand times ten thousand angels sang praises to the lamb (Revelation 5:11).

Four angels were given power to hurt the earth (Revelation 7:1–2).

Angels sealed the servants of God in their foreheads (Revelation 7:3).

All the angels fell on their faces and worshipped God (Revelation 7:11).

The saints' prayers ascended before God from the angel's hand (Revelation 8:4).

The seven angels prepared themselves to sound the trumpets (Revelation 8:6).

The angel of the bottomless pit was king over the locust army (Revelation 9:11).

Four angels were loosened to slay one-third of men (Revelation 9:15).

An angel had the open book, announcing the end (Revelation 10:1–2, 6).

Michael and his angels fought against the dragon (Revelation 12:7).

A flying angel preached the gospel to the nations (Revelation 14:6).

John got a revelation from the angel of the holy city of Jerusalem as to when it would come down from heaven, and we with it, after the seven years of tribulation. We will rule and reign with Yeshua for a thousand years. *And there came unto me one of the seven angels which had the seven vials full of the seven last plagues, and talked with me, saying, Come hither, I will shew thee the bride, the Lamb's wife. And he carried me away in the spirit to a great and high mountain, and showed me that great city, the holy Jerusalem, descending out of heaven from God* (Revelation 21:9–10).

I Yeshua have sent mine angel to testify unto you these things in the churches. I am the root and the offspring of David, and the bright and morning star (Revelation 22:16).

The question is, did the churches really apply this truth and teach it to their parishioners?

Because Lucifer, who is also called Satan, wanted to be like God, his unexpected fall was unavoidable in Ezekiel 28:15–19,

Thou wast perfect in thy ways from the day that thou wast created, till iniquity was found in thee. By the multitude of thy merchandise they have filled the midst of thee with violence, and thou hast sinned: therefore I will cast thee as profane out of the mountain of God: and I will destroy thee, O covering cherub, from the midst of the stones of fire. Thine heart was lifted up because of thy beauty, thou hast corrupted thy wisdom by reason of thy brightness: I will cast thee to the ground, I will lay thee before kings, that they may behold thee. Thou hast defiled thy sanctuaries by the iniquity of thy traffic; therefore will I bring forth a fire from the midst of thee, it shall devour thee, and will bring thee to ashes upon the earth in the sight of all them that behold thee. All they that know thee among the people shall be astonished at thee: thou shalt be a terror, and never shalt thou be any more.

Now let us look at the fallen angels. Certain angels have influence over nations. Such an angel was the ruling prince of Persia, who tried to keep the Israelites from returning to their homeland. If that already took place, as described in the Tanakh, we should assume that demonic armies are still opposing God's work in the heavens as well as here on earth.

The angel Gabriel tells of his dilemma in Daniel 10:12–13,

Then said he unto me, Fear not, Daniel: for from the first day that thou didst set thine heart to understand and to chasten thyself before thy God, thy words were heard, and I am come for thy words. But the prince of the kingdom of Persia withstood me one and twenty days: but, lo, Michael, one of the chief princes, came to help me; and I remained there with the kings of Persia.

The angel Michael is described as one of the chief princes. He rules and guards the activities of Israel. Michael and Gabriel both fought with the prince of Persia in order to get through to Daniel. Afterward, he became the prince of Greece.

Then said he, Knowest thou wherefore I come unto thee? And now will I return to fight with the prince of Persia: and when I am gone forth, lo, the prince of Grecia shall come. But I will shew thee that which is noted in the scripture of truth: and there is none that holdeth with me in these things, but Michael your prince (Daniel 10:20–21).

For if God spared not the angels that sinned, but cast them down to hell, and delivered them into chains of darkness, to be reserved unto judgment (2 Peter 2:4).

Here are some facts about demons. Demons are disembodied spirits who can enter people and animals. When dealing with demons, you must operate as a blood-washed believer and with the Word of God. Demons have knowledge. They know who Yeshua is. They know of their future. They know that we have power over them.

But we must be in the Word, prayer, and personal cleansing if we take them on. Yeshua told in Mark 9:29, *And he said unto them, This kind can come forth by nothing, but by prayer and fasting.* Yeshua also tells in Matthew 12:43-45, *When the unclean spirit is gone out of a man, he walketh through dry places, seeking rest, and findeth none. Then he saith, I will return into my house from whence I came out; and when he is come, he findeth it empty, swept, and garnished. Then goeth he, and taketh with himself seven other spirits more wicked then himself, and they enter in and dwell there: and the last state of that man is worse than the first. Even so shall it be also unto this wicked generation.*

Demons have willpower and fight to resist us. James 4:7, *Submit yourselves therefore to God. Resist the devil, and he will flee from you.* When Yeshua was tempted in the wilderness for forty days by the devil he told him: *"Satan, it is written"* meaning, written in the Bible.

Because demons are under our feet, We can bind them and cast them out in the name of Yeshua. Demonic activity in the spirit of man includes consulting the dead, witchcraft, sorcery, Satanism, wizardry, or spells put on people. These are in the religious realm and deal with the spirit part of man. Demons can also enter through the occult that opens the door for demonic activity including fortune telling, numerology, palmistry, Tarot cards, Ouija board, astrology, belief in reincarnation, sorcery, tea-leaf reading, crystal ball gazing, crystals, hypnotism, automatic writing, E.S.P. and many more. A Christian cannot be demon possessed. If generational curses effect us, we can be delivered from them.

Many more pages could be written about this subject. Should this not wake us up so that we let the Holy Spirit guide us daily?

CHAPTER 8

The Difference – Heaven or Hell

Heaven or hell—Yeshua or Satan: The choice is ours.
Merriam-Webster's Collegiate Dictionary defines heaven as:

1. The sky or universe as seen from the earth; firmament.

2. The dwelling place of the Deity and the blessed dead.

3. A place of condition of utmost happiness.

4. A spiritual state of everlasting communication with God.

The Bible defines heaven in the following Scriptures: atmosphere, space, heaven, the universe—we call our home.
The firmament:
In the beginning God created the heaven and the earth. And God called the firmament heaven (Genesis 1:1, 8a).

And God said, Let there be lights in the firmament of the heaven to divide the day from the night; and let them be for signs, and for seasons, and for days, and years: and let them be for lights in the firmament of the heaven to give light upon the earth: and it was so. And God made two great lights; the greater light to rule the day, and the lesser light to rule the night: he made the stars also. And God set them in the firmament of the heaven to give light upon the earth, and to rule over the day and over the night, and to divide the light from the darkness: and God saw that it was good (Genesis 1:14–18).

O Lord our Lord, how excellent is thy name in all the earth! who hast set thy glory above the heavens. When I consider thy heavens, the work of thy fingers, the moon and the stars, which thou hast ordained; what is man, that thou art mindful of him? and the son of man, that thou visitest him? (Psalm 8:1, 3–4).

Thus said God the LORD, he that created the heavens, and stretched them out; he that spread forth the earth, and that which cometh out of it; he that giveth breath unto the people upon it, and spirit to them that walk therein (Isaiah 42:5).

I knew a man in Christ above fourteen years ago, (whether in the body, I cannot tell; or whether out of the body, I cannot tell: God knoweth;) such an one caught up to the third heaven (2 Corinthians 12:2).

The heavens declare the glory of God; and the firmament sheweth his handy work (Psalm 19:1).

He stretcheth out the north over the empty place, and hangeth the earth upon nothing (Job 26:7).

The dwelling place of God:

Harken thou to the supplication of thy servant, and of thy people Israel, when they shall pray toward this place: and hear thou in heaven thy dwelling place: and when thou hearest, forgive (1 Kings 8:30).

But our God is in the heavens: he hath done whatsoever he hath pleased (Psalm 115:3).

Unto thee lift I up mine eyes, O thou that dwellest in the heavens (Psalm 123:1).

Thus saith the LORD, The heaven is my throne, and the earth is my footstool: where is the house that ye build unto me? and where is the place of my rest? (Isaiah 66:1).

After this manner therefore pray ye: Our Father which art in heaven, Hallowed be thy name (Matthew 6:9).

Now of the things which we have spoken this is the sum: We have such an high priest, who is set on the right hand of the throne of the majesty in the heavens (Hebrew 8:1).

The place of happiness:

But as it is written, Eye hath not seen, nor ear heard, neither have entered into the heart of man, the things which God hath prepared for them that love him (1 Corinthians 2:9).

If any man serve me, let him follow me; and where I am, there shall also my servant be: if any man serve me, him will my Father honor (John 12:26).

Rejoice, and be exceeding glad: for great is your reward in heaven; for so persecuted they the prophets which were before you (Matthew 5:12).

Then shall the righteousness shine forth as the sun in the kingdom of their father (Matthew 13:43).

Who will enter:

And they that be wise shall shine as the brightness of the firmament; and they that turn many to righteousness as the stars for ever and ever (Daniel 12:3).

Then shall the King say unto them on his right hand, Come ye blessed of my Father, inherit the kingdom prepared for you from the foundation of the world (Matthew 25:34).

And if children, then heirs; heirs of God, and joint-heirs with Christ; if so be that we suffer with him, that we may be also glorified together (Romans 8:17).

He that overcometh shall inherit all things; and I will be his God, and he shall be my son (Revelation 21:7).

Who will not enter:

Not every one that saith unto me, Lord, Lord, shall enter into the kingdom of heaven; but he that doeth the will of my Father which is in heaven (Matthew 7:21).

Then said one unto him, Lord, are there few that be saved? And he said unto them, Strive to enter in at the strait gate: for many, I say unto you, will seek to enter in, and shall not be able. When once the master of the house is risen up, and hath shut the door, and ye begin to stand without, and to knock at the door, saying, Lord, Lord, open unto us; and he shall answer and say unto you, I know you not whence ye are: Then shall ye begin to say, We have eaten and drunk in thy presence, and thou hast taught in our streets. But he shall say, I tell you, I know you not whence you are; depart from me, all ye workers of iniquity. There shall be weeping and gnashing of teeth, when ye shall see Abraham, and Isaac, and Jacob, and all the prophets, in the kingdom of God, and you yourselves thrust out. And they shall come from the East, and from the West, and from the North, and from the South, and shall sit in the kingdom of God. And, behold, there are last which shall be first, and there are first which shall be last (Luke 13:23–30).

Know ye not that the unrighteous shall not inherit the kingdom of God? Be not deceived: neither fornicators, nor idolaters, nor adulterers, nor effeminate, nor abusers of themselves with mankind, nor thieves, nor covetous, nor drunkards, nor revilers, nor extortioners, shall inherit the kingdom of God (1 Corinthians 6:9–10).

This Scripture tells us that all who live immoral lives—idol worshippers, adulterers, homosexuals, thieves, greedy people, drunkards, slanderers, and robbers—will have no share in the kingdom of God. Don't fool yourselves by assuming that you are exempt, that God will treat you differently than He had declared in His Word. It is confirmed in Revelation 21:8, *But the fearful and unbelieving, abominable, and murderers, and whoremongers, and sorcerers, and idolaters, and all liars, shall have their part in the lake which burneth with fire and brimstone: which is the second death.*

Merriam Webster's Collegiate Dictionary defines Hell as:

1. A nether world in which the dead continue to exist; the nether realm of the devil and the demons in which the damned suffer everlasting punishment

2. A place or state of misery, torment, or wickedness; a place of state of turmoil or destruction

3. An extremely unpleasant and often inescapable situation

The Bible defines Hell in the following manner.
The grave:
O death, where is thy sting? O grave, where is thy victory? (1 Corinthians 15:55).

And death and hell were cast into the lake of fire. This is the second death. And whosoever was not found written in the book of life was cast into the lake of fire (Revelation 20:14–15).

A place of torment:

And thou, Capernaum, which art exalted unto heaven, shalt be brought down to hell: for if the mighty works, which have been done in thee, had been done in Sodom, it would have remained until this day (Matthew 11:23).

The son of man shall send forth his angels, and they shall gather out of his kingdom all things that offend, and them which do iniquity; and shall cast them into a furnace of fire: there shall be wailing and gnashing of teeth. Then shall the righteous shine forth as the sun in the kingdom of their Father (Matthew 13:41–43).

The same shall drink of the wine of the wrath of God, which is poured out without mixture into the cup of his indignation; and he shall be tormented with fire and brimstone in the presence of the holy angels, and in the presence of the Lamb: and the smoke of their torment ascendeth up for ever and ever: and they have no rest day nor night, who worship the beast and his image, and whosoever receiveth the mark of his name (Revelation 14:10–11).

And the devil that deceived them was cast into the lake of fire and brimstone, where the beast and the false prophet are, and shall be tormented day and night for ever and ever (Revelation 20:10).

For whom reserved:

The wicked shall be turned into hell, and all the nations that forget God. For the needy shall not always be forgotten: the expectation of the poor shall not perish forever (Psalm 9:17–18).

Therefore hell hath enlarged herself, and opened her mouth without measure: and their glory, and their multitude, and their pomp, and he that rejoiceth (in sin), shall descend into it (Isaiah 5:14).

The sinners in Zion are afraid; fearfulness hath surprised the hypocrites. Who among us shall dwell with the devouring fire? Who among us shall dwell with everlasting burnings (Isaiah 33:14).

The Bible tells us that we must choose whom we serve. It is while we are living that this choice results in where our eternal destination will be. If you decide to follow Yeshua and make Heaven your eternal home, you will be among those who will accompany Him when He triumphantly returns to rule the world from Jerusalem. There is also another choice—to reject Yeshua. The Bible tells us that if we are not *for* Yeshua, then we are *against* Him and our eternal destination will be hell, where there is weeping, great misery, and torment in a burning lake of fire with Satan and his cohorts. In the following Scriptures, you will find examples of the great difference between these two masters.

The Name of Yeshua

And the angel said unto her, Fear not, Mary: for thou hast found favor with God. And, behold, thou shalt conceive in thy womb, and bring forth a Son, and shalt call His name, JESUS (Luke 1:30–31).

And she will have a Son, and you shall name him JESUS (meaning Savior), for he will save his people from their sins ... (Matthew 1:21–25).

This will fulfill God's message through the prophets. Listen! The virgin shall conceive a child! She shall give birth to a son and He shall be called Emmanuel, which means God is with us. But she remained a virgin until her son was born. Joseph (her husband) named Him Jesus.

And when eight days were accomplished for the circumcising of the child, His name was called JESUS which was so named of the angel before He was conceived in the womb (Luke 2:21).

He said unto them, But whom say ye that I am? And Simon Peter answered and said, Thou art the Christ, the Son of the living God. And Jesus answered and said unto him, Blessed art thou, Simon Barjona: for flesh and blood hath not revealed it unto thee, but my Father which is in heaven (Matthew 16:15–17).

He was telling Peter that this information had not been given to him by any human source. He supernaturally discerned it.

Then Simon Peter answered him, Lord, to whom shall we go? Thou hast the words of eternal life. And we believe and are sure that thou art that Christ, the Son of the living God (John 6:68–69).

Let not your heart be troubled: ye believe in God, believe also in me, In my Father's house are many mansions, if it were not so I would have told you. I go to prepare a place for you. And if I go and prepare a place for you I will come again, and receive you unto myself; that where I am there ye may be also. And whither I go ye know, and the way ye know. Thomas saith unto him, Lord, we know not whither thou goest; and how we know the way? Jesus saith unto him, I am the way, the truth, and the life: no man cometh unto the Father, but by me. If ye had known me, ye should have known my Father also, and from henceforth ye know him and have seen him. Philip saith unto him, Lord, show us the Father, and it sufficeth us.

Jesus saith unto him, Have I been so long time with you, and yet hast thou not known me, Philip? he that hath seen me hath seen the Father; and how sayest thou then, Shew us the Father? Believest thou not that I am in the Father, and the Father in me? the words that I speak unto you I speak not of myself: but the Father that dwelleth in me, he doeth the works. Believe me that I am in the Father, and the Father in me: or else believe me for the very works' sake. Verily, verily, I say unto you, He that believeth on me, the works that I do shall he do also, and greater works than these shall he do; because I go unto my Father. And whatsoever ye shall ask in my name that will I do, that the Father may be glorified in the Son. If ye love me, keep my commandments. (John 14:1–15).

And Pilate wrote a title, and put it on the cross. And the writing was, JESUS OF NAZARETH THE KING OF THE JEWS (John 19:19).

Ye men of Israel, hear these words; Jesus of Nazareth, a man approved of God among you by miracles and wonders and signs, which God did by him in the midst of you, as ye yourselves also know: him being delivered by the determinate counsel and foreknowledge of God, ye have taken, and by wicked hands have crucified and slain: Whom God hath raised up, having loosed the pains of death: because it was not possible that he should be holden of it (Acts 2:22–24).

Therefore let all the house of Israel know assuredly, that God hath made that same Jesus, whom ye have crucified, both Lord and Christ (Acts 2:36).

By stretching forth thine hand to heal; and that signs and wonders may be done by the name of the holy child Jesus (Acts 4:30).

And with great power gave the apostles witness of the resurrection of the Lord Jesus: and great grace was upon them all (Acts 4:33).

When we consider the character of Yeshua as portrayed throughout the Scriptures, we know He is holy, righteous, good, faithful, true, just, guiltless, sinless, spotless, innocent, blameless, undefiled, able to resist temptation, obedient in all things, zealous, humble, lowly of heart, merciful, patient, compassionate, benevolent, loving, self-denying, submissive, and forgiving.

Satan—The Devil:

Encyclopedia Britannica says that Satan is the English translation of the Hebrew word for *adversary* in the Torah. With the definite article, the Hebrew word denotes the adversary par excellence. His task is to roam through the earth, seeking out acts or persons to be reported adversely. His function thus is the opposite of that of the eyes of the Lord, which roam through the earth strengthening all that is good. Satan is cynical and disinterested about human goodness and is permitted to test it under God's authority and within the limits God sets. Satan, too, belongs to the spiritual and supernatural world. He is spoken of as the prince of evil spirits, the inveterate enemy of God and of Yeshua, and takes the disguise of an angel of light. He can enter a man and act through him by his subordinate demons.

Satan can take possession of men's bodies, (except the true believer in Yeshua) afflicting them or making them diseased. According to John's vision in the Book of Revelation, when the risen Christ returns from heaven to reign on earth, Satan will be bound with a great chain for a thousand years, then released, but almost immediately will face final defeat and be cast into eternal punishment. The devil is also called Abaddon, Apollyon, Beelzebub, Belial, and Satan.

We are warned in 1 Peter 5:8, *be sober, be vigilant; because your adversary the devil, as a roaring lion, walketh about, seeking whom he may devour.*

He that committed sin is of the devil; for the devil sinneth from the beginning. For this purpose the Son of God was manifest, that he might destroy the works of the devil (1 John 3:8).

He is fallen from heaven. *The serpent was the craftiest of all the creatures the Lord God had made* (Genesis 3:1). As a serpent, he causes the fall of man.

And the Lord God said unto the serpent, Because thou hast done this, thou are cursed above all cattle, and above every beast in the field; upon thy belly shalt thou go, and dust shalt thou eat all the days of thy life (Genesis 3:14).

He was the tempter of Yeshua.

And when the tempter came to him, he said, If Thou be the Son of God, command that these stones be made bread. But he answered and said, It is written, Man shall not live by bread alone, but by every word that proceedeth out of the mouth of God. Then the devil taketh him up into the holy city, and setteth him on a pinnacle of the temple, and saith unto him, If thou be the Son of God, cast thyself down: for it is written, He shall give his angels charge over thee: and in their hands they shall bear thee up, lest at any time thou dash thy foot against a stone. Jesus said unto him, It is written again, thou shalt not tempt the Lord thy God. Again, the devil taketh him up into an exceeding high mountain, and sheweth him all the kingdoms of the world, and the glory of them; and saith unto him, *All these things will I give thee, if thou wilt fall down and worship me. Then saith Jesus unto him, Get thee hence, Satan: for it is written, Thou shalt worship the Lord thy God, and him only shalt thou serve* (Matthew 4:3–10).

And he was there in the wilderness forty days, tempted of Satan; and was with the wild beast; and the angels ministered unto him (Mark 1:13).

And the serpent said unto the woman, Ye shall not surely die (Genesis 3:4). He lied to Eve and all mankind even unto this day.

Jesus said unto them, If God were your Father, ye would love me; for I proceeded forth and came from God...Ye are of your father the devil, and the lusts of your father ye will do. He was a murderer from the beginning and abode not in the truth, because there is no truth in him.When he speaketh a lie, he speaketh of his own: for he is a liar, and the father of it (John 8:42 & 44).

He is the prince of devils and the god of this world.

And you hath he quickened, who were dead in trespasses and sins;Wherein in time past ye walked according to the course of this world, according to the prince of the power of the air, the spirit that now worketh in the children of disobedience (Ephesians 2:1–2).

In whom the god of this world (universe) hath blinded the minds of them which believe not, lest the light of the glorious gospel of Christ, who is the image of God, should shine unto them (2 Corinthians 4:4).

For they are the spirits of devils, working miracles, which go forth unto the kings of the earth and of the whole world, to gather them to the battle of that great day of God Almighty (Revelation 16:14).

And I heard a loud voice saying in heaven, Now is come salvation, and strength, and the kingdom of our God, and the power of his Christ: for the accuser of our brethren is cast down, which accused them before our God day and night (Revelation 12:10).

And no marvel; for Satan himself is transformed into an angel of light. Therefore it is no great thing if his ministers also be transformed as the ministers of righteousness; whose end shall be according to their works (2 Corinthians 11:14–15).

For if he that cometh preaching another Jesus, whom we have not preached, or if ye receive another spirit, which ye have not received, or another gospel, which ye have not accepted, ye might well bear with him (2 Corinthians 11:4).

The character of the Devil is depicted throughout the Bible as daring, proud, powerful, wicked, malignant, subtle, deceitful, fierce, and cruel.

Yes, Satan is real and powerful, but we read in 1 John 4:4, *Ye are of God, little children, and have overcome them: because greater is he (Yeshua) that is in you, than he (Satan) that is in the world.*

Therefore, I no longer need to speak of fear because *God has not given us the spirit of fear; but of power, and of love, and of a sound mind* (2 Timothy 1:7).

I no longer need to speak of doubt because Yeshua said, *If thou canst believe, all things are possible to him that believeth* (Mark 9:23).

I no longer need to speak of weakness. *For the joy of the LORD is our strength* (Nehemiah 8:10).

I no longer need to speak of unworthiness. *For he has made him to be sin for us, who knew no sin, that we might be made the righteousness of God in him* (2 Corinthians 5:21).

I no longer need to speak of defeat because *God always causes us to triumph in Christ* (2 Corinthians 2:14).

I no longer need to speak of poverty because *My God shall supply all your need according to his riches in glory by Christ Jesus* (Philippians 4:19).

I no longer need to speak of failure. *And this is the victory that overcometh the world, even our faith* (1 John 5:4).

I no longer need to speak of insecurity. *But safety is of the LORD* (Proverbs 21:31).

I no longer need to speak of discouragement because *I can do all things through Christ which strengtheneth me* (Philippians 4:13).

I no longer need to speak of cares and worries. *Casting all your care upon him; for he careth for you* (1 Peter 5:7).

I no longer need to speak of loneliness. *For he hath said, I will never leave thee, nor forsake thee* (Hebrews 13:5).

I no longer need to speak of discontent. *For he satisfieth the longing soul, and filleth the hungry soul with goodness* (Psalm 107:9).

I no longer need to speak of ignorance. *If any of you lack wisdom, let him ask of God, that giveth to men liberally, and upbraideth not; and it shall be given him* (James 1:5).

I no longer need to speak of death because Yeshua said, *I am come that they might have life, and that they might have it more abundantly* (John 10:10b).

I no longer need to speak of hate. *Because the love of God is shed abroad in our hearts by the Holy Ghost which is given unto us* (Romans 5:5).

I no longer need to speak of condemnation. *There is therefore now no condemnation to them which are in Christ Jesus, who walk not after the flesh, but after the Spirit* (Romans 8:1).

It should be simple to see our downfall if we follow Satan, who will have us join him in hell. I hope you are disgusted with his deception and turn your life over to Yeshua, the Savior of the world who has guaranteed us a mansion in heaven! This is the reason we witness and share Yeshua with everyone we encounter. Sometimes they call us Jesus freaks, but when they are close to dying, many remember what we told them earlier and call on us for prayer. The following is from an unknown author:

To my friend. A letter from Hell.

I stand in judgment now, and feel that you're to blame somehow.

On earth, I walked with you day by day, and never did you point the way.

You knew the Lord in truth and glory, but never did you tell the story.

My knowledge then was very dim; you could have led me safe to Him.

Though we lived together on the earth, you never told me of the second birth. And now I stand this day condemned, because you failed to mention Him.

You taught me many things, that's true, I called you "friend" and trusted you.

But now I learn that it's too late, you could have kept me from this fate.

We walked by day and talked by night, and yet you showed me not the Light.

You let me live, and love, and die, you knew I'd never live on high.

Yes, I called you a "friend" in life, and trusted you through joy and strife.

And yet on coming to the end, I cannot, now, call you "My Friend."

Let not one of us be guilty of this accusation!

CHAPTER 9

The Names of Satan

Satan is portrayed in the Bible as the foremost enemy of God and humanity. His appropriate definition is "adversary." Known by a host of names that serve to identify him as the source of all dimensions of evil, Satan began his earthly career with the temptation of Adam and Eve. The prophet Ezekiel portrays Satan as a created being who once resided in heaven in a perfect, blameless state.

However, he grew proud and desired to be like God and even rule over Him. Because of his flawed ambition and self-deification, Satan was thrown out of heaven. This is how the adversarial relationship between God and Satan began—good and evil, holiness and sin, life and death.

He is most commonly known by the name Satan, which appears fifty-two times in the Bible. Another frequent name is the Devil, by which he is referred thirty-five times. He is also called by many other descriptive names that help to identify his nature and work.

The ruler of the power of the air:

Wherein in time past ye walketh according to the course of this world, according to the prince of the power of the air, the spirit that now worketh in the children of disobedience (Ephesians 2:2).

The god of this world:

In whom the god of this world hath blinded the minds of them which believe not, lest the light of the glorious gospel of Christ, who is the image of God, should shine unto them (2 Corinthians 4:4).

The ruler of this world:

Now is the judgment of this world: now shall the prince of this world be cast out (John 12:31).

Day star, son of Dawn:

How are thou fallen from heaven, O Lucifer, son of the morning! How art thou cut down to the ground, which didst weaken the nations (Isaiah 14:12).

The dragon:

And there was war in heaven: Michael and his angels fought against the dragon; and the dragon fought and his angels, and prevailed not; neither was their place found anymore in heaven (Revelation 12:7–8).

Abaddon or Apollyon:

And they had a king over them, which is the angel of the bottomless pit, whose name in the Hebrew tongue is Abaddon, but in the Greek tongue hath his name Apollyon (Revelation 9:11).

Beelzebub:

But when the Pharisees heard it, they said, This fellow doth not cast out devils, but by Beelzebub the prince of the devil (Matthew 12:24).

Belial:

And what concord hath Christ with Belial? Or what part hath he that believeth with an infidel (2 Corinthians 6:15).

The evil one:

The field is the world; the good seed are the children of the kingdom; but the tares are the children of the wicked one; The enemy that sowed them is the devil; the harvest is the end of the world; and the reapers are the angels (Matthew 13:38–39).

The tempter:

For this cause, when I could no longer forbear, I sent to know your faith, lest by some means the tempter have tempted you, and our labour be in vain (1 Thessalonians 3:5).

The accuser of our comrades:

And I heard a loud voice saying in heaven, Now is come salvation, and strength, and the kingdom of our God, and the power of his Christ: for the accuser of our brethren is cast down, which accused them before our God day and night (Revelation 12:10).

An angel of light:

And no marvel; for Satan himself is transformed into an angel of light. Therefore it is no great thing if his ministers also be transformed as the ministers of righteousness; whose end shall be according to their works (2 Corinthians 11:14–15).

He is a murderer and the father of lies:

Ye are of your father the devil, and the lusts of your father ye will do. He was a murderer from the beginning, and abode not in the truth, because there is no truth in him. When he speaketh a lie, he speaketh of his own: for he is a liar, and the father of it (John 8:44).

Although Satan is without the powers of God, he has the ability to seduce the human race. The struggle between Satan and humans is a constant theme throughout the Bible. However, the Bible teaches that Satan's ultimate power was broken through the work of Yeshua on the cross, as described in Hebrews 2:14, *Forasmuch then as the children are partakers of flesh and blood, he also himself likewise took part of the same: that through death he might destroy him that had the power of death, that is the devil.*

The victory over sin and death was won by Yeshua then, but the final defeat of Satan, his angels, and his followers will not be realized until after the final judgment, as told in Revelation 20:10–11 and 14–15,

And the devil that deceived them was cast into the lake of fire and brimstone, where the beast and the false prophet are, and shall be tormented day and night for ever and ever. And I saw a great white throne, and him that sat on it, from whose face the earth and the heaven fled away; and there was found no place for them. And death and hell were cast into the lake of fire. This is the second death. And whosoever was not found written in the book of life was cast into the lake of fire.

Until then, Satan will continue his attempts to destroy God's plan and usurp his position. But do not fear, we have read the last chapter. Yeshua tells us in Revelation 22:12–13, *And, behold, I come quickly; and my reward is with me, to give every man according as his work shall be. I am Alpha and Omega, the beginning and the end, the first and the last.*

Are you looking forward to His soon return?

CHAPTER 10

Who Are the Two Witnesses?

While I was working on a different chapter, all at once the Holy Spirit prompted me to write the following, which I received supernaturally through His inspiration.

Many people are of the opinion that Moses is one of the two witnesses. The word *revelation* describes the function of the two witnesses in the Book of Revelation. It is a Greek translation of *apocalypses*—a disclosing of a reality not previously perceived. We read in Revelation 1:1–3,

> *The Revelation of Jesus Christ, which God gave unto him, to shew unto his servants things which must shortly come to pass; and he sent and signified it by his angel unto his servant John: who bare record of the word of God, and to the testimony of Jesus Christ, and of all things that he saw. Blessed is he that readeth, and they that hear the words of this prophecy, and keep those things which are written therein: for the time is at hand.*

John saw the following in Revelation 11:1–12,

> *And there was given me a reed like unto a rod: and the angel stood, saying, Rise and measure the temple of God, and the altar, and them that worship therein. But the court which is without the temple leave out, and measure*

it not; for it is given unto the Gentiles: and the holy city they tread under foot forty and two months And I will give power unto my two witnesses, and they shall prophecy a thousand two hundred and threescore days, clothed in sackcloth. These are the two olive trees, and the two candlesticks standing before the God of the earth. And if any man will hurt them, fire proceedeth out of their mouth, and devoureth their enemies: and if any man will hurt them, he must in this manner be killed. These have power to shut heaven, that it rain not in the days of their prophecy: and have power over waters to turn them to blood, and to smite the earth with all plagues, as often as they will. And when they shall have finished their testimony, the beast that ascendeth out of the bottomless pit shall make war against them, and shall overcome them, and kill them. And their dead bodies shall lie in the street of the great city, which spiritually is called Sodom and Egypt, where also our Lord was crucified. And they of the people and kindreds and tongues and nations shall see their dead bodies three days and an half, and shall not suffer their dead bodies to be put in graves. And they that dwell upon the earth shall rejoice over them, and make merry, and shall send gifts one to another; because these two prophets tormented them that dwelt on the earth. And after three days and an half the Spirit of life from God entered into them, and they stood upon their feet; and great fear fell upon them which saw them. And they heard a great voice from heaven saying unto them, Come up hither. And they ascended up to heaven in a cloud, and their enemies beheld them.

What else does the Word of God say about this subject? We read about Moses in Deuteronomy 34:1–6,

And Moses went up from the plains of Moab unto the mountain of Nebo, to the top of Pisgah, that is over against Jericho. And the LORD shewed him all the land of Gilead, unto Dan; and all Naphtali, and the land of Ephraim, and Manasseh, and all the land of Judah, unto the utmost sea, and the south, and the plain of the valley of Jericho, the city of palm trees, unto Zoar. And the Lord said to him, This is the land which I sware unto Abraham, unto Isaac, and unto Jacob, saying, I will give it unto thy seed: I have caused thee to see it with thine eyes, but you shall not go over thither. So Moses the servant of the LORD died there in the land of Moab, according to the word of the LORD. And he buried him in a valley in the

*land of Moab, over against Beth-peor: but no man knoweth of his sepul-
chre unto this day.*

If we believe in the Scriptures, Moses could not possibly be one
of the two witnesses. Let's confirm it in Hebrews 9:27, *And as it is
appointed unto men once to die, but after this the judgment.*

It was Enoch and Elijah who were both taken alive by God. *And
Enoch walked with God: and he was not; for God took him* (Genesis 5:24).
Later we read in Hebrews 11:5, *By faith Enoch was translated that he
should not see death; and was not found, because God had translated him: for
before his translation he had this testimony, that he pleased God.*

What about Elijah? He, too, was taken into heaven by a whirlwind, as explained in 2 Kings 2:11, *And it came to pass, as they still went
on, and talked, that, behold, there appeared a chariot of fire, and horses of
fire and parted them both asunder; and Elijah went up by a whirlwind into
heaven.*

I believe that the confusion comes from the following Scriptures
in Matthew 17:1-3, *And after six days Jesus taketh Peter, James, and John
his brother, and bringeth them up into an high mountain apart, and was
transfigured before them: and his face did shine as the sun, and his raiment
was as white as the light. And, behold, there appeared unto them Moses and
Elias talking wit him.*

Here, the Scriptures make reference to Moses the Law-giver,
and Elijah the Prophet for a different purpose. Both are examples of
Yeshua's redemptive mission.

The high mountain mentioned is Mount Tabor. There are beautiful
murals on the walls and ceiling in the Church of the Transfiguration,
including the appearance of Yeshua with Moses and Elijah. It displays
the scene of the disciple's experience with Yeshua, which helped
them later to stand their ground for the gospels' sake and withstand
all the persecution they were subjected to. They could say with cer-
tainty, "We were there with Him, we saw it with our own eyes!" Let's
read it in the Bible in their own words.

*Then answered Peter, and said unto Jesus, Lord, it is good for us to be here:
if thou wilt, let us make here three tabernacles; one for thee, and one for Moses,
and one for Elias. While he yet spake, behold a bright cloud overshadowed
them: and behold a voice out of the cloud, which said, This is my beloved Son,*

in whom I am well pleased; hear ye him. And when the disciples heard it, they fell on their face, and were sore afraid. And Jesus came and touched them, and said, 'Arise, and be not afraid.' And when they had lifted up their eyes, they saw no man, save Jesus only. And as they came down from the mountain, Jesus charged them, saying, 'Tell the vision to no man, until the Son of man be risen again from the dead' (Matthew 17:4–9).

For the steadfastness of the apostles' faith and belief in what they experienced with Yeshua, most of them had to die gruesome deaths. Their willingness to give their lives for the truth of the gospel should be an inspiration to us. No one wants to die for a lie. Many countless millions have followed them in martyrdom through the centuries. I will mention a few. Peter was crucified upside down in Rome in about 66 AD. James, the son of Zebedee, was beheaded in Jerusalem in 44 AD. Matthew was burned at the stake in 90 AD. Philip was crucified in Phrygia in 54 AD. Paul was beheaded in Rome in 67 or 68 AD.

I hope by printing these Scriptures, it will bring clarity to the subject.

Who do you believe the two witnesses are?

15839951R00133

Made in the USA
Charleston, SC
23 November 2012